Advance praise for

COWBOY IMPERIALISM *and* HOLLYWOOD FILM

"Mark Cronlund Anderson responds to Hollywood movies in exactly the ways mass media doesn't want us to: with shrewd cultural analysis of the film industry as propaganda machine. While blockbuster hits aim to mesmerize spectators to unthinkingly identify with the heroes and absorb ideological messages through osmosis, Anderson reminds us that we have a responsibility and the right to interpret manufactured culture and to talk back. This book examines how our sense of history and intercultural relations are informed by Hollywood, one of the main storytellers of consumer culture. This interdisciplinary approach to film criticism encourages us to think about what is at stake in contemporary culture. Anderson's witty and accessible language will appeal to anyone interested in history, mass culture, and world politics, and even to those who thought they were only interested in movies and pop culture...."

Martha Nandorfy, Co-Author of
Eduardo Galeano: Through the Looking Glass
and The Concise Guide to Global Human Rights

"Mark Cronlund Anderson 'epoch-marks' and makes a film-history 'cross-pollination' by delving deep into and probing beneath the Hollywood tinseldom and its subtle didactiveness in iconoclastically attributing the role of the history teacher to Hollywood. Pathbreakingly, this text aims to bury 'five fathoms deep' the filmic images and archetypes of imperial building, neo-kingdoms expanding and frontier myth-making. It is definitely a rewarding text which does not disappoint nonspecialists but proves to be an insightful one for academia, particularly for critical humanities and critical film, historical, and political studies."

Susaimanickam Armstrong,
Department of English, University of Madras, India

Cowboy Imperialism and Hollywood Film

PETER LANG
New York • Washington, D.C./Baltimore • Bern
Frankfurt am Main • Berlin • Brussels • Vienna • Oxford

Mark Cronlund Anderson

Cowboy Imperialism and Hollywood Film

PETER LANG
New York • Washington, D.C./Baltimore • Bern
Frankfurt am Main • Berlin • Brussels • Vienna • Oxford

Library of Congress Cataloging-in-Publication Data

Anderson, Mark Cronlund.
Cowboy imperialism and Hollywood film / Mark Cronlund Anderson.
p. cm.
Includes bibliographical references and index.
1. Western films—United States—History and criticism.
2. Motion pictures—Political aspects—United States.
3. Frontier and pioneer life—United States. I. Title.
PN1995.9.W4A53 791.43'6278—dc22 2006101480
ISBN 978-0-8204-9545-3

Bibliographic information published by **Die Deutsche Bibliothek**.
Die Deutsche Bibliothek lists this publication in the "Deutsche Nationalbibliografie"; detailed bibliographic data is available on the Internet at http://dnb.ddb.de/.

Cover art courtesy of Carmen Robertson
Cover design by Sophie Boorsch Appel

29 Broadway, 18th floor, New York, NY 10006
www.peterlang.com

Table of Contents

Acknowledgments

I wish to thank Carmen for her artistry and Dagmar and Madelaine for inspiration. Also, thanks to Heidi Burns for her faith in this project. Finally, a variety of students in several classes have helped make my arguments clearer, at least clearer to me. And so I thank them, too.

Chapter One

A Theory of American Evolution: Origination of a Chosen People

While this America settles in the mould of its vulgarity,
heavily thickened to empire,
And protest, only a bubble in the molten mass, pops and
sighs out, and the mass hardens,
I sadly remember that the flower fades to make fruit, the
fruit rots to make earth…

—Robinson Jeffers[1]

The past becomes eternally present, as long as the film lasts.

—Thomas Flanagan[2]

The continuity and persistence of particular genres identifies a culture's deepest and most persistent concerns, because it reflects repeated and continuing attempts, over several years and generations, to formulate a mythic response to political and social crisis.

—Richard Slotkin[3]

Think about the best history teacher you ever had. Granted, maybe he was old and musty, clad in a tweed jacket and smelling vaguely of coffee, mints, and cats. Even so, wasn't he brilliant somehow? Or, maybe she was youthful, charismatic, full of energy, making the past come alive in the classroom. Putting it all together for you. Good teachers come in many shapes and sizes. Perhaps, more likely, she or he was not all that great. Maybe your best history teacher was not so wonderful at all. And maybe you never took a history class after they stopped being compulsory in high school because history bored you to tears, all those impossible names and irrelevant dates and boring battles.

Nevertheless, you still know it. Whether you studied it or not, you know history. You know what gladiators looked like. You can tell the difference between cowboys and Indians. You have seen World War Two soldiers in action. You saw the Titanic go down. You have seen the Middle Ages dressed up as Middle Earth. You have even seen Jesus Christ, Moses, and possibly God.

You know these things because you have been to the movies. Hollywood has been your history teacher. Hollywood has been your best history teacher—because it is what you remember.

Hollywood teaches history. It does so all the time, reflexively, automatically, whether it intends to or not and whether we know it (and like it) or not. Consider, for a moment, how you visualize cowboys and Indians. In all likelihood you have never seen a real cowboy. You have most certainly never witnessed firsthand an Indian war party, the cavalry charging, a shootout at high noon, the western frontier, or a circling of the wagons. Yet you know them because you have seen them on film. In truth, if your mental image of the old west has not been fashioned by film, you probably were not alive in the twentieth century. Movies serve as our broadest and most pervasive, though by no means our best or only, history teachers. This occurs on many levels.

To begin with, the movies depict past lives. Examples abound. Think of *Elizabeth,*[4] *Citizen Kane,*[5] *Nixon,*[6] *A Beautiful Mind,*[7] *Bill and Ted's Excellent Adventure,*[8] or *Malcolm X.*[9] They, and many, many other Hollywood productions, attempt directly to tell you stories about historical personages, events, processes, and so on. The fact that frequently they are not especially accurate or nuanced is beside the point. Interpretation rests in the eye of the beholder (and is generally limited to what can be crammed into two hours of film).

Movies also portray past events of historical significance—say, *The Birth of a Nation*[10] and its portrayal of the era of Reconstruction in the postbellum United States, *JFK*[11] and the Kennedy assassination, or *Platoon*[12] (and before it, *The Green Berets*[13]) and the visceral experiences of the Vietnam War. Again, accuracy does not really matter here. Why? Because money, not historical "truth," is the driving force and, at least in part, because historical truth is almost always contested.

Additionally, deliberately or not movies translate the past for us into intelligible images and paradigmatically meaningful dialogue, in films such as *Glory*[14] (about slavery, the Civil War, and the indomitability of the human spirit, among other things), *The Sting*[15] (loosely informing us about life in the Roaring Twenties, but also about the archetypal shenanigans of handsome rogues Paul Newman and Robert Redford), *Annie Hall*[16] (and the fashions of witty but neurotic New Yorkers in the late 1970s). The possibilities here are nearly endless. Indeed, one might generate additional lists, which themselves cross-pollinate in any number of ways, charting the many ways in which Hollywood serves as a history instructor to and for moviegoers, for us all. However, the basic truth need not be overstated: movies teach us about the past.

Even so, there are many pasts, that is, competing visions and versions of what went on before today. History is not just one thing. This observation holds true for professional historians as well as for how movies teach filmgoers about the past. The result is that in all cases some manner of interpretation provides the key to unlock the various, frequently competing historical truths related in popular films, thus blurring the line between historical accuracy and legitimate differences of interpretation. I am not here thinking about how critics read films (more about that later), but how movies express the views of those whose hands made them. In other words, films teach us about the past by infusing them with intended ready-made meaning for us (how we actually apprehend them is another matter). In so doing, Hollywood acts as a sort of collective mirror, telling us a lot about moviemakers and their imagined sets of audience beliefs but also, importantly, much about ourselves, the culture(s) in which we live, and about change (and continuity) across time. For example, *Birth of a Nation* champions alleged black inferiority—as unacceptable a notion today as it was routinely embraced by white Americans a century ago when the film was released, including President Woodrow Wilson who applauded the film enthusiastically when it aired at the White House.

So, in addition to what the filmmaker has to say, moviegoers bring their own baggage to the theater. They tend in mainstream North America to share certain cultural precepts—say, farts are funny, Brangelina are gorgeous, Muslims are dangerous—while individually maintaining their own interpretations within the greater whole. Further, the ways in which audiences understand films may reflect their educational experiences (maybe you took a film class), expectations of a film (conceivably, you love *all* Emma Thompson movies), exposure to advertising (Ebert gave it a thumbs up), word of mouth (your best friend recommended it), and such. Plus, audiences may hold conflicting and contradictory views on a given film (loved Diane Keaton but did not love Jack Nicholson). These attitudes may change dramatically after the film is long gone from theatres (try to remember exactly what you felt the first time you saw *Star Wars*[17]; better yet, watch it again and see how it makes you feel).

Woody Allen once said that box office success almost by definition equated with poor quality. Maybe so; but it is also easier to say this when your movies are perennially modest fiduciary successes. At any rate, reduced to a slogan this book operates on a basic assumption: if it sells, it speaks. What I mean by this is that, to paraphrase Homer Simpson, popularity counts. It matters. Popularity matters because movies reflect us as well as frame various suggestions—contestable and sometimes contradictory—for how we should perceive the present, the past, and even how we might anticipate the future—all while being immersed uneasily in the eternal present.

Films are not, of course, monolithic. They connote different things to different people, including those who make them. Yet, reasonably, to make sense of their implications we categorize and label them. We call these genres.

Westerns, famously, casually and prematurely declared dead by Pauline Kael, the doyen of American film critics at the *New Yorker* magazine, in 1974, though admittedly out of fashion these days, still serve as the most transparent example of the movie-*qua*-teacher in the history of cinema. How else would any of us have more than passing familiarity with that loaded phrase "cowboys and Indians" or of the old west? Further, the many dozens of Western films produced, for example, in the 1950s speak volumes about then common mainstream notions concerning race, gender, masculinity, Manifest Destiny, and so on, as well as providing a modest dose of empirical accuracy about life in the old west.

What About Trained Historians?

Of course it is also the business of specialized experts to teach history. But the playing field is not level. Filmmakers have all the advantages and will win any competition hands down. Historians plainly cannot compete with Hollywood. They do not have the resources or the saleable products to reach millions of people. Further, much if not most of what they write is quite plainly boring. Pick up a copy of any scholarly historical journal and you've got a sure-fire cure for insomnia (yes, you and the on-average seven other people who read a typical scholarly article).

This is not to say that the work that professional historians do is unimportant. Not at all. In fact, movie makers such as Oliver Stone and Steven Spielberg frequently rely on scholarly study or on academics themselves in attempts to get it right when they interpret the past. The results are mixed, of course (where were you in '62?), and I do not want to suggest that academic history is not, in the first case, interpretation. It is as it necessarily must be. The same can be said for film. Just consider the controversy generated by Oliver Stone's *JFK* or Mel Gibson's *Passion of the Christ*.[18] Both films sent droves of would-be true believers to howling at the moon.

My point is simply that movies teach most Americans more about the past than trained historians are able to. Natural advantages—such as far greater financial resources and audience interest, favor Hollywood. Further, the nature of the media—historians write stuff, whereas Hollywood works and plays in moving pictures—provides film with another big edge. Moreover, Hollywood aims to entertain (and it shows), whereas academics do not (and it shows).

Finally, and of much importance to this book, because myth, that is, how a culture perpetuates self-perceptions to, of, and about itself, is dealt best, for the increasingly visual culture that we inhabit, in rendered visual images, movies would seem to have a natural lock on the public imagination when it comes to teaching about the past. In short, in this day and age Hollywood images trump history prose. Again the western comes to mind, tied as it has been to mythic American lore.

This book engages an exploration of such traditional American wisdom as it relates to film and the frontier myth. Any quick perusal of the offerings at Amazon.com will amply demonstrate that the western (alive and well in its own right in literary form, judging by the numbers of new western novels published last year, or in any recent year) has been studied a lot. The frontier, too, both as a historical subject and as an American cultural artifact (frontier myth), has received close, though not frequent, examination. Yet the linkages—that is, between the empirical frontier and mythical frontier—especially as they pertain to the promotion of American imperialism (rooted squarely in candied Manifest Destiny—and the cultural attributes of this process and how it relates to, derives from, and reinforces ongoing notions about the mythical frontier) have been overlooked in the study of American film. These are the focus of this study.

This neglect stems from two basic sources. First, only recently have historians, among the last to arrive at the banquet, begun to appreciate the centrality of film to U.S. culture in the past century. A quick glance at how films are reviewed in historical journals (say, the *American Historical Review*, the mother of all American historical publications) reveals just how shaky, dull, and flat academic film criticism can be. The flipside is that most film critics, and there are, lamentably, few exceptions, generally exhibit scant knowledge of U.S. history, and certainly even less about the frontier myth, apart from a predictable handful of ultimately misleading knee-jerk half-truths and nods to the seminal writing of Frederick Jackson Turner. Roger Ebert, for example, while indisputably the most popular film critic in America, appears to be poorly informed about much of the nation's past (a point taken up later in the book).

Finally, most of what little has been written about the mythical frontier-film relationship has been altogether superficial, ignoring the dark (and empirical) side of the frontier myth—that is, its apology for and promotion of cowboy imperialism, Manifest Destiny, and all that this cultural doctrine implies.

This work is not a history of the western. It is instead an exploration of the domestic, cultural waging of U.S. colonialism, as promoted by the frontier myth, and readable in popular film. It argues that the traditional western has been miscast—and subsequently misunderstood—as joined at the hip with the frontier myth. I agree with those who hold that the western has served as a sort of arena for debating the merits of competing visions of Americanness,[19] but as it is normally conceived, it certainly remains far from the only filmic vehicle to promote the frontier myth. The western becomes too unwieldy, a blunt instrument, when conceived of as one-size-fits-all (see chapter two).

However, neither is this work a full examination of the frontier myth.[20] That is a huge and different topic. Instead, I argue that the myth should be understood as a cultural recipe for various avenues of U.S.-style colonialism—mostly, versus people of color (in particular those with indigenous roots)—and how these cultural visions emerge again and again and yet again in Hollywood. In fact, the images spoon feed apple-pie imperial Americana to audiences and serve, subsequently and consequently, to constitute the very base cloth upon which Hollywood embroiders.

My interest primarily draws on two types of films. The first I refer to as frontier westerns because they represent the invariably aggressive, though frequently (and often cleverly) projected psycho-progeny of the frontier myth (films such as *Full Metal Jacket,*[21] *Red River,*[22] and *The Big Lebowski*[23]). In whole or in part frontier westerns relate the mythical frontier narrative. Second, you have also got your garden variety westerns, which are effectively once-removed from their mythical frontier birthplace, which I simply refer to as traditional westerns. In other words, they do not bother with the frontier myth as such, though they may have a look and feel otherwise apparently identical to the frontier western. That said, I do not mean to suggest that all traditional westerns share anything more in common than to say that they are not frontier westerns. Additionally, I want to stress that that the ground between the frontier western and the traditional western is not represented by a clearly fenced border but rather tends to reflect a shared, overlapping region of mutual occupancy. Traditional westerns include flicks such as *Silverado,*[24] *High Noon,*[25] and the spaghetti westerns that starred Clint Eastwood (e.g., *A Fist Full of Dollars,*[26] *The Good, the Bad, and the Ugly*[27]). They have been dealt with elsewhere in detail.

Frontier westerns, the subject of this work, include standards such as *Dances with Wolves,*[28] *Far and Away,*[29] *Full Metal Jacket, The Green Berets, Man in the Wilderness,*[30] *The Man Who Shot Liberty Valance,*[31] and *Posse.*[32] However, because the mythical frontier in film is not limited to westerns (despite what many critics and scholars suggest and/or imply; a point I take up in the next chapter and throughout the book thereafter), this work also considers a variety of films not normally considered to be westerns at all, such as *Alien,*[33] *The Ballad of Little Joe,*[34] *The Big Lebowski,* John Sayles's *Lone Star,*[35] *Raiders of the Lost Ark,*[36] *About Schmidt,*[37] *25th Hour,*[38] and others. These flicks are unequivocally frontier westerns but are not easily classified as traditional westerns because they lack the standard conventions by which the genre is known, such as horses, Injuns, sixguns, sage brush, saloons, those sorts of things (a topic explored at some length in the next chapter).

This book is divided into eight chapters, six of which are introduced by a discussion of one of the chief characteristics of the frontier myth, followed by an examination of three films, which in turn relate specifically to one of the key themes drawn from the frontier myth and its promotion in film of American empire building. For example, chapter two explores the western *qua* genre, briefly considers its scholarship and its critics. Additionally, it charts the shores of the frontier myth, in particular, as it was spelled out by Frederick Jackson Turner in his famous and profoundly influential essay, "The Significance of the Frontier in American History." The thesis, which may be understood as an articulated myth, presents a blunt recipe for U.S. colonialism, Manifest Destiny. Importantly, film scholarship and western criticism has largely ignored this less palatable region of the frontier narrative, especially as it serves to promote American-style imperialism; and has instead tended to fixate on the imagined cause-and-effect relationship between the existence of a frontier and, say, rugged individualism.

Chapter three examines the perplexing yet centralizing determinism of the frontier myth and its relation(s) to Manifest Destiny. By nearer magic, the narrative relates, the very experience of enduring frontier hardship bred John Wayne-style proto-Americans. Stanley Kubrick's *Full Metal Jacket* vigorously and brilliantly dissents from this view whereas Ron Howard's *Far and Away* embraces and revels in it like a hungry dog on a fresh bone. *Man in the Wilderness* promotes a mild revisioning of the myth-in-film in order to accentuate anti-Vietnam War tropes.

Chapter four explores the mythical assertion that the historical frontier served as a stage for the epic struggle between civilization and savagery. Frontier westerns have tended to relate this idea via affirming tales of whiteness conquering retrograde, backward, uncultured territories in order to render them suitable for occupation and domination by the sorts of characters from television series such as the twerpy *Little House on the Prairie* or the obnoxious *Bonanza*. Director John Ford's enthralling, yet ultimately mythically dissatisfying film, *The Man Who Shot Liberty Valance*, establishes a meditative frame and sketches sober borders from which to approach the mythical theme of cross-cultural contestation. Howard Hawks's *Red River* takes the myth's exaggerated masculinity to the point of near pathological homoeroticism. Kevin Costner's *Dances with Wolves* swarms with putatively revisioned Indians while simultaneously exalting a touchy-feely frontiersman as a liberal superstar and feather-haired lord of all that he surveys.

Chapter five asks how the frontier myth might account for the fact that the United States is more or less, as Gore Vidal has argued, perpetually at war.[39] Even when not physically engaged *mano a mano* (e.g., Desert Storm, military strikes aimed at Grenada or Libya or Sudan, extra-legal conflict with Nicaragua, not very secret wars waged in El Salvador, Guatemala, and Honduras, governments toppled in Argentina and Chile, invasions of the Dominican Republic and Vietnam—and all this only since 1960), the United States uses the language of armed conflict domestically (e.g., Wars on Terrorism, Drugs, Poverty, and so on). John Wayne's dreadful (yet now campy) *Green Berets* presents probably the last great, unaffected simple frontier western. Like *Full Metal Jacket* and *Red River*, Clint Eastwood's *Heartbreak Ridge* [40] thoughtfully plumbs the frontier myth's homoeroticism as played out in American foreign policy. While it is not especially subtle, it is awkwardly, sometimes grandly, humorous. Like *Dances with Wolves,* Steven Spielberg's riotously unfunny *Raiders of the Lost Ark* tears a page from the mythical yarn. The uncanny parallels between the two flicks ought to disturb anyone unconvinced by George Bush's defense of the war on Iraq. While *Raiders* is unquestionably a terribly exciting film, it also affords Arabs the nineteenth-century Indian treatment à la Manifest Destiny. The myth helps explain why.

Chapter six proceeds from the observation that some of the key phenomena of the 1960s, such as the Vietnam War, Civil Rights, the rise of feminism, and so on, led not to the death of the western (as Pauline Kael claimed), but to a creative resurgence in the ways in which the frontier narrative expresses the ideals and goals of Manifest Destiny in Hollywood. In other words, while the traditional western has nearly disappeared, the frontier western continued and continues to thrive. Ridley Scott's genre-bending *Alien* takes not only the mythical frontier to space but conjures up a female hero as archetypal frontiersman. Mario Van Peebles's *Posse* strikes out as a back frontier western, despite much ambition. Maggie Greenwald's delightful and surprising *The Ballad of Little Joe* turns the myth sideways by grubstaking a female disguised as a frontiersman in the dreamed old west.

Chapter seven asks you to remember the Alamo and then to consider the ways in which Hollywood has remembered it on your behalf. Interestingly the results bear no small resemblance to the war in Iraq: select a weak opponent whose resources you covet, accuse him of all manner of depravity and injustice, provoke a conflict, then kick some ass in the name of righteousness and self-defense. Predictably the results are by turns truly ridiculous—as in John Wayne's *Alamo*.[41] Released in 1960 and directed by the Duke himself, Wayne starred as Davy Crockett in this preposterously preachy version of the great Texas land grab for slavery. The new *Alamo*, released in 2003 and starring Billy Bob Thornton as Davy, fares even more poorly. Awkwardly it aims, and ultimately fails, to revision the tale. Meanwhile, to be fair and consistent one must consider Disney's Davy Crockett films. Okay, so ten million coonskins hats could not have been all wrong, could they? It begs the question, what on earth were they thinking?

Chapter eight explores three recent financially and critically successful films, *About Schmidt*, *25th Hour*, and *Hidalgo*.[42] Each in its own way, these films illustrate the vitality of the frontier myth early in the twenty-first century in Hollywood as well as speak to the depth and breadth of its contemporary reach. *Schmidt* aims for humor by playing ironically against well established frontierisms (e.g., woodmen vs. frontiersmen), whereas Spike Lee's *25th Hour*, his best film since *Do the Right Thing*,[43] considers 9-11 profoundly as a frontier event, while *Hidalgo* revisits *Raiders'* Muslim-bashing territory in a sort of onanistic colonial fantasy.

Chapter Two

The Imperial in Residence: Who's Your Daddy

> So she became, and her process of becoming was like most of ours: she developed a hatred for things that mystified or obstructed her; acquired virtues that were easy to maintain; assigned herself a role in the scheme of things; and harked back to simpler times for gratification.
>
> —Toni Morrison[1]

> ...holding the line, riding the cyclical nature of things are what this country's all about, and thinking otherwise is to drive optimism into retreat, to be paranoid...
>
> —Richard Ford[2]

> His dilemma is that of the dwarf. With his pineal eye he sees his silhouette projected on a screen of incommensurable size. His voice, synchronized to the shadow of a pinhead, intoxicates him. He hears a roar where others hear only a squeak.
>
> —Henry Miller[3]

It starts with a story. It is a tale that you already know pretty well because, in its many guises, it suffuses American popular culture (and thereby the world). It begins with a plucky immigrant. Say, an Irish lad. Imagine Tom Cruise. Having fallen on misfortune not of his own making, one fine (yet typically desperate and latently sanguine) day Tom sets out for the world of opportunity, a land of milk and honey, where nothing more is required of a good lad than honesty, decency, a strong back, a clever mind, and a hearty disdain for the whiff of authority and the stench of things aristocratic. A certain athleticism does not hurt, either. It comes in handy if you know how to use your dukes in America, especially when you wind up on the mythical frontier, that American cultural dreamscape where this narrative unfurls.

What happens to Tom after he arrives? Adversity. Heaps and heaps of it. Then, though, in time—and we can tell by his ebullient integrity, the pluck of an outraged handsome eyebrow, the quick toothy grin thrown blessedly to a despairing child in need of a hero, the determination of a set jaw and steely dancing eyes—the immigrant lad prevails, as he must, cleverly, violently, sexually; and in so doing he becomes Americanized and comes to personify America. In his victory he emerges as the all-American lad. A poster boy for the American Dream.

Incidentally, this story should make you feel good insofar as one expects to identify with a protagonist—not the clunky rendition presented here so much as the timeless, essentialized frontier narrative it houses.

Another version of the tale begins with an easterner, say someone from Boston, Philadelphia, or New York. Imagine Jimmy Stewart, moving west to the frontier. Again, it helps that if by predilection the protagonist, our hero Jimmy, exhibits stubborn resistance to authority, exudes valiance and goodness, is inherently nimble of mind, and exhibits a fierce individualism.

This variation of the yarn, as is the case with Tom's story, should be as predictable to an American audience as a Greek tragedy was in long-ago Athens. On the mythical frontier our hero is put to the test—challenged by Indians, money changers, harlots, overbearing toughs, ruffians, corrupted lawmen, rapacious ranchers, nature herself, whatever you got. Take your pick. You get the picture. These stories are westerns, normally set on the mythical frontier, that special location where American goodness takes root, blossoms, and prevails.

Tumbleweeds and Apple Pie

But what specifically makes them westerns?

Moreover, what exactly is the connection to the mythical frontier?

The answers to these questions overlap. As a discrete genre the western does not hold water very well. For some scholars, critics, and film reviewers the rubric goes consciously undefined, implicitly acting on the idea that a definition of the western may well be unnecessary. After all, doesn't everyone already know what a western is?[4] As it turns out, the answer is an emphatic no. The experts disagree. As the scholar Edward Buscombe asks, "[H]ow do we know which films to look at until we know what a western is?"[5]

How do we know what a western is until we have seen a few?

Perhaps the easiest thing is to close your eyes and imagine, if you will, then, a western. This is a cinch, right? You've got your cowboys, Indians, horses, saloons, fallen women, shootouts, lawmen, and tumbleweed. You may have stagecoaches, barroom brawls, and teepees. The setting may be Arizona's Monument Valley, a Texas border town, or the badlands of Alberta. Because it is always, eponymously, played out in the occidental United States, in a sense the props invite themselves.

These lists are not inclusive, nor do all westerns necessarily involve all or even many of the characteristics noted above. Nevertheless, you know a western when you see one, don't you, as Buscombe suggests? The genre maintains a form of cultural currency of the highest order, does it not? I mean, by the age of five my daughters could identify westerns readily (and eagerly, too, for that matter). So the critics are on to something: we know what westerns are in the sense that one may loosely ascribe a collection of attributes to them. Westerns deal in cultural currency.

However, is this all? Is this what makes a western a western? Some semblance of the above lists?

That is the problem. The western does not bear close scrutiny as a readily explicable genre because all it amounts to apparently are a bunch of conventions that may or may not be found in a given film. That is, must a western include a cowboy? An Indian? A saloon? What to leave in, what to leave out! Where does one draw the line?

More problematic is that for those writers who have sought to explicate the meaning of the term, responses vary considerably from a simple wish list of western symbols—say, cowboys, Indians, whores and such (see above)—to the allegation that the western, because it incorporates many well-traveled characteristics—say, desert scapes, sixguns, and saloons (etc., etc.)—has become so broad a narrative device as to: a) more or less tell any story, and/or, b) defy (or transcend) definition. Obviously, neither of these positions helps us much. In the former case, to argue that the western has become broad enough to tell most any filmic tale amounts simply to a copout, fashioning a definition too sweeping to be of any real value. While the latter is akin to simply throwing up one's hands in despair.

The western clearly cannot tell any tale. It cannot, for example, tell the story of *Titanic*[6] or *Serpico*[7] or *Alice in Wonderland*[8] or *Barney's Great Adventure.*[9] Even worse, though, is the notion that the western escapes definition. At the very least, in this way, not only does it skirt meaning(s) nearly altogether but dangerously repudiates accountability for its signification (which, as we shall see, derives in the first instance from the mythical frontier). However, this does not stop some writers from waxing on about it as if it were nothing, after all, but airy entertainment, harmless mind-candy. The scholar Lee Clark Mitchell responds to Buscombe by affirming that if there is a cowboy and he is out west, then it is a western.[10] But does this really resolve the question? Is it true? What does he mean by "cowboy"? Where and what does he mean by the west? Is the location geographic, metaphoric, or processural?

Some years ago John Cawelti observed that the "Western's capacity to accommodate many different kinds of meaning...have made the formula successful as popular art and entertainment over many generations."[11] Buscombe meanwhile provides a typical list of (what else?) genre attributes. First, he identifies the requisite setting, which may be outdoor—"deserts, mountains, plains, woods"—or indoor—"saloons, jails, courtrooms, ranch houses, hotels, river boats, brothels," appropriate for "those who live an outdoor and/or wandering kind of life."[12] Buscombe's continuing list of characteristics—clothes, weapons, horses, and "miscellaneous physical objects" such as trains with cow catchers—is similarly too capacious to be of much use, especially when he notes that *any* combination of these elements may suffice to define a film as a western.[13] Greater precision, he says, is not necessary because these elements in themselves fashion a "formal structure" that (incredibly) limits the sorts of stories that a western might tell. As if this was not confusing enough, Buscombe's explanation ultimately lapses into a sort of reverse tautology when it goes on to argue that westerns suitably narrate stories about man versus nature, and feature virile, violent men and sexually objectified women—except when they do not.[14]

Academic Andrew Tudor explores this question by leading us back to square one: "From a very early age most of us have built up a picture of a western. We feel we know what a western is when we see one," he writes. "Genre notions are sets of cultural conventions."[15] In this way, genre (and the Western) become hazily undefinable yet intrinsically recognizable—a way of saying, well, come on, you know what I mean, don't you? You know what I'm talking about, right?

The thing of it is, most of us do. Westerns deal in cultural currency.

However, this statement merely takes us back to where we started—we know what dog shit is when we step in it. The question is, why does it smell so bad?

What Makes It a Western?

Writer Stuart Kaminsky offers this take: "A body, group, or category of similar works; this similarity being defined as the sharing of a sufficient number of motifs that we can identify works which properly fall within a particular kind or style of film."[16] This assertion only reaffirms the idea that this genre may serve most any narrative end, providing a story can be told with a selection of the identified genre icons, and within a "repertoire of stock situations," adds Richard Collins.[17] This may well be descriptively accurate, but again, what does it mean? If it is on the mark, you may well ask, as I have, what is the point of genre at all?

The trouble, ultimately, is that the experts too often sketch this genre as form without content, trace a body outline as if it were a stick figure, present characters without evident motivations (as if they might be inferred by the conventions—say, a black hat or "red" skin). Douglas Pye writes that the "best that can be achieved in genre criticism is to identify and analyze tendencies within the tradition and to consider the variations developed by particular films or groups of films."[18] Well, whatever. Try again. Harris M. Lemtz writes that "The genre is populated by cowboys and Indians, wagon trains and settlers, desperados and Texas Rangers, and other figures both historical and fictional."[19] Similarly catch TV star Tom Selleck waxing emptily, as if his celebrity memories might be mistaken for ideas, in the preface to the *Encyclopedia of Westerns*.[20] In summary, study leaves us no better off than where we started. Indeed, I would wager a bet that your average adolescent, if pressed, might come up with analyses as useful as what we get here from historians and film critics on this topic. To be fair, in pop-postmodern terms you might say that many critics find themselves in the unenviable position of attempting to describe a paradigm wholly from a position *inside the box*.

Enter the Myth

There is of course a catch. As it is commonly understood, the western has been conflated and held to be roughly synonymous with (or at least reflect) the mythical American frontier.[21] In other words, what makes a western a western? The frontier myth does, stupid. The western's direct power of signification is delimited by the power and suggestiveness of what it brings to the table—its conventions, and these derive their form and essence from the mythical frontier (though are not entirely bound to it).

The western should not then simultaneously be viewed both as more expansive *and* more restrictive than the mythical frontier narrative. Bigger, possibly, because it can allegedly tell any story (it cannot, and neither can the frontier myth); yet smaller because it educes its power of signification from the mythical frontier (its parent), which is certainly not infinite. This is where study of this genre—the most popular and permissive in film history—breaks down and why a close look at the western *qua* genre is vitally important. The traditional western, a repository of clichés and time-worn conventions to be sure, as a system of meaning amounts, borrowing from Roland Barthes, to a second-order semiological system, one stage removed from its proper birthplace.[22] It is the mythical frontier that provides narrative content (the guts, the motivations) most commonly identified with the western. It is the mythical frontier content that lends the western its cultural probity (as in, say, *Far and Away*), its power of irony (as in *High Noon* or *Unforgiven*[23] or *Blazing Saddles*[24]), its archetypes (e.g., John Wayne so many times or the Marlboro Man or Clint Eastwood or Indiana Jones). The frontier myth is triumphantly American; thus, as a consequence, the frontiersman is also consummately, archetypically heroically American (e.g., John Wayne, Gary Cooper, Clint Eastwood, Han Solo, Rambo, Arnold, and so on).

To sum up, scholars and/or critics have collectively not ably defined the western as a stand-alone genre. However, there is a hitch. It is that the western has at the same time been widely conflated with the mythical tale that narrates the settling of the American historical frontier. The frontier myth, in other words, in the first instance supplied the conventions—that is, the conventions drew their essence from the mythical frontier narrative.

The results are two related sets of films—the frontier western, which relates the mythical narrative in whole or in part, and the traditional western, borrowing and applying conventions that derive their character from mythical conventions but are not hidebound to the narrative. Frontier westerns may or may not employ standard western symbols.

In this way the frontier western is like a set of fraternal twins. Imagine them also, if you will, both as first-born children, adhering conservatively to their roots. Both personify some aspect(s) of the frontier myth. One takes place out west on the mythical frontier of the past (e.g., Texas, Colorado, Wyoming), whereas the other twin may take place anywhere, anytime (e.g., space, the future, Vietnam). They share a connection through the mythical narrative but only one necessarily employs the conventions of the western genre as we have come to know it. *Shane,*[25] for example, fits the former whereas *Alien* fits the latter.

Second, there exists the traditional, non-mythical western, a sort of latter-born, more rebellious child. It employs the symbols of the frontier western as widely as it likes but is not directly beholden to in any way retell an aspect of the mythical frontier tale. *High Noon* is a good example. It says nothing about the mythical frontier as such (but says a lot about McCarthy's America in the early 1950s). Film critics often mistakenly conflate these two variations derived from a common parental theme—the result being, as we've seen, a genre uneasy under the glare of close inspection.

The traditional western, in short, is not synonymous with the myth but merely happens frequently to borrow from its lengthy list of signifiers. It is the frontier western that embodies the frontier myth, providing a mythopoeic narrative and not simply a collection of disconnected conventions. To reamplify Barthes, here lies the basic issue: who would argue that *High Noon* or *The Oxbow Incident*[26] are not westerns? But they are clearly not frontier westerns inasmuch as they make no attempt to relate a mythical frontier story (why should they?). They are once-removed, second-order semiological systems. Further, many films about the mythical frontier bear scant iconographic resemblance to traditional westerns. Here *The Big Lebowski, Starship Troopers,*[27] *African Queen,*[28] or many others, come to mind.

To sum up, from this perspective the traditional western emerges as a collection of genre conventions unstuck from the historical and cultural context from which the conventions themselves emerged. The context, the motor force—that is, the mythical architecture—is plainly missing in the traditional western.

The Timeless Frontier Myth

Since the time of the Puritans *the* central American cultural vision has portrayed the frontier as a special, enchanted place, a veritable cauldron of primal Americanization—in this way the historical frontier begets the mythical frontier.[29] It provides the rosiest reflection of Americana. This is where America peers into the mirror and is delighted to find some guy like John Wayne grinning back, aw shucks, dilly dilly. Today he might be a younger, harder, sexier male than the Duke (as my students are all too quick to point out), but this archetype stems largely from the culturally espied characteristics of the modern-day frontiersman.

However, popular culture, like film critics, has tended to embrace westerns without closely considering the fuller implications of the frontier myth. The talk centers on the conventions, conveniently ignoring their source. A recent collection edited by two well known American cultural studies professors, Peter C. Rollins and John E. O'Connor, promisingly titled, *Hollywood's West, The American Frontier in Film, Television, and History*,[30] provides a good example. Like many Americans, the editors clearly love the genre. Fair enough. But such adoration is not a substitute for analysis. Such ignorance, whatever its source, is precisely what has allowed the mythical frontier's darker recesses to escape detection and examination. This variety of collective amnesia makes mythic sense, too. After all, the western-as-mirror functions to make you feel euphoric, not lousy. It is something you can enjoy, not think about. It champions Americana, not paradigmatic treason. One result is that all challengers will be met, all critique stifled, dismissed as so much leftist junk.[31] Such work belies the assertion that academics have turned their backs on Turner.[32]

This should come as little surprise since the scaled underbelly of the myth speaks directly to issues of American imperial behavior and the Othering of those who do not fit the core American culture model. In the latter case I mean those who do not see (or pine to see) John Wayne in their own reflection—you know, Injuns, liberals, half-breeds, womenfolk, hippies, sidekicks, the gender-challenged, and such like. It should come as less surprise, then, that the western suddenly began to disappear in the late 1960s, precisely the point at which America's colonialist behavior, because of the Vietnam War, and emerging Civil Rights campaigns, pushed its way forcefully into public awareness.

Headwaters of the Myth

That said, the historical frontier has been the place that has given birth to what, according to this cultural vision, amounts to American exceptionalism and sense of superiority.[33] Again, in so doing the historical frontier is supplanted by the mythical frontier. In other words, the experience of a liminal edge of white settlement set against the backdrop of hostile and foreign Other land—espied as savage, uncivilized, pagan, not white, and so on—has been the defining feature in American history, according to the myth. And what makes America culturally unique (that is: better than you) is, then, according to this view, the determining influence of the historical frontier. This idea may be dated to the earliest days of settlement in the United States.

So when historian Frederick Jackson Turner penned that most famous and influential of all American historical essays, "The Significance of the Frontier in American History,"[34] in 1893, he neither invented nor discovered anything original. However, in championing his "frontier thesis," as it came to be known, he articulated a long-standing vision of American cultural "evolution" that had and has seldom been challenged effectively until recently. In fact, it is to Turner that the experts normally turn to explain the western as a mythical frontier vehicle.[35] Trouble is that the Turner thesis's apple-pie do-goodism has generally been bought into hook, line, and sinker by popular culture. Turner's thesis *is* the very embodiment of the frontier myth. Then when Hollywood gets its hands on it, it becomes the frontier western.

However, Turner was wrong. All wrong.

No concerted effort to take Turner to task for a whole series of groundless claims made in the thesis, yet supported and reflected in popular thinking, especially in film for the last century or so, began in earnest until the 1950s[36]; and it was not until the 1980s that such work gained any significant support in the American academic community.[37] Remarkably, though, while scholars have begun in recent years to accept that the thesis/myth as dished up by Turner errs badly on its major points,[38] the myth so capably articulated by Turner remains alive and well in Hollywood.[39]

Today its principal guardian and occasional critic, historian Patricia Nelson Limerick, has likened it to the Pillsbury Doughboy: you can poke it all you want, but it always resumes its cheery, resilient shape.[40] That is both the beauty and folly of myth: an unerring, maddening plasticity. And the mythical frontier remains at work seemingly everywhere in mass culture. Just think about how many advertisements you have seen that are set somewhere in the mythical west—for cigarettes, SUVs, beer, mountain bikes, shampoo, cell phones, pizza, you name it. Presidents invoke it for political purposes.[41]

Turner's thesis argues that the experience of frontier made American culture unique, exceptional, and superior, and that its endemic violence was redemptive and restorative.[42] His analysis worked this way. When immigrants came to America (remember Tom's story?) they tended in large proportion to flock to the outside edge of white settlement, way out west. Once there, the severe and exacting environment had the effect of stripping them bare of retrograde, corrupted European culture and then, if they survived, recasting them.[43] This is fundamental. Turner, alternatively identifying the frontier as a place and a process, referred to what happened then as a "perennial rebirth."[44] "From east to west," he asserted, "we find the record of social evolution."[45] Further:

> The frontier is the line of most rapid and effective Americanization. The wilderness masters the colonist. It finds him a European in dress, industries, tools, modes of travel, and thought. It takes him from the railroad car and puts him in the birch canoe. It strips off the garments of civilization and arrays him in the hunting shirt and the moccasin...In short, at the frontier the environment is at first too strong for the man. He must accept the conditions which it furnishes, or perish...The fact is, that here is a new product that is American.[46]

The personal characteristics required for American-style success—even, survival, on the frontier—honesty, hard-work ethic, rugged individualism, cleverness, Protestant virtue, mental dexterity, physical toughness, and so on—emerged spontaneously as the frontier worked its inexplicable deterministic magic, according to Turner:

> ...to the frontier the American intellect owes its striking characteristics. That coarseness of strength combined with acuteness and inquisitiveness; that practical, inventive turn of mind, quick to find expedients; that masterful grasp of material things, lacking in the artistic but powerful to effect great ends, that restless, nervous energy; that dominant individualism working for good and for evil, and withal that buoyancy and exuberance which comes from freedom—these are traits of the frontier, or traits called out elsewhere because of the frontier.[47]

Once stripped down, the man is rebuilt—again, in and by Edenic nature. What emerges is a neoteric man, a prototypical model American—clever, brave, flexible, adaptable, rugged, democratic, and so on. Successive waves of this process, Turner held, populated the continental United States, fashioning in the wake, a fresh and improved society of democracy-loving rugged individualist democrats (imagine *Hondo*,[48] even the Marlboro Man). It is easy enough to conjure up images here of John Wayne, a younger Clint Eastwood, Eastwood's hero Gary Cooper, even Ronald Reagan (that is, in the minds of his many political admirers), or countless other western stars. But you might also consider *Alien*'s Ripley, Arnold Schwarzenegger's action heroes, Han Solo from *Star Wars*, Walter from *The Big Lebowski*, Rambo from *First Blood*,[49] and, insofar as he is a mediated construction, George W. Bush in the weeks immediately following September 11.

Turner also suggested that the frontier operated as a safety valve for the intense social pressures exerted by late nineteenth-century industrialization in eastern cities (e.g., Jimmy's story). Once on the frontier these newcomers (and we are meant to understand these as white males) are beaten down by the demands exacted by the new, harsh environment. This environment in effect reduces the man to his barest essence: American man (not woman) *cum* Adam. Those who resist this process simply expire. End of story. Those who endure are born again as proto-Americans. What you've got is very much America's secular creation story.

Trouble in Paradise

Even so, there is something wrong with this picture. Nearly everything. To begin with, immigrants did not flock to the frontier. They quite simply could not afford to purchase the land let alone the costs incurred to journey to get to it. Alas, the historical Tom likely ended up working in a factory, lived poorly, and died early.

Second, and following from this, the new settlement in the west was not peopled by immigrants with European cultural baggage, but with Americans proudly carrying cultural torches picked up in the American East. This culture was not stripped away. In fact, the best historical scholarship demonstrates that it was this eastern baggage that gave rise to democracy in the West. It was Jimmy's story: he brought democracy and other WASP trappings with him.[50] In other words, Turner had the process of democratization backwards. In reality, democracy in the west grew from eastern seeds. However, Turner mistakenly writes:

> But the most important effect of the frontier has been in the promotion of democracy...As has been indicated, the frontier is productive of individualism. Complex society is precipitated by the wilderness into a kind of primitive organization based on the family. The tendency is anti-social. It produces antipathy to control. The tax-gatherer is viewed as a representative of oppression...The frontier individualism has from the beginning promoted democracy.[51]

Further, the frontier was not unoccupied. It belonged either to American Indians or, in the greatest land-grab in the history of the Americas (after initial European invasions), to Mexico (i.e., Mexican-American War of 1846–1848). This point is crucial because the key foreign policy undercurrent of the frontier thesis is its concurrent apology for and promotion of American expansionism, imperialism. The thesis sugars Manifest Destiny, the nineteenth-century idea that the United States had a divinely sanctioned mission to expand its continental borders and to assimilate or, if necessary, to crush other cultures in its wake, all draped in a syrupy cloak of academic, intellectual legitimacy. In short, Manifest Destiny and the premise upon which the frontier thesis is based—that is, imagined American exceptionalism and virtuosity—are one and the same.[52]

In circular fashion the myth champions and rationalizes American expansionism as unavoidably good because territorial expansion produces and promotes Americanization, a self-evident good, according to mythical Americana.[53] A Marine general in Stanley Kubrick's *Full Metal Jacket* put it this way while explaining why the United States was involved in the war in Vietnam in the first place: "Inside every gook there is an American trying to get out." U.S. Indian policy in the nineteenth century for decades followed a similar dictum in its efforts to "civilize" the red man: kill the Indian to save the man. This begins with land theft. But it is not really theft, I guess, when God implores you to take it.

Additionally, immigrants and easterners did not flock to the west as a safety valve for the same reason that immigrant workers seldom went west—they had neither the funds to get there nor the skills needed for farming life. Although the land in some cases technically was free, travel to it was not, nor were draft animals, farm equipment, seed, food, housing and such.[54]

Turner erred further by suggesting that once stripped down the white male newcomers would participate in their own rebuilding by adopting the ways of the Indian. But what of the Indian? If the stripping-down process was universal, as Turner claimed, then surely Indians would have been reborn? Indians, however, did not really count. A paragon of Social Darwinist times, Turner avowed that the land was, after all, there for the taking and more or less empty to boot. Paradoxically, Turner argued that the land both was and was not—at once—occupied. Empty of civilized beings is what you are meant to understand.[55]

Here at the darker reaches of the thesis we find a recipe for and rationalization of Manifest Destiny and U.S. imperialism in the twentieth century. Turner has proven to be prophetic in this regard, explicitly countenancing such a future for the United States.[56] His sanctioning of Manifest Destiny has provided a gloss of sorts for aggressive American foreign policy since 1898, the year when the ostensibly anti-imperialist United States went to war with Spain so that it might free (that is, in reality, claim) Cuba, among a variety of islands struggling for autonomy, as its own, and later from incursions in Mexico in 1914 and 1916, incessant meddling in Central America (including military occupations), forays into Chile and Brazil, all the way to the recent unconstitutional invasion of Panama to capture and incarcerate Panama's head of state (and former CIA asset) Manuel Noriega, a media-fashioned bad guy if ever there was one.[57] Probably the seminal event in American imperialism and frontier delusionism of the twentieth century, though, came with the failed U.S. involvement in the Vietnam War.

Here is what the mythical logic of Manifest Destiny reasons. Expansion—territorial, economic, and Christian—is desirable and necessary because it had created and creates, had promoted and promotes a better (that is, mainstream WASPY American) culture. Others would do well to be exposed to or taught by it (e.g., Indians, Mexicans, Vietnamese, Iraqis). Is this not at least in part George Bush's justification for the war in Iraq? Further territorial growth (say, war vs. Mexico of 1846–1848) or economic expansion (doing the basic business of capitalism) or simple interference in the affairs of other nations (say, Cuba in the 1910s or Honduras in the 1980s) was by definition, then, ideal because it was being conducted by superior beings acting out a process of divinely sustained self-improvement.

Big Little Man

You might wonder, though, why would the stripping down not have engendered anarchy rather than democracy (a question *Full Metal Jacket* explores)? Here the key points to remember are that Turner believed that Indians and Mexicans were inferior to whites and that the thesis therefore not surprisingly provided a mellifluous prescription for imperialism.[58] Insofar as the frontier thesis proclaimed universality it really only was meant to apply to whites of European descent.

Culturally, what Turner postulated had long been standard thinking in the United States (and still is, if film and political behavior is any barometer). That is why the thesis was and remains popular, plausible, and durable. Turner's powerfully persuasive version of events sounds very much like what Americans had long been reading about themselves in the novels of James Fenimore Cooper, written decades before Turner, or later in the westerns of John Ford, or still later in space adventure films such as *Apollo 13*.[59]

Turner's essay is especially useful because it lays out the myth so clearly and instructively. Moreover, that Turner was a university professor gave his enunciation of the well-traveled myth enhanced credibility. Scholars have been reacting to it for more than 100 years; and despite the fact that nothing from Turner's essay has borne itself out empirically, the myth survives in Hollywood and popular culture (and the Bush White House). In short, as verifiable history it is wrong. As cultural history, on the other hand, it is nearly perfectly on the mark. Culturally, the Turner essay expressed what scholar Eldon Kenworthy has aptly called America's "foundation myth,"[60] myth serving as fusion, to quote Henry Nash Smith, of a "concept and emotion into an image."[61] Myths serve as the glue that binds a society together.[62] Here is how a recent article in *Newsweek* discussing oil development in Alaska put it:

> America's founding myths are largely about taming wild places. The frontier shaped the American character even as we shaped it, moving from the Allegheny Mountains to the Mississippi, and onward to the Missouri, the Rocky Mountains and the Pacific. But the frontier is all but gone now [in 2001], and what remains occupies a unique place in the American psyche.[63]

Ira Progoff suggests that myth amounts to an animate, waking dream.[64] You might say that the frontier myth is the American Dream through a glass darkly.

The Myth and the Western

The conflation of the frontier myth with the western genre has created two basic problems. First, for the purposes of analysis frontier westerns have unfortunately tended to be subsumed by the more generic traditional western. This grants the latter, where the signifiers have become unstuck from their source, as critics have correctly yet shortsightedly noted, a wide license for creativity—but at the expense of critical and/or historical accountability. In fact, it effectively serves to cloak imperialism. Consequently, the western has served as a slippery, guileless vehicle for promoting and justifying colonialism, mostly because it so capably sublimates and projects the American historical experience of frontier as its own opposite in much the same manner that President George W. Bush surely was not consciously framing mythic motifs when he struck imperial poses in the days immediately after the terrorist attack on the WTC in New York City (that is, the western's "wanted: dead-or-alive," the binary of "you're with us or with the terrorists," a Manifest-Destiny-esque termed "Crusade").

Second, there are those hard to decipher frontier westerns, which are frequently ignored and almost always misunderstood by film critics. For example, *Full Metal Jacket* has been all too predictably lumped in by critics as just another Vietnam War flick, albeit an excellent one, when it is best viewed as a frontier western, with director Stanley Kubrick likening the western and its mythopoeic associations to homo-imperialistic masturbation. That said, do not expect Ebert and Roeper to have picked up on the transparency of how this theme frequently dominates the picture. (It is not that they are lousy critics but that they operate within fairly narrow discursive limitations established by the dictates of American popular culture.) Likewise, *The Big Lebowski*, tossed dismissively by critics upon the heap of the quirky and (un)recognizably madcap, bristles unequivocally as a frontier western, a lampoon of the 1989 Gulf War in which imperialism finds its domestic counterpart in 10-pin bowling.

Another way to think about the Turner thesis/frontier myth is to invert the imagined American characteristics that the frontier experience allegedly gives rise to. In this way, rugged individualism becomes childlike dependency, honesty becomes deviousness, the work ethic becomes sheer laziness, Protestant becomes pagan (or Roman Catholic), white becomes un-white (pick a color—red, brown, black, yellow; you know, John Wayne becomes an Indian or a lesbian or a commie). We are talking here obviously of the "Other," the projected binary inversion of what mainstream Americana, however unrealistically, treasures about itself. Reading Turner this way suggests that the existence of the Other justifies, while at the same time the stereotyped actions of the Other invites, American expansionism. Approached this way colonialism has become reworked as a polite response to an invitation to colonize. In short, white American Anglo-Saxon colonialism becomes a necessary thing, even a duty, an American white man's burden.

Imperial Delusions: A Summary

At one extreme in traditional westerns, in the absence of the mythical frontier narrative, you simply have free floating symbols, which at best cast shadows of the frontier myth. However, as a second-order semiological system this traditional western form has redoubtable powers. In some of these cases, to be sure, the west is just the west. But in many cases not. There is no magic formula. Every film should be assessed based on its own particular merits.

Dissociated from their mythic source, these genre conventions of the traditional western, especially because they are allowed frequently to stand in for the genre as a whole, offer the form a wide latitude for application, as noted, while inscrutably absolving the genre of the sins of the promotion of the many aspects of Manifest Destiny (as will be argued in some detail throughout this book). In this way, nearly anything goes because of the genre's popular divorce from historical connectedness. On the other hand, link them—that is, connect the traditional western to the frontier myth—and you end up with full-blown colonialism: the frontier western. Full frontal imperial hegemony, though, has been unpopular since at least the 1960s (though it has resurfaced in the Bush White House), hence the virtual disappearance of the traditional western (not the frontier western) from popular radar. Americans, it would seem, prefer the illusion that the results of Manifest Destiny really are in the best interests of those upon whom it is forced (another theme of Kubrick's *Full Metal Jacket*). Nobody likes bullies, after all. (And, as an aside, what the hell kind of egg-headed commie notion is hegemony anyway?)

In a country that through the mid-1990s had established a two-century legacy of continental imperialism (versus indigenous peoples and blacks and Mexico/ans) and neo-colonialism (interventions in Mexico, Guatemala, the Dominican Republic, Honduras, Vietnam, El Salvador, Afghanistan, Iraq, and so on), it is not hard to imagine why the frontier western, which sublimates and sugars imperialism by standing it on its head and proclaiming it to be the opposite of what it actually is, has endured, if unevenly, in recent years. Empirical reality, like academically trained historians, plainly cannot compete. Put simply, films about cowboys and Indians have inebriately displaced the moral ambivalence of empire, which is what the mythical narrative is all about. Cowboys and Indians may be less popular than they once were but the frontiersman soldiers on as do Indians, recast as Muslims, blacks, aliens, Others, whatever.

When the traditional western is divorced from the mythical frontier it exists liminally, in the way of quicksand. You bog down. You cannot get through it. You are not supposed to get through it. In effect, it dismantles the empirical frontier and its "legacy of conquest"[65] in favor of the mythical frontier—where imperialism is inverted as the sweet land of John Wayne and the Marlboro Man.

Film critics are a lot like Sunday morning talk show regulars—self-important, yes, but also gassily ignorant on many of the very issues upon which they are called to comment. Their particular lack of knowledge about American cultural history is especially unsettling. So let's get serious. The mythical frontier endures, comfortably fatted, feted, fetid. The frontier western lives, even thrives, and sometimes lurks, and occasionally skulks all over Hollywood. Make no mistake, though, the mythical frontier western is all about conquest and control.

Forked Paths

How does one explain the divergence between the traditional western and the frontier western, especially why has the former overwhelmed the latter? On one hand, we are taught *how* to see the western in mythical terms. This is the most basic Americana. (By the way, if it did not work for you, you are not normal.) Additionally, the ground between them sometimes is slippery, ambiguous and unpredictable. Plus, something nearly unthinkable inhabits the frontier western, like in one of those dreams that are so real that they rouse you to fright. The frontier western performs the magic of psychological projection. Uneasily yet with certainty the frontier western cuts too close to home, its mirror reveals more than American core culture can bear to see in itself.

Americana has loved westerns because there the Other lurks, tucked comfortably and safely away in its place at the same time as reminding us how wonderful it is not to be like them. Just circle the wagons, dude! Moreover, the myth frames aggressive, expansionist American-style capitalism in such a way as to suggest liberation, edification, common sense, and sex appeal. So come on! The business of

America is business. Just relax, have a cocktail, watch a football game, buy an SUV, go shopping, pop a Tylenol.

The implications of the frontier western say much, too much, and are resisted, to borrow from Adorno and Horkheimer, because they "actually confirm…that the real point will never be reached, that the diner must be satisfied with the menu."[66] The western has been that menu.

Let's eat.

Chapter Three

The Empire's New Clothes: Getting Naked

> A way of life is the combination of patterns of thought and action that, as it becomes habitual and institutionalized, defines the thrust and character of a culture and society.
>
> —William Appleman Williams[1]

> To the frontier the American intellect owes its striking characteristics.
>
> —Frederick Jackson Turner[2]

> I wanted to see exotic Vietnam, the jewel of Southeast Asia. I wanted to meet interesting and stimulating people of an ancient culture and kill them.
>
> —Private Joker, *Full Metal Jacket*[3]

The basic trouble with Marxism, if we are to believe popular culture, and what is also sometimes referred to as vulgar Marxism by academics, is that it appears to reduce most human social behavior to material conditioning. This (still) radical view seems to heap together all identifiably objectionable behavior and then claims that the determining influence of the material conditions of one's life (that is, capitalism) made it that way. In short, your day-to-day existence and even the consciousness that guides it are, necessarily, products of the conditioning effects of exposure to one's day-to-day reality. In other words, you are what you do.

Few outside academia take this seriously. In fact, not even those inside academia who might be considered to be soft on Marxism would accept such a simplistic reading of the canon. In truth Marxism, for better or worse, has morphed into a wide variety of more subtle and sophisticated colors. One way or another, so pervasive have its influences been that it has touched everything from the study of behavioral psychology to the environmental movement to rock and roll to the corporate theology employed by the founders of Ben and Jerry's ice cream.

Like for Curly (played with serpentine jocularity by Jack Palance), who in the movie *City Slickers*[4] claimed that the meaning of life was, "one thing, just one thing," popular Marxism has been fairly tarred with oversimplifying reality. From Marx to Freud to Kafka to Chaplin, this has been one of the classic underpinnings of modernism, hanging it all up on the idea of one thing. Just one thing.

The world is obviously more variegated, but not on the mythical frontier, another spot where determinism rules, and not in Hollywood, which celebrates simple notions and easy commercial formulas. This makes for a nearly perfect marriage.

Turner's frontier thesis is every bit as reductionist as popular Marxism, condensing, for example, its imaginary model American to a series of impossibly and grossly unrealistic archetypal characteristics. To put it in contextual perspective, while no right-thinking person would reasonably allege that *all* American business owners are capitalist pigs (that is, that they have been conditioned to be so by market forces), incredibly Hollywood and its audiences have long heartily embraced the mythical frontiersman, that hunky creature fashioned on and by the American dreamscape (imagine the Marlboro Man or Dirty Harry or Rambo or Indiana Jones). My point is not to query why one set of conditioning fashions alleged capitalist devils and proletarian dupes and false consciousness and the like, while another spews out surreal, non-quiche eating men in the mold of the cinematic John Wayne or the mythical frontiersman of American lore. Instead, I want modestly to contend that such an environmentally determined character—the frontiersman—is as alive and well in contemporary Americana as ever it was. And why not? After all, the frontier myth continues—just think about the meta-narrative inherent in the U.S. reaction, especially from the White House, to September 11—to serve as America's foundation story. Perpetual war effectively guarantees perennial rebirth. In this way, in any case, one might argue that Americana remains stubbornly modern in an increasingly postmodern world.

However, let me add a caution before going further. It is all too easy to conclude that the results of the supposed conditioning effects of the mythical frontier are in fact patently absurd and have no basis in reality. For the most part they do not, I agree (and so does a generation of sound scholarship). However, the imagery (what some might call the imaginary) persists in American film and, in addition, it is singularly *not* devoid of meaning. It should not be mistaken purely for empty entertainment. While it sometimes offers nothing more than noxious sensory candy (I mean, did anybody ever take *Rambo* seriously?), both American domestic practices and foreign policies are rife with the empirically nonsensical but culturally essential mythical frontier. In other words, *Rambo* was thoroughly ridiculous at an empirical (and artistic) level but comforting, even reassuring, at a mythical level, as evidenced not only by its embrace of the myth but by its wide popularity, which inspired several additional equally vapid serial installments.

Like Tarzan, Lord of the Apes and King of the Jungle, the frontiersman archetype is born and comes of age on the untamed frontier.[5] The mythical frontier strips him down, reduces him to his mythical human essence, then refashions him as a prototypical democratic individualist. Baby Lord Greystoke becomes Tarzan, Joe Redneck becomes Rambo, Clark Kent becomes Superman, via the frontier Tom the Irish lad becomes Tom the model American cock. Real-life fantasies, in short, fuse with and stand in for cultural realities.

As noted earlier, and because it is worth repeating, Turner famously opined that:

> ...to the frontier the American intellect owes its striking characteristics. That coarseness of strength combined with acuteness and inquisitiveness; that practical, inventive turn of mind, quick to find expedients; that masterful grasp of material things, lacking in the artistic but powerful to effect great ends, that restless, nervous energy; that dominant individualism working for good and for evil, and withal that buoyancy and exuberance which comes from freedom—these are traits of the frontier, or traits called out elsewhere because of the frontier.[6]

Hollywood has traditionally shaded this creature as extraordinary, personifying the best of what Americana desires to see when it peers into the looking glass. In other words, physical reality takes a backseat to the imaginary. This guy can run faster, jump higher, shoot straighter, love more earnestly, be joined at the hip with truth and Protestant virtue. He can kick colored ass all day long and fuck hard all night long.

Getting Naked

The process of fabricating this character begins with the stripping down. It may take as many forms as creativity may allow. Further, no film that I know of is devoted entirely to the process. For example, while *Full Metal Jacket* comes about as close as any to exploring this idea in full splendor, the film also has a lot of other things going on, only some of which connect back to the mythical narrative.

Further, the process is often understated in Hollywood, as in *Far and Away* (starring Tom the Irish immigrant lad, played appropriately enough by Tom Cruise). Here, by nature Tom seems primed for transformation, a necessary setup in most stories; besides, a smoldering love story (Tom and Nicole Kidman) grips the audience. Is it not possibly nothing more than just a steamy and predictable love story set on the historical frontier? (No.) Similarly, in 1971's *Man in the Wilderness* a bone-hardened, vengeful, self-made trapper/scout (played more or less wordlessly by Richard Harris) is unmade by an encounter with nature, a grizzly bear, and left to die. Even so, against all odds he survives. In so doing, he is reborn on the mythical frontier only to learn the value of forgiveness and the palliative currency of love (while remaining hard and self-made), all set against the backdrop of the fever of the (real-time) Vietnam War.

I want to stress that I aim not to measure a film by how closely it adheres to Turner's thesis, but ask whether it is a frontier western in the first case and, if so, if and in what ways it speaks to the issues of American colonialism. In this regard think of Turner's essay as the Holy Bible of the frontier hallucination, not literally, empirically accurate as such, yet culturally dead-on.

The World Is a Stage

Like the Bible, the myth may be studied discretely in any of its constituent parts. In the case of *Far and Away*, for example, the imperial project appears relatively benign at first glance, a counterpoint to Kubrick's *Jacket*. *Hondo*, eponymously played by an almost youthful John Wayne, on the other hand, presents a classic case of the frontiersman who has slipped well beyond the pale of civilization but lingers near its margins, presenting a theme of stages of development common also in films such as *Shane*, *The Man Who Shot Liberty Valance*, and, again, *Full Metal Jacket*.

Stages of development correspond to the various characters fashioned by the mythical frontier's magical stripping and subsequent rebuilding processes—assorted shadings of the all-American boy upon whom the frontier has worked its business, in reverse order typically represented as some variety of gunfighter (often signifying the area beyond the frontier, savagery) or rancher (and here all bets are off, from rancher as unredeemed in, say, *Shane*, or our lovable, if slightly gruff, hero as in *Open Range*[7]) or farmer (living in a cleansed state near or possibly on the frontier, fully capable, when roused, of embracing just, redemptive violence—but only once a measure of stripping down has occurred).

In many cases, however, as audience we are simply presented with a given stage of development as a film begins (e.g., Shane rides into town an already fully developed gunslinger, but we soon discover that his stage of development is dying off, moribund, a point the film stresses again and again; Shane himself even says so). Then there is the man who was stripped but never delivered (normally and morally the bad guy, in other words, for example, take the character of Liberty Valance). Then there is the man who needs transformation to occur in the course of the narrative development (see Jimmy Stewart, the easterner who embraces mythical values and in so doing becomes Americanized through just and necessary violence in *The Man Who Shot Liberty Valance*).

The three films explored here are all devoted in important ways to the process of stripping down and the ways in which this quality of mythical Americanization may take place.

Striptease

Imagine a western, and director Stanley Kubrick's name is not likely to come to mind. Not one of his films has been identified as such.[8] However, Kubrick's penultimate work, 1987's *Full Metal Jacket*, is rife with western conventions—Americans in uniform, noble savages and debased savages, whores, phallic weaponry, a character named Cowboy (if not an actual cowboy), verbal invocations of John Wayne, General George Armstrong Custer, Indians, and so on. However, according to critics, *Jacket* belongs alongside *Platoon, The Deer Hunter,*[9] and *Apocalypse Now*[10]—Vietnam War flicks[11]—none of which have been termed westerns.[12] Yet *Jacket* exhibits not only many traditional western and mythic signifiers but, equally important, it embodies key elements of that most fundamental of frontier westerns—the myth itself.[13] *Jacket* delivers, in short, a provocative meditation on the cultural yarn that derives from America's creation story,[14] albeit posed from Kubrick's point of view. In fact, in *Jacket* Kubrick inverts key aspects of the frontier myth to drive home one of the common, misanthropic themes of his *oeuvre*—the contemptible corruptibility of the human soul.[15]

The film bifurcates the experiences of Marine Private "Joker" (played by Matthew Modine) through boot camp on Parris Island and, then, "in the shit" in Vietnam. The first of two acts earned high marks from commentators, even from those who expressed disappointment with the remainder of the work.[16] Writing in the *New Yorker,* Pauline Kael asserted that "after the first part reaches climax, the movie becomes dispersed, as if it had no story. It never regains its forward drive."[17] Echoing this idea, Roger Ebert called it "strangely shapeless."[18]

Ebert also complained that *Jacket* lacked "the awesome reality of *Platoon, Apocalypse Now* and *The Deer Hunter.*"[19] Others, including me, find Ebert's view here shallow and unconvincing. For example, Robert Castle and Stephen Donatelli wrote that "Kubrick approaches his audience with too much candor and maturity to pretend that a representation of the soldiers' experience is possible. It is not."[20] The dreamed frontier, as it has been portrayed in American literature and film, too, is also not "realistic" but that does not mean that it, or the way *Jacket* deals with it, is not culturally—even, at times, disturbingly—real.[21] Mario Falsetto claims that "The macho, bullying and humiliating behavior of the Marines has never been depicted with such precision."[22]

Kubrick takes the thesis to task over three basic issues: 1) the alleged alchemic cauldron of masculine Americanization; 2) the process of forging mythical characteristics; and, 3) the frontier *qua* Eden. Like Turner, Kubrick approaches these themes as interrelated, yet discrete enough (for the purposes of analysis) to weigh more heavily at certain points. Both stylists also make ready use of metaphor.

Social Death and American Rebirth

The pith of the Turner thesis holds that the frontier served as the laboratory of effective Americanization. Turner takes the liminal, ever-shifting geographic edge of anglo-American settlement and recasts it, as noted, as "the meeting point between savagery and civilization" (though he also identifies land beyond white settlement as essentially empty; can land by itself be savage?).[23] However, the frontier proved to be especially harsh, withering, even lethal for those who refused to bend to its demands. The survivors, on the other hand, experienced the benefits of a divine transformation and so on, said Turner. The frontier stripped immigrants (i.e., white males) of their cultural (i.e., corrupted eastern) baggage and then it rebuilt them as quintessential, prototypical Americans, Turner asserted.

Kubrick takes up this central mythical theme of stripping down and rebirth both during the boot camp sequences as well as while in-country, the two halves that cleave the flick. The boot camp sequence seemingly occurs as an isolated, out of context application of Turner—that is, there is no geographical frontier here. Instead we are greeted in the first instance with would-be Marines, to begin with, being shorn, and then in their barracks, standing at attention in uniformed underwear. This might immediately strike one as suggesting that stripping down (literally, they've taken their clothes off) does not produce individuals, but, rather, fashions likeness and conformity[24]—and that the process accelerates as it becomes more successful (i.e., being shorn: from hair to hairless, a common-enough biblical signifier of masculinity; and, from clothed to nearer nakedness in their underwear). Kubrick reinforces this point in an exquisite scene where the camera rotates slowly round and round the bunkhouse following the delightfully vulgar drill sergeant (dialectically and provocatively named Hartman and played brilliantly by Lee Ermey), suggesting a ritual, circular monotony to the process. Hartman declares disingenuously, "The Marine Corps does not want robots...The Marine Corps wants to build indestructible men." However, you cannot have it both ways. The Marine Corps either really does want robots or does not know the difference between robots and men.

Sgt Hartman (Lee Ermey) berates Private Pyle (Vincent D'Onofrio) in a scene from *Full Metal Jacket*.

Hartman endeavors to trim the cultural baggage from the new recruits as so much flab, the prospective apostles of the goodness of the American word. Hartman informs them that "if you survive...you will be a minister of death praying for war." To be sure, this first act systematically strips the young men down.

Turner also insisted that the process created the American nation, generated "the American people" as we know them from politicians' lips today. To suggest that Kubrick scoffs at the simplicity of such a notion would be to severely understate his position. Kubrick focuses here on one Private "Gomer Pyle," a baby-faced, flaccid, undisciplined recruit (played by Vincent D'Onofrio) who seems incapable of doing anything to Hartman's satisfaction. Still, despite humiliation heaped upon insult, Pyle succeeds—that is, he becomes stripped down. Turns out that he has a gift with a gun.

So Drill Inspector Hartman thereby appears to carry the day, after all. His abusive treatment of Pyle ultimately uncovers Pyle's natural gift: marksmanship with a rifle (or, inverted rifle: "the only pussy you people are going to get," Hartman refers to the weapon). Hartman's words reinforce the sexual connotation when he congratulates Pyle homoerotically on his success, "You are definitely born again hard." Though Pyle strips/breaks down, he does not rebuild, as Turner would have it; no, Kubrick's vision is darker, yet more sensible. Once stripped of cultural baggage, social conditioning, Pyle has become what Kubrick suggests that we all are beneath our social masks—imperfect, dark-hatted menacing replicas of Natty Bumppo or John Wayne, brutish, nasty beasts. In other words, you take culture away from a human being and what you are left with is an animal, driven and directed by base instinct. Whereas Turner's frontier fashions Marlboro Men and characters like Hondo, Kubrick reinterprets the process to birth a dehumanized killer. And kill he does, in a murder-suicide in the latrine that remains a shocking bit of theater no matter how many times you see it.

Turner finds enchantment in being stripped down. Life becomes free, uncluttered, bursting with possibility. Kubrick concludes, in contraposition, that stripping down leads not to purity of spirit but to psychopathology. In this way, then, Pyle, stripped of culture (intimacy, love, nurturing) becomes a killer, shooting both the Drill Instructor and himself. A primordial beast lies beneath our socialization, Kubrick stresses, not warm and fuzzy Americana. Unlike Turner, Kubrick posits culture as our necessary friend.

Moreover, whereas Turner identifies the process as forging real men, Kubrick presents it as basically, fetishistically homosexual (which may, in turn, reflect a subtle homophobia on Kubrick's part). This theme is so often reinforced in the first act of the film that it provides an erotic cadence to the early scenes. Hartman threatens to "fuck them up," "fuck them" in various ways, accuses them of homosexuality, commands that "you will give your rifle a girl's name because this is the only pussy you are going to get" (as if rifles stand in for vaginas), proclaims that "your days" of heterosexuality are over and "you will be faithful" to the transformation because "your ass belongs to the Marine Corps." Even God, after all, "had a hard on for Marines." In short, Kubrick takes the position that sexuality is socially constructed. Stripping it away for the purposes of training soldiers (phallus warfare?), in effect, crossing several frontiers, not just emasculates but replaces it with homosexualized killers. No surprise, then, that such creatures find themselves constantly "in the shit," a crude reference to male homosexuality.

The Garden and Hellfire

The frontier myth should be seen as an apology for American expansionism and aggressiveness.[25] It glorifies Manifest Destiny and candies American expansionism, a historical process that, from a more sober light, saw the United States colonize Indian nations and engage in a war of unmitigated aggression toward Mexico in 1846–1848, 1914, and 1916, war with Spain in 1898, intervene in Honduras in 1907, 1911, 1924, occupy Nicaragua 1912–1933, wrestle Panama from Colombia in 1903, occupy the Dominican Republic, 1915–1934, maintain Cuba as a dependency from 1898 through 1959, meddle in Brazil in the 1960s, Chile in the 1970s, and on and on. At the close of his seminal essay, unwittingly yet accurately Turner prophesied:

> He would be a rash prophet who should assert that the expansive character of American life has now entirely ceased [in 1893]. Movement has been its dominant fact, and, unless its training has no effect on a people the American energy will continually demand a wider field for its exercise.[26]

On the other hand, of course, to the extent that one buys into the frontier thesis, expansion, because it Americanized the West, was righteous.[27] Thus, naturally, then, American empire building, defined by the *Oxford American Dictionary* as "the process of deliberately acquiring extra territory or authority," also was good.[28] This process of expansionism is what William Appleman Williams means when he speaks of America's "way of life."[29] In political terms, Noam Chomsky sums it up this way: "The first principle of U.S. foreign policy...is to ensure a favorable global environment for U.S.-based industry, commerce, agribusiness and finance."[30]

The United States has always been expansionist, and the Turner thesis serves as a recipe and a justification for it. American history has, first, been one of territorial increase and, second, (as if joined at the hip) of economic expansion. This dynamic reflects nothing more than sound business practice, from a capitalist (say, Hamiltonian) position. Moreover for the nationalist (Jeffersonian) position, growth is good because America is by nature good.[31]

All foreign policies, including one premised on Manifest Destiny, contain these three elements: self-interest (what is in it for me?), pragmatism (will it work?), and morality (is it the right thing to do?). While Manifest Destiny may not in itself be pragmatic (for example, you might miscalculate and lose, as was the case in Vietnam), in another sense it has lent to the United States constancy in behaviors. For example, that Vietnam War era desire to "win their hearts and minds" has long been a tenet of justifying pacification efforts. Has it ever worked? Anywhere? The answer is no. I mean, there is not one example in American history where this has succeeded; yet there are many where it went disastrously wrong—with American Indians, Cuba, Guatemala, Haiti, Vietnam, Iran, and, in all likelihood, Iraq, and so on. The results are always similar—brown-skinned people do not appreciate being warred upon, and so they fight back. They fight back because the expected results (from the American side) are falsely premised upon the idea that a mythically grounded frontier foreign policy will deliver the goods of Americanization just as surely as it did for Americans themselves. Hoever, because this sequence of events never happened for America, as the historical literature has shown clearly, it should come as no surprise that it will not work elsewhere.

Likewise, a mythically driven foreign policy conflates self-interest with morality, generally denying the notion that America stands to gain directly in favor of the assertion that it is for the good of the colonized. In this way naked aggression (for example, the two centuries of imperial warfare directed at America's indigenous population or the war in Iraq)—which cannot be sanctioned as such (that is, we want their land or we want their oil)—is reframed mythically. In this way, U.S. expansionism is cast as beneficial for, say, Indians or Iraqis; even going so far as to suggest that the sensible among them desire it.

The chief reason that mainstream American culture persists, even in the new millennium, in *not* espying American international behavior as frequently imperialist is that the United States was born mythically on the frontier and additionally as a violent expression of anti-imperialism in its own revolutionary war with Britain. It has identified itself throughout its history as doggedly, righteously opposed to empire-building and, correspondingly, supportive of national self-autonomy—except, notably, in the case of the American Confederacy and the various other imperial wars already noted.

Anti-imperialists do not, by definition, engage in imperialism. End of story. Besides, the United States was not really engaged in imperialism—which requires and promotes corruption and vice, in the mythical view—but, rather, in the Americanization of, first, the frontier, which, as Turner would have it, begets and reflects an entirely benign and uplifting process. Turnerian syrup ("To the frontier the American intellect owes its striking characteristics") represents a stridently positive affirmation of Americana. Second, those savages living/not living on the frontier might benefit (or be destroyed, if necessary) by exposure to Americana.

Thus America's role as an international aggressor becomes indispensable, just, and hearty—irrespective of the cold war that compounded American excuses for the intervention in Vietnam. It was *indispensable* because America, by definition, expands. It always has; and the growth of capitalism is (consequently) self-evidently virtuous. It was *just* because, as the myth explains, America breeds democracy—another self-evident rationalization because American-style democracy (George Bush's tainted victories notwithstanding) is the best. Finally, the imperial increase is *hearty* because it promotes the spread of Americana, chirps Turner. The Vietnam War, of course, was all frontier: full of colored savages, amok with pagans, glistening with economic opportunity, portending strategic importance. Because, by definition America always expands to new frontiers, intervention in Vietnam was culturally irresistible.

Frontiers Without Borders

Kubrick's frontier is not empty, devoid of human life like Turner's, but it is instead occupied precisely like Turner's—filled largely with faceless, expendable savages. The only Vietnamese characters depicted in *Jacket* are whores, pimps, snipers, and probable Vietcong (used for target practice from a chopper). However, Turner suggested that the process of stripping and reconstructing was universal. Should Vietnam not have been processed in this way? Yet Turner's process apparently did not work for Indians, who simultaneously both were ("arrays him in the hunting shirt and the moccasin...and the birch canoe") and were not present ("the existence of an area of free land") on Turner's frontier. Kubrick's bitter commentary, conflating and reflecting Turner's observation about the frontier as a "meeting point between savagery and civilization" with the stripping down/rebuilding process, may be witnessed at various places "in the shit." As a Marine colonel explains to the ambivalent narrator-protagonist, Private Joker, "Inside every gook there is an American trying to get out."

For his own part Joker, too, suffers a variety of processural transformation. Surviving the tour in-country with a peace sign button pinned over his heart and the words "Born to Kill" etched on his helmet, explained away to that same Marine colonel as "the Jungian thing, sir," (and waxing briefly about the "duality of man") Joker comes face to face with near-death at the hands of a sniper who killed three of his comrades. As the ragged remainder of the troop stand over her once she has been shot but not eradicated, she does something the viewer does not expect—she prays. Then she begs to be shot.

Joker finally pulls the trigger, leaving the audience to wonder whether it was done simply in bestial anger (i.e., he is now stripped to the level of an animal) or out of mercy. Kubrick's lighting suggests an answer: as the camera returns for an upper-body shot of Joker after he offs the sniper, a shadow cast from his head obscures the peace button, again reifying the notion that once stripped down we're essentially beasts, raw animals. It makes perfect sense, then, at this point that command of the unit has passed to the character Animal Mother. In fact, the devolution of command speaks directly to the frontier myth.

In Turner's story, after the stripping down concluded the American was rebuilt through a series of stages: frontiersman (representing nearer animalism), rancher (signified by the cowboy), farmer (getting closer to home), American urbanite (reflecting superior organization, purified civilization). However, rather than having the frontier resprouted from frontiersman through cowboy through to democratic city-dweller, Kubrick's frontier literally kills the chain of command in reverse order: the lieutenant (civilization) falls first, followed by Joker's buddy Cowboy (but only after Animal Mother had effectively usurped his command), and then to Animal Mother. Thus, we return to first principles in the second act of *Jacket*, in a sense, where we left Act One: civilization not so much peeled off as scraped painfully, violently away. To reinforce the point, Kubrick equates his reordering with masculinity: Animal Mother gets to have first sex with the prostitute, Animal Mother explains that the war is about "poontang," Animal mother packs the biggest phallus-weapon, hung beneath matching, strapping testicles (hand grenades) on his chest and over his heart.

Although we never see it, Animal Mother is unlikely to be rebuilt à la Turner. As the soldiers stand and pay homage to their fallen comrades after dispensing with the sniper, Joker's buddy Rafterman notes, "At least they died for a good cause."

Animal Mother: "What cause was that?"

Rafterman: "Freedom?"

Animal Mother: "Flush out your head gear, new guy. You think we waste Gooks for freedom? This is a slaughter. If I'm gonna get my balls blown off for a war, my word is poontang."

You Want Custard?

Perhaps Kubrick's most obvious invocation of anti-Turner sentiment comes from a scene where the remnants of the troop are filmed by a television news crew, each character commenting quickly as the camera pans by. Joker's reflexive ambiguity has him query, "Is that you John Wayne?" Then, as the camera rolls horizontally, before the scene ends we hear in turn from different characters:

"I'll be General Custer."

"Who'll be the Indians?"

"Hey, we'll let the Gooks be the Indians."

George Armstrong Custer, of course, was a noted American Indian killer (but not the first; Andrew Jackson used similar notoriety to ride himself to the presidency in 1828) whose enduring hubris eventually cost him his life. He is nothing if not the most perfect enduring symbol of Manifest Destiny.

Yet *Jacket* provides more than a simple excoriation of Manifest Destiny. Kubrick stresses the socially constructed nature of gender, inasmuch as American masculinity allegedly has been engendered by the experience of frontier. Even so, it is to social construction that we owe our imperfect civilization. The key, oddly, both for Turner and for Kubrick seems to be balance—"the Jungian thing, sir," (Joker's words) for Kubrick, whereas for Turner the frontiersman walks that line, as in the composite John Wayne/Jimmy Stewart character fashioned in John Ford's *The Man Who Shot Liberty Valance* (1962). The difference is that Kubrick is neither a nationalistic booster nor an imperialist. Turner was both. Kubrick plays sober pessimism to Turner's punch-drunk, aggressive optimism. No wonder that Joker emerges self-described as "unafraid," marching ever forward to the relentlessly glib theme song from the Mickey Mouse Club.

Tom Tom and the Music of Empire

The mythical vignette I sketched in the previous chapter about the Irish immigrant lad who made good in America has many Hollywood versions. I suppose one could fashion a genre in its own right on the subject of immigration, from *Coming to America*[32] to *Moscow on the Hudson*[33] to *Titanic* even to include films such as (another Vietnam War flick) *Coming Home.*[34] In any event, the Tom I was thinking about was actually *the* Tom Cruise in the Ron Howard film *Far and Away,* released in 1991.

As befitting Howard's style, the film generally is mawkish, excessively earnest, and boyishly transparent in its attempts to push your buttons.[35] "It isn't a movie, it's a cartoon," opined reviewer John F. Kelly, in the *Washington Post.*[36] In some ways Howard is very much a watered-down, weepy John Ford for his generation, all pureed Americana.[37] As Roger Ebert aptly put it, "Howard is tiptoeing around in John Ford country when he should be wearing bigger boots."[38] Writing in *People,* Joanne Kaufman agreed and dismissed *Far and Away* as "a disappointment of epic proportions."[39] Actor Tom Cruise is clearly the boy-man for the job as the Irish lad, reflexively handsome, anxiously athletic, his rugged eagerness tinged with the self-same desperation typifying Howard's movies.

The setting is the west coast of Ireland, 1892, where the rotten aristocrats have been gouging the poor farmers yet again. It is an age-old story here on majestic wind-swept shores. But one lad, an unusual youth in that he is hardy, industrious and ambitious, stands ready to fight for what is right. He is Joseph Donnelly (that is, Tom Cruise), the good son (his two older brothers are drunken layabouts) to a tired, beaten-down, aged father. Joseph is also a scrapper, a none-too polished vengeful lad who, after the father is killed accidentally in the course of taking part in a collective challenge to the evil agents of the landlord, sets about gaining his just reward, delicious revenge.

Turns out that the landlord, one Daniel Christie (played with disaffected relish by Robert Prosky), is a good fellow too, though a slightly pathetic caricature of a man who parades his self-disappointment at having inherited a fortune as opposed to having earned it (you know, the American way). So he drinks, thereby at least making himself popular; and even our hero Joseph ultimately cannot resist his charms. However, before that Joseph has a blood debt to settle with old Christie, or so he thinks. It turns out that with Horatio Alger-esque providential interference, Joseph, instead of killing Christie, falls for his love interest, Shannon, Christie's willful daughter (and Cruise's then real-life love, Nicole Kidman).

Shannon and Joseph are alike in that they are both fighters, intractable, attractive, head-strong, and ambitious. Thus, she improbably spirits him away across the Atlantic Ocean to the rat-infested tenements of Boston (and this intrigue effectively drives the love story, the feints and the jabs and the inevitability of it all). Posing alternatively as master/servant and sister/brother, they reach the promised land. America. She is hell-bent to be modern, she says; and he, though reluctant, appears destined to achieve the "miracle" his father had prophesied on his deathbed. The audience of course is savvy to all of this, even if the characters are not, and this is certainly what is intended to fuel us onward—like the thrill of the babysitter who goes upstairs when the audience knows something that she does not. In this way, when Joseph and Shannon inevitably fall into each other's arms a couple of tired hours later, the audience is mildly rewarded at an emotional level for having known something obvious all along. Yes, but that is Hollywood and that is Ron Howard.

What about the mythical frontier and the mood of empire?

The allure of America operates, first, as a place of destiny to which to escape, as the thesis implies. Joseph puts it plainly when he says, "I think I like America...Look at the welcome we got." Later, and here we are supposed to nod our heads in affirmation, he adds, "Maybe this is my destiny." Of course, immigrants want to come to America—in this case they crave freedom measured in homestead land and by the concept of modernity. Furthermore, they are driven to America on the run from aristocratic anti-modernism and by aristocratic vice and corruption. Joseph and Shannon want these things—

she, modernity and he, land—and both, as noted, seek freedom. She entices him, "they've got so much of it they give it away for free," referring to the Homestead Act of 1865. "You said you wanted land...Come with me," she teases him.

Joseph (Tom Cruise), the Irish immigrant lad, duking it up in *Far and Away*.

And so the land of plenty (of land) beckons, in short, an urge, both a push and a tug, that cannot be resisted. The audience recalls, too, that on his deathbed Joseph's father admonished his son that "without land a man is nothing," though neither the father himself nor apparently any of the other Irish locals had ever owned any.

"A miracle, that's what you want," the father, dying, rasps out to Joseph. He is talking about America, of course, and we all know it. Not to worry. Joseph is a good lad and we know he will make it. The question is really a matter of how well he is able to display the characteristics of the all-American boy in winning his victory, and not whether he'll gain his victory. Victory is his destiny.

Far and Away is an important frontier western because it exemplifies a common characteristic of mythical frontier films—it launches the mood for empire. Joseph sets the mood for empire. By this I mean that his character establishes and reinforces the frontier ideology upon which America has been causally structured. I do not mean to suggest that this movie on its own promotes, say, U.S. imperial policy in Columbia's drug war or egged George W. Bush to frame the hunt for Osama bin Laden in frontier terms (you may recall Bush's infamous, "wanted, dead or alive," crack) anymore than it served as an apology for U.S. involvement in Vietnam. Rather, it contributes to a larger, more elliptical cultural project, the outcome of which presages, soothes, and serves up imperial behavior. *Far and Away* does this in at least three ways.

First, Joseph is our hero. Joseph is also a frontiersman. Nearly to the letter does he embody the traits of the rebuilt proto-American. In fact, he embodies and personifies mythical Americana.

But wait. Is he not all of these things before the stripping down gets underway? Yes and no.

Joseph certainly has the potential to achieve Americanness, as we witness through his randy, pugilistic, vengeful behavior in Ireland. That said, he gains by it nothing more than near death after his attempt to confront and dispense with old Christie (his father-in-law to-be). In America, in the sweat and the grime of tenement Boston, as Turner undoubtedly imagined, he began to win his stripes. Here again he appears to prosper by violence (bare-knuckled boxing and defeating men twice his size in semi-professional pub fights). However, the apparent success is tempered by clouding his thirst for land. In fact, he becomes less free insofar as his vision is set aside temporarily and to the extent that he becomes enamored of suits and fancy hats.

The mythical frontier will have its way with Joseph, however. For not only does he ultimately get his land (mounted atop the wildest steed available), nab his girl (a feisty filly, in her own right), defeat his rival (another overdressed, excessively-mustached aristocrat, of course), but he dies in so doing. Literally, Joseph dies. He is stripped of life itself, at the very instant that he has overcome his vanity, his aristocratic junky self-love of the East, learned to measure his violence, reined in his animalism yet harnessed its energies for the goodness of Americana.

He dies—and then he is reborn. In fact, this is the second way in which the film delivers up a mood of empire.

Here is what happens. The camera pans upward and away, via which we are meant to understand by filmic convention that he has expired, Shannon mutters something about loving him, and then the camera pauses. Oh my God, you wonder, she has finally admitted to it. She loves him! She really loves him! Upon this not-so shocking realization (the audience has always known it, after all, even if it was not apparent to our heroes) the camera pans back down, back to earth. Presto, just like that, Joseph is back. Alive. And better than ever. Better because the mythical frontier has promised it to be so; and so we, as by association as witnesses, are also delivered into the promised land. We believe it because we have always believed it. Because the mythical frontier has always promised it and kept its word. However, if you do not believe it, just go to the movies and see for yourself. We are reaffirmed through the frontier, as Joseph tunes in his rival, "You're not in Ireland anymore you insolent bastard...This land is mine. Mine by destiny."

Third, and finally, *Far and Away* sets the mood of empire in the wells of indomitable presence and aggressive strength it imparts to its heroes. If America is the frontier and Joseph and Shannon are its agents, then they, too, are America. In turn, then, America is them. So what are they? Youthful. Sexy. Angry. Violent. Proud. Dangerous. Ambitious. Hard-working. Aggressive.

Is this the America of the 1990s? I mean, is this the way contemporary America desires to perceive itself?

More or less, yes.

Imperialists take land away from others—Others, say, to choose one example from among many, the United States grabbing half of Mexico's land in 1848 (as Spain/Mexico had earlier taken it from Indians). What about Joseph and Shannon? The free land in the film is empty, seemingly there for the taking. It was empty for Turner, too. In reality, much of Oklahoma, the setting to which the film advances ultimately, apparently was unoccupied. But it was never empty in the sense that no one could be said to own it. Indians owned it. They owned it differently, to be sure, from how ownership is today conceived in North America, but it was theirs. Indeed, it had been theirs for thousands of years.

While Ron Howard, naturally, as a director is not necessarily responsible for historical accuracy, nor compelled to portray or account for historical actors who were not there (that is, the Indians), the film contributes to the promotion of the mood of American imperialism in its meta story by echoing closely the mythical frontier narrative. The absence of Indians fits this mood, but surely does not define it in this film. In this way the film commits an act of omission, not commission.

Just Say No to Vietnam

Indians, though, are omnipresent in the 1971 minor classic, *Man in the Wilderness*, which aims a querulous eye at the mood and enterprise of empire. Stripping-down in this film leads to revisionist conclusions that might be summed up in that old slogan: make love, not war. Even so, in some basic ways Joseph Donnelly shares key traits with Mr. Zachary "Zach" Bass, the English immigrant-scout, played by Richard Harris, whose story is related in the anti-Vietnam War movie *Wilderness*.

Wilderness is not solely a frontier western. Where *Far and Away* flirted uncertainly with romance and was all thumbs with romantic comedy, and Kubrick's *Jacket* with black humor, *Wilderness* explores (without much success) the nature and role of Christianity and serves as a wise, if preachy, reminder of the bountiful yet fruitless carnage of the Vietnam War. Crosses are omnipresent in the movie, for example, and Zach is framed as an eternal son, Christ-like, of his father figure/captain, played straight ahead by John Huston. The captain explains to the crew:

> Gentleman, you will learn that man is expendable. We're exploring a new frontier and must always push on, give our lives, if need be. This is more than a trapping mission. We're here to explore the new America, dig into its pagan regions, and we can't afford to fail. A man must be prepared to sacrifice. A father should give his son's life gladly. Zach was like a son to me.

Early in this film we are presented with Zach as an accomplished frontiersman, neatly and nearly stripped down, arrayed in buckskins, lean, edgy, a man of few words who would rather let his actions do his talking. He is part of a trapping expedition that has filled the hull of an 1820s' ship with two years' catch of valuable furs. "Them beaver pelts are solid gold," one of the crewmen explains. The ship sits on wheels, being towed overland in an effort to reach the waters of the Missouri River with the aim of then taking the cargo on to market.

Although Zach is quite naturally an excellent marksman, a young colleague who accompanies him on a short hunting trip is not. The result is that Zach is horribly mauled by a Grizzly. Though near death, Zach refuses to die because of his toughness. Still, the captain instructs two men to stay behind and bury Zach.

But he is not dead, someone complains.

Then kill him, the captain intones, for there is no chance for survival given the gravity of Zach's injuries.

But the two commissioned to kill and bury Zach fail to do so because just then the group of Indian warriors that has been shadowing the ship and her crew is too nearby for them to risk taking a shot and thus being revealed. So they abandon him to death, to the wilderness. You can guess the rest. Of course Zach does not die physically—instead he is reborn. To survive he must adopt the ways, quite literally—and this is unadulterated, mythically Turnerian—of the Indian. He scavenges buffalo marrow from a wolf kill, fashions deadly weapons by his own hands, learns to survive in that stark empty quarter beyond the edge of white settlement.

Zach is no Indian, though. He stands as a rebirthed Briton cum American. For not only has he suffered social death, he is reborn in the determined manner of his survival. Unlike Turner's assertion that this experience inevitably produces Joseph Donnelly-like characters or Kubrick's darkened inversion of Turner's vision, in *Wilderness* Zach emerges as very much the liberal for his times (1971), for in his rebirth he embraces *amore*, not anger, forgiveness, not vengeance, and learns to eschew violence.

That said, while *Wilderness* offers a revisionist take on the processural outcome of the myth, it does not challenge the centrality of the rebirthing experience. Very much the opposite, in fact. It embraces the idea. America, it recognizes, is already all about empire and violence—but *Wilderness* promotes an alternative end product, a kinder, gentler version. Thus, Zach is going home to love his young son as a father should and must. The frontier has taught him this. Why? Because love is better than war. Why? Because it is just so, self-evidently, no explanation being proffered or required in 1971.

What about empire and Manifest Destiny? The film here is pessimistic, simply assuming the existence of an ongoing empire-in-the-making. Zach does not so much provide an alternative as he does an antidote. That Indians lose is a given, despite the film's sympathetic, slightly romantic treatment of them. What can and should be different, however, the film suggests, is America's frontier-driven compulsion to expand beyond its continental borders.

Zach (Richard Harris) as frontiersman in *Man in the Wilderness*.

Ultimately, this posits a confused reading of the myth. On the one hand, the film accepts the frontier as the fount of mythical rebirthing. At the same time, however, it denies what the innate logic of the myth implies: rebirth leads to empire-building. It is difficult to imagine how you can have the first without the second. Then, too, Lyndon Johnson's domestic policies—the Great Society—also flew in the face of his foreign policy—upping the U.S. involvement in Vietnam. In this way, like Johnson's style of governing, the film is classically post-WW II liberal, wanting things both ways (that is, make love *and* war) but failing to accept the consequences of its own logic/illogic.

Chapter Four

Being Not It! (And Other Teleological Silliness)

> Splitting constitutes an intricate strategy of defense and differentiation in the colonial discourse. Two contradictory and independent attitudes inhabit the same place, one takes account of reality, the other is under the influence of instincts which detach the ego from reality. This results in the production of multiple and contradictory belief...Splitting is then...a strategy for articulating contradictory and coeval statements of belief.
>
> —Homi Bhabha[1]

> The American lives on the very edge of the now, always ready to leap forward to the future. The country's foundations are in the future, not in the past. Or, rather, its past, the act of its founding, was a promise of the future, and each time the United States returns to its source, to its past, it rediscovers the future.
>
> —Octavio Paz[2]

> *Teacher*: "We're not changing anything. We're just trying to present a more complete picture."
> *Parent*: "And that's what's got to stop."
> *Teacher*: "Look, there's enough ignorance in the world without us trying to encourage it in the classroom."
> *Parent*: "Now who are you calling ignorant?"
>
> —an exchange in *Lone Star*

The mythical frontier is all about the contestation between civilization and savagery, celebrated right and alleged wrong, white and non-white. It is all about conquering uncultured territory in order to render it suitable for occupation and/or economic exploitation and/or geo-political strategization. It implies assimilation (that is, a softer variety of cultural genocide), in the best case, outright genocide (we have to destroy the village in order to save it), in the worst, for those already living beyond the pale. This is precisely what the myth promotes and, in fact, is precisely what the historical continental frontier was actually about, too: Americans taking Indians' land, grabbing half of Mexico's national territory, stealing Hawaii, buying Alaska in a sleazy colonial real estate deal, seizing the day in the name of Manifest Destiny.

Neverthless, for all the exaggeratedness of the myth, the historical frontier was a dangerous place, if not quite as formulaically as supposed by its imaginative chronicler, Frederick Jackson Turner. Where historical reality and the myth part company is discernible in the way that they differently characterize the nature of the dangers and the motivations of those who engendered them. For example, Indians did indeed threaten settlers on the historical frontier and vice versa; and on either side many died in pitched battles between the groups of whites and Indians, conflicts that sometimes also reflected the various ways that they allied themselves (e.g., French-Indian War). On both sides much of the fighting might be considered inhuman by today's standards (but really no worse than, say, the carpet bombing of southern Iraq during the first Gulf War or the use of napalm in Vietnam or the brutalizing crime that goes down in many neighborhoods in American cities every single day). Moreover, settlers had good reason to fear aboriginal peoples. After all, Indians often aggressively and violently defended their lands. I mean, and why not? Wouldn't you? It is called self-defense. Settlers and, notably, the American Army proved equal to the challenge, however.

Not always, though, and it is certainly no more accurate historically to paint Indians as violent any more than it would be to cast settlers (or trappers or miners or ranchers) as mindless, sadistic land poachers.

Indians and whites struggled for land, territory that both saw as rightfully belonging to themselves. Put plainly, the basic aboriginal case was built upon the assertion that Indians were there first. They were. Further, that the land belonged to them first. It did. Should that not have been enough? Well, yes, but things turned out differently.

Among other issues, white Americans felt that the Indians were not using the land efficiently or properly. Moreover, from a centered Anglo perspective, Indians were not.[3] That is, they did not farm for profit, did not raise cattle, did not fence land or even understand Anglo conceptions of private property rights, did not work nose to the grindstone saving for rainy days, and so on. From this point of view whites were right to usurp the land. The Indians simply were not employing it in ways that made any real sense to European-Americans. Moreover, Indian behavior (for example, permissive child-rearing or excessive sharing) seemed to confirm Anglo notions about alleged Indian inferiority that, in turn, invited corrective reaction. Further, both whites and Indians felt justified in using violence and war as means to exercise their incompatible claims to land usage and ownership (even though the issue of ownership is more complicated than mere occupancy).

In other words, a historical case may be constructed to explain competing motivations, intercultural misunderstandings, cross-cultural confusion, and habitualized and aggressive ethnocentrism on the part of white Americans. That is the basic historical tale.

But not according to the myth. According to the imagined frontier, Indians and whites clashed, to be sure. But the root of the problem lay in Indian savagery, inferiority, backwardness, aggressiveness, and other ineluctable traits. Apparently, on the brighter side, the myth contends, virtuous, brave, democratic white Americans were compelled to fight back in the names of civilization, decency, and Coca Cola. In short, they were fighting a defensive offensive. To have done less would have been unmanly, ungodly, un-American.

Complex historical motivations, in other words, are perniciously simplified, dumbed-down, laid to waste by the myth. The result is that historically complicated peoples are reduced to near cardboard characterizations—whites as upstanding, trusty heroes, Indians (and espied other non-whites such as Mexicans, blacks, whomever) more or less as treacherous, sneaky devils.

The mechanism via which these imagined characterizations operate is deceptively crude, too—Othering. Again, as noted in chapter one, if you fashion a list of mythical American attributes as personified by the frontier thesis, you'll end up sketching the frontiersman (say, John Wayne, Natty Bumppo, or Indiana Jones). Invert or reverse those model elements and you get the Other, that is, the imagined Injun, Nigger, Latin American Greaser, Vietcong, Soviet communist, or even plain old lesbian. It is not only a matter of constructing a simple binary code, rather it is binarism gone collectively crazy. The mechanism is facile enough—I am this (hurrah!) and you are the opposite (for shame!); but the grab bag of characteristics allows for much flexibility. For example, a great range of choices exists among stereotypes applicable to Indians. In the very best case you can sketch the Noble Savage—the stoic (simplistic), strong (too moronic to notice pain), silent (got nothing to say), wise (yeah, smart like a child). In short, the stereotyping operates on a slippery slope, which makes it durable and handy, as well as a useful tool for keeping Others firmly at bay, at least, figuratively.

Meanwhile, Manifest Destiny, that is, unadulterated imperial American cultural nectar, provides the story America tells itself about itself to explain the processes of its history of uncompromising land-grabbing. The myth says the frontier experience created superior white beings, it contends that the process was good for all concerned, that God himself wanted it so (and here I freely invoke the *Simpsons'* deity, the old white guy with flowing robes and an imposing snowy beard, the same fellow I imagine Jerry Falwell and Pat Robertson and John Ashcroft supplicating to). America *is* expansion. America *is* good. Therefore, expansion *is* good.

Expansion is good.

And necessary.

Indeed, it is even inevitable insofar as a Protestant God wants His variety of goodness, now available for purchase and export at Wal-Mart, to prosper.

So mythical frontiersmen by nature reside on the edges of civilization, the frontier, where they do battle to render it safe for occupation. Alternatively, they may wage an ongoing rearguard action to protect the civilized side from the savage side, which, in the style of the captivity narrative popular in fiction and film, is aggressively hostile, too. At any rate, the frontiersman is our hero. He serves as our model.

Yet, strumming music sweet to liberal ears, frontier-style heroes also battle for basic American virtues—love of generic freedom, clinching democracy, in-your-face individualism, and such, don't they? I mean, the frontiersmen certainly do not present themselves as harbingers of a vicious, occasionally psychotic colonialism anymore than your typical settler grappled with the moral implications of Manifest Destiny. (And this is one of several points where I see the applicability of Homi Bhabha's notion about "splitting," a sort of post-colonial having-your-cake-and-eating-it-too.) It is the willful refusal of dreamed Americana to accept, plainly put, the bath water with the baby that augurs trouble.

Most of those actively and typically unthinkingly engaged in the promotion of Manifest Destiny—settlers and/or policymakers—were likely good, well-mannered human beings of a certain stock, but they were also imperialists. It is possible to be both. Their experience was not so very different from how it has been for the Brits or the French or the Russians or the Japanese to be both. Look it at it this way: if America had not engaged in empire-building, how did it get all that land? America is the just dessert of a land grab.

In turn, then, via the myth the imagined American is scrubbed squeaky clean while the actual aggressive, would-be uncivilized componentry of the model (i.e., historical American) is not only denied (splitting again...) but projected on to the Other, thereby assuaging culpability for loutish and even murderous behavior by displacing it, and the historical actors being Othered (I know you are but what am I?) are systematically, as a result, stripped of their humanity. It is a common enough psychological phenomenon, after all, like the classic homophobe who projects a sublimated fear of his own complex sexuality (or, more abruptly, his attraction to other males) on to homosexuals. At one and the same time, he may deny the reality of his own longings while doubling the scorn he feels for those "guilty" of what he cannot abide in himself. It is quite clearly as if, in order for the imaginary (white American) to feel safe itself (himself), it (he) usurps all right and heaps all wrong upon its (his) binary (Othered) reflection. This may be a crude instrument, agreed, but it is also highly effective. It is also flexible and porous, not monolithic. So you'll get your white savages on film all right (you know, the ones wearing the cliché black hats, dressed like dandies, sporting scars and slightly menacing facial hair), as well as your Noble Savages. The line may on occasion be fuzzy but it is still that, a line—even if we understand it as an interstitial region, a liminal area, a slippery slope.

Stereotypes, after all, are not automatically bad things. In fact, they are necessary insofar as they allow us to process raw data into useable, intelligible, simplified chunks. If I stereotype robins as the birds who eat worms after a rain or automobiles as polluters or the sky as blue, how is the world any worse off? It is not. However, when applied to human beings, stereotypes obviously may present all sorts of problems. At least they do if we accept that the society in which we live ought really to be about some of the core values ostensibly promoted by the mythical frontier—egalitarian freedom, democracy, liberty, decency, tolerance, and so on. The trouble is that these virtues traditionally have been accorded only to the mainstream hardcore, those occupying the cultural center, rather than to those Others dwelling on the periphery, the margins.

One of the beauties of the frontier tale derives from its conflation of narrative and geography, its simultaneous stripping down (that is, shedding corrupted, retrograde Euro-Otherness) and subsequent rebirthing (that is, figurative death and nearer Indianness) and regrowth (that is, like a rough flower in the desert, say, a cactus rose). Stanley Kubrick in *Jacket* alludes caustically to these stages of ostensible American social evolution neatly in the shaping of characterizations—Lieutenant/Cowboy/Animal Mother. Nowhere is this process more exquisitely examined and promoted than in John Ford's last and possibly best frontier western, *The Man Who Shot Liberty Valance.*

Doing John Wayne

At one level Ford's film relates the simple story of two men grappling over a woman, and only one man can prevail. Jimmy Stewart plays the bony, upright newcomer to the western town of Shinbone, one Ransom Stoddard, fresh and somewhat too eager from law school (though he must be about 50 years old here). John Wayne plays the guy (another 50-ish oldster), Tom Doniphon, who has got the girl for now. She is Hallie, played by Vera Miles, an illiterate blonde waitress of high temper and virtue. Doniphon has been waiting to complete the extra room on his modest ranch house before popping the proverbial question to Hallie. Doniphon's the toughest man in the territory, of course—and may well have been styled on the now obscure, but formerly noted American soldier and Indian tamer/killer Colonel Doniphan, colleague of Stephen Kearney during the Mexican-American War in 1846.[4] However, he has a rival, the low-down villain Liberty Valance, played nearly perfectly by Lee Marvin.

Valance and his gang of thugs hold up Ranse's stage coach as he comes to town at the beginning of the extended flashback that constitutes the bulk of the film. Ranse is beaten savagely by Valance partly for the sheer hell of it but also for trying to protect an elderly woman's necklace, given to her by her "dead husband."

"What kind of men are you?" Ranse bellows in protest.

"This kind, dude," Valance declares, striking him down. "Now, what kind of a man are you?" Not a *real* (or is that *reel*?) man, at any rate. A man who cannot protect himself let alone an elderly female.

All he has are words and what good are they in a world of deeds? The frontier covets action.

A lover of constitutional law and such, and though beaten to within an inch of his life, Ranse is determined to bring Valance to justice, put him behind bars. Yes, but this is the west, where primitive notions about such things, settling scores, prevail—as Valance intones before commencing on the primary beating, "I'll teach you western law." Bam, smash, boom.

Ranse appears to stand little chance against Valance. Tom Doniphon stands between the two men, a strong, self-reliant, gallant, wholesome, literate westerner—my God, he is literally John Wayne—but cannot protect Ranse directly, as such, because to do so would break one of the rules of masculinity that Liberty, Tom, *and* Ranse all agree upon—a man fights his own battles. Some things are universal.

Still, Ranse has certain qualities. First, he is unafraid, so he has the potential makings of a real man. Second, he is effectively stripped down by Valance in a variety of frontier rape. He is beaten, robbed, but not fully emasculated (though that is hinted at later, when he is compelled to wear an apron). These attributes when taken together grant him a virile frontieristic potentiality. It is the old mythical frontier story again. Like adult sex, it is one that we know all about but suspend judgment on so that we might take pleasure in what we know will climax eventually. The buildup is mere foreplay.

Ultimately, Liberty calls Ranse out and Ranse of course must go. "Now you stay out of this, Doniphon," Valance warns Tom off. "He's been hiding behind your gun long enough." Again, the code requires that Tom stand down. "You got a choice, dishwasher," Liberty then menaces Ranse. "Either you get outta town or tonight you be on that street alone. You be there."

What develops is your basic western cockfight, shootout on the sidewalk. Ranse is overmatched. Accepting the challenge from Liberty Valance, while manly, is as good as a death sentence. Still, Ranse does not run. So then that night Liberty, staggering from the saloon viciously drunk and gaily evil, fires off a round into a potted plant near Ranse's head. The pot explodes wetly on to Ranse's shoulders. A mere warning shot. Then he blasts Ranse in the shooting arm, guffawing handsomely crazy all the while. Then, as skinny Ranse resiliently picks up his pistol with his left hand, right bleeding, Liberty tells him,

"Okay, dude, this time right between the eyes." Liberty takes careful aim but then Ranse fires first and Liberty Valance falls dead.

So hurray for goodness, and why not? Along the way Ranse had promoted a free press in town, started schooling children not only on how to read but about the glories of American republicanism. He even teaches the prettily raw Hallie; Tom's girl wants to learn so that she might read the Bible. Not only that, but Hallie falls for him hard. Plus, Ranse's virtue and learning make him a leading candidate for the political forces (that is, good settlers vs. bad ranchers) pressing for the territory to earn statehood. In fact, he is selected to go to Washington to carry the territory's torch.

But he will not go. He will not go because his opponent's camp tags him as a killer. Albeit the death was Liberty Valance's, killing is killing and it is wrong. Ranse accepts the logic of the eloquently delivered rebuff (by John Carradine). However, as you likely know, and in what must have shocked moviegoers when the film was released in 1962, Ranse never actually killed Liberty Valance. Tom Doniphon did. Tucked into the shadows across the street that fateful evening, we learn from Tom, that Tom himself had fired the fatal bullet from a Winchester repeating rifle. Ranse had had guts enough, but Ranse could not hit anything. End of that story. In the shadows Tom did the dirty, the necessary work. Meanwhile Ranse gets the girl, Ranse gets to go to Washington, Ranse ultimately becomes a senator. A pestering prickly decency, a Jimmy Stewart trademark, prevails over darkness.

This movie concludes in an unsatisfying manner somehow, unless one gets off on Tom's ennobling self-sacrifice.[5] Ranse, after all, is not only utterly humorless, he is a dork, a dweeb, a nerd. He does not know when to lay off, when to shut up. He is gangly, awkward, and preachy. His decency is good for little old ladies, perhaps, but it borders on the shrill. He hectors from every excitable pore. On the other hand, John Wayne as Doniphon is at his playful, manly best, relaxed and impish like a lumbering ox.

So what about the guy in the middle? Sandwiched between extremes—Liberty and Ranse—what about Tom? John Wayne is left dangling. He had the girl in the first place. He was decent-like, too, honorable, and he was good. He was tough. He was a frontiersman of the highest order. Hell, he could kick Jimmy Stewart's ass to hell and gone. Why did he get dumped on?

The answers are several. To begin with, this is no common frontier western; and while it *is* steeped in archetype and stereotype, and while it does champion the frontier myth in virtually every frame (come on, this is a John Ford job of work here!), so too is it an admirable piece of filmmaking, a "thoughtful masterpiece,"[6] one scholar has fairly tagged it, and about as meditative as westerns get. Director Ford uses the film to explore the stages of development wrought by the mythical frontier in its inexorable (alleged) fashioning of the American nation.

So let me back up slightly. The movie proper is the reminiscence of Ranse in old age. He, now a wise old senator, former governor of the state, and diplomat, and Hallie (a good wife? We can only assume; at any rate she dresses well and holds herself in an upright fashion) have come back to Shinbone on the railway to bury Tom in the twilight of their lives. The local newspaper compels Ranse to tell the story that composes the film—and he does, hence the extended flashback, and thus we meet the stagecoach and a youthful Ranse and Liberty Valance.

Ford hints at his intentions plainly enough right from the start. The film opens with a train chugging into Shinbone, like some John Sargent canvas of the nineteenth century dinging the bell for humankind over nature, signifying the arrival of mechanized civilization, colonization in its finest hour. That is a big picture, and that is what has happened in a lifetime. As Hallie says, "Look at it. It was once a wilderness. Now it's a garden." This has been noted frequently by commentators.[7] However, what has gone unnoted is Ford's specific take on the myth in this film. In fact, this is surprising given that it is the driving force behind the tale.

The various espied Turnerian stages are housed in the principal characters: Ranse is the over-civilized bristly easterner, from the city, educated and proudly effete and all that; Tom's John Wayne presents, as Wayne's characters frequently did, "Manifest Destiny on the hoof," as historian Garry Wills has cleverly remarked,[8] though Wayne's comfortable performance is very nearly a brilliant self-parody; Liberty Valance serves as a reminder of what happens when you go too far, past the frontier, when you succumb, like some western Pinnochio, to its dark compulsions. To become whole, a real man, an American, Ranse needs to strip down and be saved. And this is precisely what happens. So it is not quite accurate or fair to say that this movie is about civilization over savagery because the former only prevails with the agency of the frontiersman (Ford grants him the gift of divination here), who serves to cleanse civilization with just violence (not altogether unlike George W. Bush's regenerative War on Terrorism). The names hint at it baldly: Ranse ransoms liberty. Is this done merely for the sake of a bunch of written words? Not quite, because the words and what they signify—Americanized civilization—are not empty. In fact, the wandering, playful yet hard, sexual tom, Tom, understands that more is needed, that Ranse needs to become a man.

In the beginning Ranse had heeded Horace Greeley's romantic admonition, "Go west, young man. Go west. And seek fame. Fortune, adventure," Ranse as senator explains. He is clearly not Tom Cruise/Joseph Donnelly, who came ready, willing, and able to scrap physically in *Far and Away*. Yet he is a fighter by nature. Problem is that he is too stuffed up with learning and such that he is slightly effeminate. He is a chappie not troubled in the least by wearing an apron, washing dishes, waiting on tables (remember, this was 1962). At one point even Hallie scoffs, "What good has readin' and writin' done you? Look at you! In an apron!"

At any rate, the dialogue in the film is transparent through and through. Ranse declares his intention to see Liberty brought to justice, to jail (though we are meant, too, to understand that eastern life is itself jail-like, imprisoning men in states in which they are over-ruled, over-governed, overburdened with a variety of civilized corruption not unlike Turner's Europeans). Tom replies, "Well I know those law books mean a lot to you. But not out here. Out here a man settles his own problems."

Ranse is taken aback. "Do you realize what you're saying to me?" he asks. "You're saying just exactly what Liberty Valance said. What kind of a community have I come to here? You all seem to know this fellow Liberty Valance. He is a no-good, gun-packing, murdering thief. But the only advice you can give to me is to carry a gun. Well, I'm a lawyer..." And with that he collapses.

Right. The battle lines are then set. The easterner promises the rule of law, but he is a sissy-pants (that is to say, not a real man, not an American). So he has got to self-improve. Got to get reborn. The westerner/frontiersman, on the other hand, has got it all—with the exception of what guarantees the enfranchisement of the conditions under which progress and manliness of a tempered sort might prosper: the rule of constitutional law. Because he is an archetypal man, a stage in the development of the essential American man, he remains the same, just dies off (though Ford fudges here by having him give up his guns at some indeterminate point in later life). Liberty Valance represents the epitome of frontiering gone wrong, too far. He is precisely what the law must rein in. White on the outside but red beneath, an inside-out apple.

Ford grants the two basic positions historical processes and actors. At the political convention where the territory must decide which interests to promote, here is how the editor of the *Shinbone Star* addresses the issue, beginning with a dig against the southern dandy stumping for the ranching interests:

> Under the spell of his eloquence I could see once again the vast herd of buffalo and savage redskin roaming over our beautiful territory with no law to trouble them except the law of survival, the law of the tomahawk and the bow and arrow. And then with the upward march of our nation came the pioneer and the buffalo hunter, the adventurous and the bold. And the boldest of these were the cattlemen who seized the wide open range for their own personal domain and their law was the law of the hired gun. But now today, today have come the railroads and the people, the steady, hardworking citizens, the homesteaders, the shopkeeper, the builder of cities. We need roads to join these cities, dams to store up water of the Picket Wire [river] and we need statehood to protect the rights of every man and woman, no matter how humble.

This is Turner all over again. First, you have got your savage Indians who cannot govern themselves properly, though they are generally as significantly absent from the film as they are from Turner's narrative. Then come the early frontiersmen, culminating in the strength, energy, and cunning of the ranchers who could begin to tame the wilderness. Lest the point not be clear enough, these are gunfighter types, a step up from Indians, but yet not civilized Americans. You do not want too much civilization, mind you, which is why Ranse needs to embrace violence (or, at least, the willingness to do violence when required). Then come the rest—farmers and, later, urbanites.

Ford employs standard western signifiers cagily in the film. You get the not-men, the timid fat slob (marshal), the dopey immigrants (Swedes), the stutterer (but proud to be an American), the eloquently goofy, endearing drunks (the editor and the doctor), the saloon (where mei and find release), the black slave (Wayne's pseudo-sidekick, Pc , played by Woody Strode, offering ironic comments on the featı American freedom), and so on. In fact, Ford's frontier vision i characters. dent explai ıe nature of U.S. politics: "The United States is a republic. A re is a state where the people are the boss. That means us. And if t shots in Washington don't do like we want we don't vote for the golly, no more."

More te hough, in a rambling, inebriated monologue, a supplication tc ıythical frontier, the editor of the *Shinbone Star* affirms, "As ou Horace Greeley, go west, old man, and grow young with untry." There lurks the pithy bit of the imperial gesture—go w aded for bear and come what may, and become American, l e America, the perennial adolescent.

The ges bides the promises of expansion, embedded pregnantly in G 's averral, go west. Hallie wants to read in order to better knov vord—and the words are go west, young man, go west. Go w man and drink of the fountain of youthfulness. Just go west. H t do it. The film is so flawlessly mythical, so tirelessly, syco cally Turnerian—and Ford, at the top of his game, knows this- the work takes on a syrupy, brackish (reinforced by the shadov ck and white film) surrealism. We loathe Jimmy Stewart, all ng, skin and bones, and self-righteously distant. He is the sort c e most anally conservative might love. Still, he wins our rationa iance because, of course, we know that he has to prevail in that we become what we are today, his mythical progeny on h, continuing to get our collective fix at the box office (or in C var reportage), if not in reality. It is Wayne, though, always Wa ho, polymorphously childlike, saunteringly sexual, and preterr ly avuncular wins our hearts. He is always an 11-year old bo gine what that felt like in 1962.

To grea t, *Shane*, the legendary frontier western of 1953,[9] is told throug yes of a young boy, eight or nine. Again, it recounts the center f mythical American evolution: sodbusters versus cattlemen, both are defended by that moribund, yet sexy breed: gunf . Clad in buckskins, the eponymous pistol packer of goodness r assically into the movie frame as if from nowhere other than the pregnant mountain landscape back dropping the picturesque agricultural flatlands.

Ranse Stoddard (Jimmy Stewart), ambiguously gendered, in a publicity still from *The Man Who Shot Liberty Valance*.

Neither less transparent than *Liberty Valance* nor less evocative of the mythical theory of American evolution, *Shane* is, however, more effective mythically as a film because its focus is narrower and truer. This is the short story of the last of a dying breed. The result is a jauntier shootout.

Homosocial Horse Opera

Matthew Garth is about 11 years old when Tom Dunson adopts him in *Red River*. John Wayne plays Dunson, though it would be a mistake to consider this or *Liberty Valance* as vehicles for Wayne's stardom in the way that *Far and Away* serves for Tom Cruise; rather, Wayne plays a bona fide role and does not just posture as a toothy celebrity, and while it may be a role that he seems to own (or maybe it is the only one he can play effectively), these are more directors' films than they are star vehicles. The story begins with Dunson pulling himself out of wagon train heading to California.

His withdrawal presages danger for the group as it passes through hostile Indian country (as if there were any other kind!) somewhere northeast of Texas. He is too good a gun to be allowed to depart. However, he warns that he is too good to be forced to stay. And so he goes; and with him goes his second, alternatively a sidekick, part-time conscience, camp cook, and latent sweetheart, Nadine Groot. Significantly, Dunson is compelled to leave his actual woman, Fen, behind while he heads south to build up the biggest cattle collection that Texas has ever seen, this being the story of the creation of the Chisholm Trail. That is his destiny because the erection of such provides the architecture for building America, another film about mythical stages of development. As usual, women folk stay behind. This is manly work.

"I decided last night," Dunson tells Fen (played by Coleen Gray) of his decision to leave.

"I decided too," she responds. "I want to go with you. I know you have work to do, Tom, but I want to be a part of it. I love you." She is earnest. "I want to be with you. I'm asking you, Tom, please take me with you. I'm strong. I can stand anything you can." She means it.

"It's too much for a woman," the Duke explains, though if what he says is true, it is hard to imagine how he thinks that sloppy, grizzled old Nadine Groot (Walter Brennan) will endure it.

"Too much for a woman? Put your arms around me, Tom," she implores him. He does. They kiss. "Hold me," she says. "Feel me in your arms. Do I feel weak? I don't, do I? Oh, you'll need me. You'll need a woman. You'll need what a woman can give you, to do what you have to do. Oh, listen to me, Tom," she implores him. "Listen with your head and your heart, too. The sun only shines half the time, Tom. The other half is night."

"I made up my mind," he says. He is John Wayne.

"Well, change your mind, Tom. Just once in your life, change your mind." But he is John Wayne. There will be no change.

"I'll send for you," he promises, pressing down on her arms, ending it.

I have quoted the dialogue at length because these opening moments and those that follow for about seven or eight minutes, which take Dunson et al. into Texas before the film flashes forward 14 years, establish not only the mythical setting but also allude to the homoeroticism suffusing this Howard Hawks classic. The film debuted in 1948, a time when it was not unusual for folks to imagine that men did certain things, some of which women could not do. Take conquering the west, for this film is unequivocally about conquest, as an example.[10] Then, get a bunch of men, only men, together for long periods of time and well, you'll get the picture. Do not drop the soap in the shower. As Fen had pointedly reminded him, women are especially useful after dark.

More to the point, no sooner are Dunson and Groot hours away from the wagon train than they spot ominous movie smoke in the desert distance, an unqualified signifier of Indian trouble in the direction they would have gone had they not decided to pull out. However, they are too far gone now to turn back and provide help. What help could they be, anyway, now? It is a brutal moment in the story because Dunson's indifference, while perhaps pragmatic, chills you to the bone. Then that night the Indians attack them anyway, which in turn provides Dunson with a measure of absolution.

Dunson and Groot are ready for the heavily stereotyped Injuns, waiting watchfully, before responding violently and cunningly. They kill several. Ultimately Dunson kills one in hand-to-hand combat after they have tussled their way into a pond. Groot tosses him a honking big knife which Dunson plunges repeatedly into his red foe. As well he should, too, for it turns out that the Indian is wearing the bracelet Tom had given his betrothed Fen when they parted. Shaken, Dunson nakedly embraces his homosexuality here in transformative wetness.

The next day it is further confirmed when from behind a bush up pops the lad Matthew Garth, a lucky survivor of the wagon train massacre. He has fallen into shock but he has also, usefully, got a cow in tow. When he proves valiant and brassy enough Dunson and Groot adopt him and continue on into Texas. Dunson takes a shine to the boy because the lad is angry, stands up for himself, is eager to be tutored, and is already quick with a pistol. "He'll do," Dunson drawls.

When at length they stumble upon land Dunson wants, they promptly lay down stakes. "This is it. This is where we start growing good beef, everything a man could want," he beams.

Alas, the land belongs to another, a Mexican, one Don Diego. Two of his employees, including a hired gun, ride up to scare Dunson and his family away. The pistolero amiably explains that Don Diego's family has held the land legally for generations. Dunson says that now the land belongs to him, and so they fight. The Mexican, naturally, dies. Dunson gets the land.

By these actions, all in the first fifteen minutes of the film, Dunson comes to own the land in much the same way the United States came to claim the land of the American southwest, by provoking Mexico to fight for territory that Mexico had swiped from Indians (and there lies your justification, as if stealing stolen property nullifies the immorality of the second theft). This is, after all, a frontier western. The land is up for grabs because Dunson is American and Mexicans are, well, at best half-breeds. That is the story of Manifest Destiny, too—here I am reminded of Woodrow Wilson's sanctimonious boast that he was going to teach Latin Americans how to "elect a few good men" not long before he sent troops to occupy Mexico's port city of Veracruz in 1914—and it is the gist of this film: Mexican (nee Indian) land is taken by force in the rancher stage of American frontier evolution, pilloried reluctantly as retrograde attire in *Liberty Valance* and *Shane* but championed here, at least at a surface level.

Even so, the film is not straight up, though director Hawks wraps it plainly in Turnerian packaging. First, the film, like other frontier westerns, has the feel of an episode in a mini-series, you know, one week it is the bootstraps myth, another week the north fought to free the slaves myth, and this week it is how the frontiersman taught the heathens a thing or two while doing them wondrous favors (i.e., taking their land, killing them, putting them on reservations, forcing spare-the-rod Christianity upon them, relegating them to second-rate governmental services, practicing unofficial segregation, and such).

This abounds in *Red River*, but in Hawks's hands a cleverly posed (if clichéd) homosensuality undergirds the narrative. *Red River*, in other words, proposes that the rancher stage of American evolution, while as necessary as adolescence (another historical fiction), was also deviant in its exclusion of women from what Dunson identifies as man's work. The result is, the film affirms, not normalcy, yet not exactly perversion either.

Dunson "reads over" the Mexican he has killed at the burial the next day, a gesture he repeats later in the film and at least on six other occasions we are meant to know, during the space covered by the 14-year flash forward. He intones, "We brought nothing in to this world and it's certain we can carry nothing out. The Lord gave and he has taken away. Blessed be the name of the Lord." So here we glimpse what drives Dunson's embodiment on the mythical frontiersman. He promotes self-making. A man is as a man does. And a real man *does*, either with his gun or by the force of having a gun. Notice, too, the divine sanction of the motivation for the killing itself, and its consequences—the "Lord gave and the Lord has taken away." It is Manifest Destiny's passing of the collection plate. Praise God, for He does not like wetbacks or Indians either. One of the cowhands ruefully notes later in the film: "Plantin' n' reading. Plantin' n' readin'. Fill a man full of lead, stick 'im in the ground and then read words at 'im. Why, when you've killed a man, why try to read the Lord in as a partner on the job?"

It never bothers Dunson.

Once that is settled, Dunson, clad early in the film in buckskins and Union trousers, builds the magnificent herd he had prophesied the coming of. "Good beef for hungry people," he exclaims. "Beef to make 'em strong, make 'em grow." Trouble is that he cannot sell the meat in the south for the Civil War has ended and the region is cash poor. That said, at least Matthew, now grown up, has returned home from the fight. That much is comforting, good news. Now Dunson plans to drive the cattle to Missouri for sale and Matt will help lead the way.

A cattle drive ensues. It is tough going but Dunson is equal to it. In fact, he is merciless in his pursuit. The cowhands grumble, the cowhands even attempt to rebel, but Dunson prevails. They get word that a nearer railroad might be found in Abilene. Dunson says no, they are headed to Missouri. At length, though, Matthew turns on Dunson because of Dunson's increasingly gratuitous cruelty and because he feels that Abilene presents a more sensible destination for the herd. Dunson never budges. His single-mindedness may be his greatest asset but it also proves to be his undoing. It drives him from frontiersman to nearer savagery, from heterosexuality to homo. He really needed that woman because he has become, as she warned him, overtaken by the night.

In an adolescent rite of passage from *Red River* Matthew Garth (Montgomery Clift) proves faster on the draw than his adopted father Dunson (John Wayne).

Of course, Matthew and friends lead the herd successfully to Abilene. Along the way Matt, too, meets a strong and alluring female, Tess Millay (acted by Joanne Dru), and then they all collide in Abilene. The denouement is one of the most famous in all of film. Wayne pushing his way through a herd of cattle as if he were sweeping a bunch cats out of the way, stepping significantly over the railway line (back to the good side of the tracks, that is, heterosexuality, financial solvency, where cooler heads prevail), calling out Matt (played by the lithely youthful Montgomery Clift, whom Wayne in real life considered to be an "arrogant little bastard,"[11] in a breakthrough performance), shooting his hat off, grazing his cheek with a bullet, belittling his weapon and throwing it down, punching him in the face. So they dance, Tess steps in angrily, blathers on about how Dunson and Matt really, really do love each other. Suddenly boyish, a Wayne trademark, they grin back at her. End of that story. Presto, things are back to normal. The west has been won (again), Mexico pushed aside, Indians killed, heterosexuality reinstated. All is well in the American empire.

Director Hawks clearly had some fun putting this together.[12] It all hangs effortlessly enough, too, on its mythical frontier architecture. Once that much is established in the early going the rest becomes a gay romp, which led many critics to agree with Bosley Crowther in the *New York Times*, who called it "one of the best cowboy pictures ever made."[13] Take the relationship that develops between Matthew and Cherry Valance, the young gunslinger (played by John Ireland who, according to Hawks, got drunk every night and smoked too much marijuana on the set[14]) who signed on for the drive. First, they meet in a confrontation over Dunson's branding any and all cattle that wander his way. It is all a preparation for the drive. While the cattle dispute is resolved, the dialogue crackles in ways only a western can.

"Who are you?" Matt asks aggressively.

"Some call me one thing, some another," Cherry laconically offers.

"What do they call you most?" Dunson pushes in.

"By my name, Cherry Valance."

"They say you're good with a gun. How good?" queries Matt.

"I manage to stay alive." Ah, the studied understatement of a dangerous man.

No surprise that the use of western conventions turns out not to be rocket science. Guns stand in rather obviously for cocks in this film. Again the dialogue.

"That's a good looking gun you were about to use back there," Cherry says as he and Matt walk off. "Maybe you'd like to see mine?"

They exchange. Matt's handle is pearly white, Cherry's dark.

"Nice, awful nice," Cherry gushes, hinting at confliction. "You know, there are only two things more beautiful than a good gun. A Swiss watch or a woman from anywhere. You ever had a good Swiss watch?"

Within days their latent romance gets downright steamy. It is in the dark evening after another tough day on the trail. Matt is seated, leaning against a wagon, legs bent at the knees, splayed open. Cherry lays next to him on his own side, propped comfortably on an elbow. The talk is casual, exploring the rumors of a route alternative to Missouri (i.e., Abilene), the framing of the scene intimate. Buster (acted by Noah Beery), the cowhand nearest queries quietly, "Cherry, how come you done joined the drive?"

"Because Matt turned me down...besides I've taken a liking to that gun of his."

Dunson disrupts the calm momentarily like a parent bursting in on a heavy petting session. Then as he strides away Cherry begins addressing Matt by noting that if he took on Dunson, "I'd have to take you on, too?"

As Matt replies he strokes his nose provocatively. But it is more than a simple Brando-esque gesticulation. He speaks, "You'd find him a handful by himself." Then he tweaks the end of his nose as if passing something off. As he does so the camera leads sneakily to Cherry's insertion of a finger to suck into his own mouth, consummating the allusion to fellatio.

However, it cannot hold. While it is not day all the time, as Fen had remarked, neither is it night. Groot comments to Matt, "Funny what the night does to a man." Matt responds, "During the day they can see." (See what?) The compulsion driving the homosensuality finds its roots in immoderation—Dunson takes Groot, and indeed they carry on like a stereotypical, nattering, bantering old married couple, because of his own excessive hardness, his erect aversion to bending, changing his mind. When he does adjust direction, though, all becomes well. Likewise, Matt and Cherry, overgrown adolescents for whom the homosocial play results from immaturity and the lack of normalcy, straighten up once a woman is introduced to fornicate Matt back to his senses.

The theme of the dangers of excess are most obviously laid out in the subplot of the cowhand who cannot keep his fingers out of the sugar bowl. Groot chastises him repeatedly. "Your sweet tooth is most as bad as liking a woman," he says on one occasion. Ultimately, the inability to rein in his passion for sugar generates a mishap that leads directly to a stampede, which, in turn leads to the death of the stuttering cowhand, Dan Latimer (another mildly drawn Other; played by Harry Carey, Jr.), which, in turn, finds Dunson set to whip the craven sugar lover. "Stealing sugar like a kid," Dunson spits at him. This, because Dunson overreacts for the last time, then leads to Matt's successful wrestling of command from Dunson. In short, they all behave like Freudian adolescents.

Does this all make the movie objectionable or offensive? Not really, Hawks plays the stereotypes as if he is conducting a western symphony. Sure, the homo bit is corny but it is not sinister or mean-spirited or vindictively Othering. Just the opposite. That such behavior signifies espied deviance in the film serves to ironize the whole concept of stages of American evolution. That is, the post homo/Chisholm Trail stage is male adulthood for America in the same way that hetero male adulthood flows from homo adolescence.

The film also has its humorous frontier moments, largely taken at the expense of the cardboard Cherokee cowhand, Quo (acted by one Chief Yowlachie), and his running dispute with Groot. Early in the film Groot loses his false teeth to the aboriginal in a table stakes poker game.

It comes as no surprise of course that Quo cannot speak fair English. "Me bet one silver dollar," he says, without apparent emotion.

Groot complains about the size of the bet.

Quo replies, "Put up or keep face closed."

"Anything's I hate is a happy Injun," Groot retorts. "Look at that gapering puss. How's a body to tell when an Indian's running a bluff or not?"

Ha ha.

The point about how you cannot tell when an Indian is bluffing because they are sneaky and shifty merely evinces a stoicism designed to mask deeper, sinister goings on.

When Quo wins the bet—and the teeth, Groot complains that he needs the dentures to eat.

"Come grub, you get 'em."

"What are you gonna do with 'em?"

"My name now Two-Jaw-Quo."

More ha ha. Silly Injun.

This cantankerous running joke continues while in the background more serious Indian trouble looms. First, there was the initial deadly attack on the wagon train followed by an unsuccessful, unprovoked assault on Dunson and Groot. Now they face similar threats on the drive northward. As Dunson warns, "There's gonna be Indians. How bad I don't know."

Groot and Quo share a wagon (where women and sissies ride, real men preferring to ride the pony), and they argue about the teeth. "If you were half human you'd give 'em back to me."

Quo, stubborn Indian, will not budge. Indians don't, do they, anymore than men who slipped over the line into nearer savagery (such as Dunson).

Savage Indians emerge again in the time between the mutiny against Dunson and the cattle drive reaching Abilene. The cowboys come upon another wagon train, headed to Nevada, where Matt meets his own woman, one Tess Millay (or is that, Tess, invoking the Thomas Hardy heroine, and "my lay"?). First, though, the group is attacked by Indians in the old circle-the-wagons shtick, you know, where Indians can hoot and holler all day long but cannot hit anything.

Lest the problem with Indians, alternatively childish and pathetic mascot-like creatures or the devilish and aggressively pesky ones, not be obvious to viewers, Matt lays it out to Tess in Turnerian terms. Talking of Dunson, he says, "See, he'd taken empty land used for nothing, made it the biggest ranch in the state of Texas, fought to keep it." So here again the common mythical themes emerge—of land empty of civilization and the staking of the right to use violence to get it and keep it. It is not clever, I grant you, but international politics—the arrogant ramblings of imperialists like Henry Kissinger notwithstanding[15]—generally adhere to the same rules as can too easily dominate playgrounds at recess. The biggest dicks decide.

All in the Interstitial Family

While the frontier myth remains grounded in certain resilient, yet frequently undulating and almost unbearably pliable presuppositions about self and Other, it rests firmly upon the architectural supports of imagined stages of development, of espied mythical American evolution. These represent the "old comfortable fictions," as Vine Deloria identifies them, a stench blowing indelibly through the imaginary frontier. Its malodor continues to waft through contemporary film where, as in, say, *Dances with Wolves*, the old fracture lines, glossing over the interstitial spaces, are allegedly relocated.

But what if things were different? I mean, what if instead of insisting on parading and championing difference, one were to promote and embrace the ways in which the experience of frontier has fashioned a unified (but not necessarily homogeneous), albeit complex and recurrently contradictory, whole? To paraphrase historian and media critic Carlos Cortés, you might not like all the traffic congesting the interstate freeways of your city, but the question is what are you going to do about it? There is no point in pretending it is not there.

John Sayles's bewitching, multi-layered *Lone Star* (1995) takes dead aim at a variety of mythical frontier clichés and offers a strikingly innovative and historically more appropriate metaphor for regarding the historical frontier in the American Southwest: incest. In this film an American lad, Sam—Sam, though not an uncle in this world—and a Mexican lass, Pilar, Spanish for pillar, they do it. They *do* it. Because, despite the mythical frontier, they must. Boy meets girl. *Lone Star* relates their hopeful story. It provides an alternative way to read Mexican-American relations, a topic that has all too often been overdubbed with mythical phrasing.[16] Peter Travers of *Rolling Stone* and Roger Ebert called *Lone Star* "great," the latter noting how "deeply and subtly" the film was made.[17] Another critic labeled it "Sayles' version of menudo, the hearty and picante tripe stew popular in Mexico's northern states."[18]

The principal tale hinges around a murder-mystery on the mythical frontier, a thoroughly contemporary revisionist frontier western set in the imagined community of Frontera, Texas, bordering the Rio Grande. Sheriff Sam Deeds, only child of the legendary Frontera sheriff Buddy Deeds, is called upon to investigate the digging up of human remains in the nearby desert. The body turns out to be that of the notorious sheriff Charlie Wade (played with tenebrous and drafty charm by Kris Kristofferson, which critic Stanley Kaufman called a "key performance" as a "son of a bitch"[19]), whom Buddy Deeds had replaced as lawman. For Sam all signs point to his father having shot Charlie in cold blood and then dumping the body. Sam's investigation, the gist of the manifest story, leads to a voyage of self and familial discovery.

Three additional narratives are woven into the fabric of the central story. First, Sam is gradually yet definitively reunited with his one true love, Pilar, now a Mexican-American history teacher in Frontera. The two had consummated a relationship as adolescents. However, their strong and authoritarian parents forcibly ended the relationship and Pilar was sent off to Catholic school.

Pilar's mother, Mercedes, had come to Frontera as a youth. Like many Mexicans before and since, she risked her life crossing the river illegally to the United States. Once there, she prospered. She runs a successful restaurant, owns an impressive home, and drives a Cadillac. Her husband, Eulalio Cruz, had been murdered decades ago by Charlie Wade (Kristofferson). Mercedes, meanwhile, has become aggressively Americanized as the result of her experiences in the United States. For example, on occasion she spots young illegal Mexicans immigrants, fresh from the Rio Grande, sprinting across her lawn. Shocked and dismayed, she calls the Border Patrol on them. "Wetbacks!" she scoffs with no visible trace of irony.

One of her employees, Enrique, challenges her, though. His lover breaks a leg while crossing the border river and then they end up in her back yard. Enrique appeals to Sra. Cruz for help. Will she continue to forget that she came to America in very much the same fashion? Didn't everybody at some point? That is the second minor tale that Sayles spins in this film.

The third revolves around a black Army colonel and the halting steps he takes to rebuild his family. The officer's father, Otis, owner and operator of Big O's, the best and only watering hole in the county for blacks, had abandoned the colonel and mother when the boy was eight. But he did not go far. O moved three doors down and took up with one of his wife's best friends.

The colonel, meanwhile, runs a tight ship in all facets of his life. Nonethless, his beleaguered teenaged son independently approaches O, who, in turn, welcomes a rapprochement. The only way this strand can resolve itself favorably is if the colonel bends, because Grandfather and grandson are willing. Ultimately, he does. In fact, the movie is relentlessly upbeat in this regard, as if Sayles is saying, look, it is possible to change course, lousy things are repairable. Can't we all just get along? The price of admission is self-knowledge. "The man knows 150 varieties of beer but can't tell a Poinsettia from a Prickly Pear...You live in a place, you should learn something about it," one of the soldiers in the film chastises a friend.

The frontier problematics, as identified in the film, include those key historical frontier issues that the myth denies, perverts, and inverts. The contemporary state of American race relations, with a Texas twist, is the result. For example, a new court house is to be named in honor of Buddy Deeds (get it—*buddy* deeds?). Some local Chicanos protest. Buddy was corrupt and bigoted, they cry. An Anglo town councilor, Fenton, complains to the mayor and to Sam, "They call everything else in the county after Martin Luther King, [and] we can't have one measly court house? ...It's bad enough all the street names are in Spanish."

Sam (acted with a brilliant melancholic intensity by Chris Cooper) responds quietly, steadily, "Well, they were here first."

"Well, then, let's call it after Big Chief Shit-in-the-Bucket," Fenton erupts, averring that Indians "had the Mexican beat by centuries."

"Nineteen out of twenty people in this town are Mexican, Fenton," Sam retorts.

A blistering parent-teacher meeting reinforces the common mutually exclusive understandings of Mexican-American history and relations presented by the ethnically divided factions. The camera pans round the group, suggesting a never-ending circularity to the arguments and its roots.

An angry blonde mother complains that Pilar's teaching amounts to, "Tearing everything down. Tearing down our heritage. Tearing down the memory of people who fought and died." She is implying unknowingly that Pilar, the pillar, is seeking to replace the old accepted truths with new. Pillar for a pillar, is what we are meant to understand. It is not so much you have got your truth and I have got mine but, rather, that a middle ground may be found if only folks would act like rational adults.

A Chicano father responds hotly, "We fought and died for this land, too." Bitterly, he adds, "We fought the U.S. Army, the Texas Rangers..."

Seamlessly the camera tracks the ensuing point, counterpoint. The gloating Anglo response: "Yeah, and you lost, buddy. Winners get the bragging rights. That's just the way it goes." A standard sort of redneck, Republican response/nonsense.

And so continues the camera round and round. Let me pick it up again with the angry blonde parent as she spits out, "You people can believe whatever you want. But when it comes to teaching our children..."

"They're our children, too," a Latina counters. Invoking another common platitude, she adds, "As a majority in this community we have the right."

On it goes. When the local Chicano political agitator, Danny, who is also plotting a corrupted run for mayor, points out sharply, yet correctly, that Texas broke away from Mexico in part so that slavery might endure and prosper there (it had been outlawed by Mexico in 1829), the heat reaches its peak.

"Yeah," he is challenged. "You call it history. I call it propaganda. Now I'm sure they got their own account of the Alamo on the other side, but we're not on the other side."

And this is the crux of the film—the Alamo and what can be learned from it. For some whites the message is clear: the United States won. And winner takes all. End of that story. Notice, too, that this position embodies the frontier myth in all its simple-mined, colonial splendor: whites rule, Others drool.

For some Mexican-Americans in the film, the balance has changed since the Alamo because numbers now favor them, hence the story must change, as if history should be qualified by quantity. But should it? How many stories are there of the Alamo that are accurate and fair? Isn't invoking numerical democracy both as a justification and a recipe for new interpretations a restatement of winner-take-all?

Sayles ultimately promotes the notion that, at the very least, any solution must first recognize that either-or dichotomies are useless, wasteful, counterproductive, and even dangerous. Far better to accept that the culture of the southwest is in reality a mixture, a marriage, familial. Part Anglo, part Latino, part Indian, and part black.

The film itself becomes both a history lesson strung together most obviously in the characterizations of the various sheriffs, that is, the law, as well as a meditation on how things should be. Sayles at once recognizes the folly of the myth's evolutionary stages yet simultaneously and carefully notes that the United States has historically behaved in a way commensurate with stages theory. In other words, the ideological pith of the myth may be nonsensical, but culturally it has held much water. And it, too, has operated on the winner-take-all approach to jurisprudence.

Take the sheriffs. Charlie Wade, signifying the oldest way of doing things, was corrupt through and through. As a lieutenant for a shady judge, he systematically and violently promoted not simple segregation but a variety of apartheid in which Chicanos and blacks knew their places *and*, importantly, greased his palms. Those who did not play ball his way faced death. He was, in short, a gunslinger. Meanwhile, it is understood that miscegenation was widespread at the time.

Buddy Deeds was different, more complicated, too. As his name suggests, old-timers from all racial groupings remember him fondly as, well, a buddy. His actions, his deeds, backed this assessment up. Buddy practiced machine politics to Charlie Wade's Anglo *caudillismo* (strong-man rule). The unwritten rules about interracial conduct had not changed much since Charlie Wade. In those days folks understood how to get along. Moreover, Buddy was fair and consistent in enforcing the conventions. Did this not represent (teleologically fuzzy liberal) improvement? Plus, he was respected deeply for it.

But not anymore. Times change and historical revisionism sets in.

Now it is Sam's turn. He is a Gary Cooper hero for our time, *sans* the self-deprecating humor. He is strong, silent, resilient, honest, earnest. And he is in love with Pilar. Always has been. She loves him back, too. Always has. In this way, by and by they are reunited and their love rekindled. Then, it turns out that Buddy had not killed Charlie Wade. Plus, it turns out that Mercedes Cruz remembers who she is and where she comes from and she is going to help those wets, Enrique and amigos, after all.

When Enrique shows up at her door, she chastises him, "You think you are doing these people a favor. What are they going to do? Either they get on welfare or they become criminals."

He dissents, "No es verdad," he implores her. It is not true. And she knows it.

Finally, the black colonel transforms. It happens during a conversation with a young black female whom he reprimands for having failed a drug test.

He challenges her commitment to the Army, but she replies that it is "their [that is, whites'] country! This is one of the best deals they offer."

The bare-knuckled truth of these words strikes him like thunder.

"How do you think I got to be a colonel?" he responds seriously.

"By being good at your job. By doing what they tell you," she stammers, accurately synopsizing the rules white America has thrust upon blacks: follow our rules, or else. But the rules do not generally make a lot of sense because they are not fair and they are not applied evenly. The Private knows this and says as much.

"With your attitude, Private, I'm surprised that you want to stay in the service."

"I do, sir."

"Because it's a job?"

"Outside, it's such a mess," she falters. Correct, idiotic or not, at least the Army's rules are predictable.

"Chaos," he agrees quietly. "Why do you think they let us in on the deal?"

"Cause they got people to fight, you know, Arabs, yellow people, whatever. Might as well use us."

Might as well?

There is, of course, a hitch to all of these near-sugary resolutions to the various conflicts in the film. And it is one that routinely makes my students squirm. Turns out that Buddy and Mercedes had another reason, beyond embracing sheer racialism and upholding community mores, for keeping the adolescent Sam and Pilar apart: they share the same father. Buddy and Mercedes had carried on a long love affair, out of which Pilar was born, shortly after Charlie Wade was killed. Buddy even used county money, $10,000 stolen by Charlie Wade, to set Mercedes up in her business, considering it widow benefits.

So Sam and Pilar's love is incestuous. They are half-siblings. The point being that the frontier is not a line at all, at least not in the sense that borders separate things, cultures. As O explained to his colonel son, Delmar, "You see, it's not like there's a border between the good people and the bad people. You're not on one side or the other." Alternatively, when Sam's investigation of the Charlie Wade death takes him to Ciudad Juárez, he meets with the witness to Wade's murder of Eulalio Cruz. "The bird flying south, you think he sees that line? Rattlesnake? Javelina? Whatever you got. You think halfway across that line they start thinking different? Why should a man?"

"Your government's always been pretty happy to have that line. The question's just been where to draw it," retorts Sam.

"My government can go fuck itself—and so can yours. I'm talking about people here. Men. Mi amigo, Eulalio Cruz was giving some friends of his a lift one day in the back of his camion. But because they're on one side of this invisible line and not the other, they gotta hide in the back como criminales. And because over there he's just another Mexican any man with a badge is his jefe."

Still, it is true love between Sam and Pilar, and true love will out in this film. She cannot have any more kids. As if the point is not obvious enough, she says, just before the camera pulls away and closes the film, "We start from scratch...Forget the Alamo." Good advice.

Remembering the Alamo

Americana, however, has not wanted to forget the Alamo. Quite the opposite. The Alamo represents a grand and lasting moral victory of imagined real men (I mean, John Wayne played Davy Crockett in the film version of it that Wayne directed) conquering lesser beings (you know, of the wetback variety), and out of the wellspring of imagined American virtues winning and winning and winning.

In frontier terms, real and imagined, the Alamo is hardly unique. In fact, it has been played out on a national scale on several occasions since—the battle of the Little Bighorn, Pearl Harbor, September 11. In fact, you might even go so far as to argue that the Alamo is always playing itself out in one version or another in America insofar as the nation always has its public enemy number one. In these cases and others, patterned mythical frontier myopia has contributed to U.S. policies that actually and invariably, unintentionally promoted violence against it. Mind you, the counter response, war vs. Mexico, Indian wars, pinko witch hunts, or war vs. Osama bin Laden is never justified in these terms. Self-interest is packaged into catchy tropes about liberal democracy and capitalism.[20] Blowback is blowback precisely because nobody sees it coming.

Instead, the United States dons its gunfighter pose, assumes the role of victim, and usurps the right not to turn a cheek. I suppose that if one places such attacks against the United States in a fishbowl for the purposes of examination, it does not seem unreasonable to strike back in anger. What else are you gonna do? But on closer inspection, from a view outside the fishbowl, to carry the metaphor, the underlying logic reeks of frontier Othering, of the persuasively insidious whisperings of the magic mirror telling us to conquer and dominate in the name(s) of an imagined unitary civilization. The fact that American behavior contributed to and encouraged violence against it is never seriously considered. To do so is to puff the breath of treason. In order to understand the Others we first simply adopt the bellying pose of American superiority. Then we deny them (that is, those who are It, not us) the right to culture as they see fit. Then we attribute to them stuff that we despise or suspect—and sublimate—about ourselves. We project our uncertainties and our deepest fears, our wildest fantasies and childish fetishes. This is the pure genius of the venture, its glorious plasticity, its liminal permeability. It achieves monolithic results by, er, Other means. In this way, it really is nearly magical (I am tempted, on the one hand, but resist on the other, to call it "black" magic, because even our common language is stacked against the Other—that is: black in what sense?).

Is American society even now still reduced to playing old-fashioned cowboy and Indian games in its race relations and foreign policy? *Lone Star* strongly suggests as much. Sam has been married before to Bunny (acted by one of the best Hollywood actresses that nobody seems to know, Frances McDormand). Bunny is, well, as she puts it, "tightly wound" (a phrase suggesting additional connotations). She is obsessed with football, especially the Dallas Cowboys, America's team. She takes in the home games firsthand but also flies to the away games. She cannot get enough of the Cowboys. When Sam visits her she is watching a college game on television, decked out in a Cowboys jersey. She is always watching—the pros, college, high school, does not matter too much to her. Football is the thing and the Cowboys are the team.

But who are these modern Cowboys, America's team as they have been known for decades? For one, they are the epitome of modern capitalism, contemporary America. As Arthur Asa Berger has noted, "One very important aspect of football is the way it socializes and encultures us. It teaches us how to get along in society, what rules to follow, what life is all about, and so on."[21] (Is this not precisely what the frontier western does?) What is it specifically, then, that football teaches us? Let me answer this briefly by asking you to note how the response parallels some of the things that the frontier myth in film teaches: that violence is good, that football is sexy (I mean, what else are the cheerleaders there for?), time is valuable (and suddenly I can see senator Ransom Stoddard checking his pocket watch, satisfied that the train has arrived on time in Shinbone, as surely as John Elway was the master of the two-minute warning), that the winner knows how to employ the rules to advantage, that rule breakers will be punished but also that rules should be tested constantly, toughness is a virtue, and so on.

Alas, Bunny, devotee of America's team is gone crazy. Football, and by extension what it represents, and in particular the ways in which it encapsulates certain aspects of frontierism *qua* some titillating escapism in the modern world, has thoroughly unbalanced her. She cannot see clearly. Neither can she breathe, she admits. Thanks to the Cowboys, capitalism's team.

The Indian presence in *Lone Star*, meanwhile, echoes a come-as-you-are fatalism tinged with lively, wise humor. In his search for the details of Charlie Wade's death Sam stops to chat with a side-of-the-road peddler, an unnamed Indian (played by Gordon Tootoosis), a sort of Trickster figure. It is here that Sam learns that Buddy had kept a mistress, though she is not identified. This scene reorients the story fundamentally as well as deepens its complexity. Plus, the way in which the Indian is presented stands as crucial. For here the Indian has been reduced to a side-show attraction, except that he is attracting apparently little to no interest at all (which seems to suit him fine, and why not, given the past?). "This stretch of road runs between nowhere and not much else," he tells Sam.

"It's a hell of a place to put a business," Sam observes dryly.

"Don't see much competition, do you?" the Indian laughs, demonstrating that he has mastered one of the key concepts of capitalism (besting the competition), but still does not quite get it. Then, though, because he has self-knowledge and he knows his community, he also does not seem fazed in the least (which in turn might lead one to ponder, who is not getting what?).

Lone Star suggests that a paradigm shift is in order, that the old cultural shibboleths are not working, in fact, that they are maddening (see Bunny). Such a shift, if frontier western war films—for example, *The Green Berets*—are any indicator, may well require tectonic movement. What sustains imperial America is its living, waking dream, the fabulous and resplendent, table-thumping self-deception that imperialism is something that America thwarts, not practices.

Chapter Five

Ritual War: The Only Good Indian

Times Change, Heroes Remain The Same.

—Advertisement for *The Virginian*[1] (2000)

It was not long ago that the western was America's pre-eminent genre. Its ethos and its codes were bound up with America's sense of itself as the nation for which no frontier was uncrossable, no enemy untamable, no mountain too high or forest too dense for conquest. In this respect, westerns were jingoistic lies...

— *New York Times*[2]

...such ideas will make sense when, and not before, Euroamerica finds it as harmless for its children to play Nazis and Jews as it always has Cowboys and Indians.

—Ward Churchill[3]

Isn't the United States constantly at war? Gazing backwards in time I espy the War on Terrorism, the War on Drugs, Desert Storm, military actions against former CIA asset (and erstwhile buddy of George Bush Sr.) Manuel Noriega. Then there were military strikes taken against Grenada, Libya, Sudan, the illegal funding of a war versus Nicaragua, not-so secret wars waged in El Salvador, Guatemala, and Honduras, governments toppled in Argentina and Chile, invasions of the Dominican Republic and Vietnam. Wars on crime and poverty and alleged communist sympathizers, the bombing of Cambodia. And do not forget the cold war, the Korean War, meddling in Brazil, various botched attempts to kill Fidel Castro. And on and on and on.[4]

This endless aggressivity is no less apparent when approaching American history from its hind end. There you find war against the British, a long period of state-sanctioned violence against African-Americans, and hostilities toward lots and lots of Indians, then against Mexico, then the nation rent by internecine conflict, then more Indians and Indians and Indians. Then, in the early twentieth century, repeated military incursions in Cuba, Haiti, Mexico, Nicaragua, the Philippines...and on and on.

Has somebody tallied the deaths here? At least half a million in Central America. More than a million in Vietnam, including 58,000 American boys. U.S. interventions led to many thousands of deaths in Chile and Argentina. Meanwhile, the toll of lives lost and cultures misshapen and destroyed in campaigns of conquest against American indigenous peoples is nearly incalculable.

And for what?

Each case has its unique characteristics yet all share a common, driving cultural explanation, reified by Hollywood and in American pop culture, redolent in mythical frontier terms. While the myth itself did not initiate any of the conflicts any more than it fully and/or satisfactorily accounts for them rationally, still the mythical frontier has framed and continues to provide a national language, sets of commonly understood meanings and signs, a ready source of quietly institutionalized cultural codes of explication. In other words, you know (that is, to borrow Bhabha's notion of splitting) what a western is when you see it, don't you? The frontier western is the spoonful of sugar for the medicine of empire.

Feathering the Colonial Nest

The historical frontier had not suddenly filled up in 1893, when Turner wrote, any more than did disappear the cultural impulses that centuries of empire building had engendered up to that point. If it had, and if they had, real and lasting democracy and equal opportunity and tolerance might well have come to the United States, the imperial expansionism might have ground to a halt. Things have not turned out that way. Not by a long shot. Instead, the mythical frontier worldview has continued to reside comfortably in mainstream thinking as surely as it continued to dominate foreign policy throughout the twentieth century up to the present day—ergo, one reason for the seemingly endless jingoism. But notice too that through psychological processes of projection and inversion the United States is never to blame for the aggression, the violence, the death. It is always the Other's fault. In particular, weak states (or would-be states, say, the Sandinistas) have picked on Uncle Sam. So the United States reacts to attack or responds to invitations to attack and in this way is ethically never to blame for a damn thing.

Take Vietnam. What else could the United States do? They started it, right? "They" being communists bent on world domination and savage, backward "Gooks" corrupted by communism, so many yellow Asian red Indians. Let us not even mention the fact that the Gulf of Tonkin Resolution, which gave the President the right to war on Vietnam, had been premised on fabricated charges of Vietnamese aggression to which the United Sates, naturally, had to respond violently and with extreme prejudice—much the same as it did in the Mexican-American War of 1846–1848, another case of completely fictitious evidence. In reality, trumped–up allegations have served as well as any gilded RSVP.

Turner wrote as a response to the conclusion that the historical frontier had officially closed by 1890. Further, the finding that the old west had been subdued was not an unreasonable assessment. The Indian Wars were over and what remained of American aboriginal peoples had generally been forced on to reservations (though this should not be seen as an acceptance of defeat on their part, any tribe will tell you today). Mexico's territory had long since been incorporated socially, culturally, and economically to the Union (though, again, not easily; and I am referring to mainstream trends, not the margins, because it is in the WASPy middle where the frontier myth is principally operative and resides most comfortably). Moreover, the land itself had been tamed—wolves and grizzlies disappearing, farm and urban communities just beginning to sprout widely.

But what about the sets of attitudes that gave rise to and rationalized the above? Did filling the west solve mainstream America's ethnocentric nearsightedness? Of course not. What about the racially tickled imperialism, the testicular craving of expansion? Did it suddenly wane with the settling of the west? Why would it have? The United States has never stopped expanding. Why should it? Expansion is good, right? Good for everybody. Capitalism could hardly continue to exist as we know it without aggressive growth. That is what capitalism does, expand. Turner's thesis was every bit as much a blueprint for future action as it was a rationalized interpretation of past and present behavior, and Turner made this explicitly clear.[5]

In mythical frontier terms, Vietnam presented a case at one level eerily similar to that presented by U.S. indigenous peoples. Like

Indians, the Vietnamese were non-white, non-Christian, spoke an unintelligible language, stubbornly clung to an ancient culture, and practiced retrograde politics. However, lots of countries did and do. What made Vietnam special was that it additionally represented a significant geo-political and economic morsel to be savored—also just like the old west. Further dumbing-down matters, the United States faced in Vietnam, it assumed, another, formidable and dangerous Other—Soviet and/or Chinese communism (another kind of red, also highly objectionable to the dreamed American model). This conflation of cold war and Monroe Doctrine with Manifest Destiny, as discussed earlier, served as one point of departure in Stanley Kubrick's *Full Metal Jacket*. Kubrick, of course, has hardly been the only one to weigh in on the idea of Vietnam presenting another, offshore frontier for Americans to vanquish.

Wayne's World

The United States methodically bumbled its way into southeast Asia as colonial France backpedaled away from the region, providing the unusual example of one imperial power handing the ball off to another. At least four seminal films have been made about the U.S. role in Vietnam's attempt to decolonize. A masterwork of American cinema, *Apocalypse Now*, released in 1979, reeks of mythical frontier themes (especially the director's cut), employing them as metaphors for the personal journey of Captain Benjamin L. Willard (played by Martin Sheen). There is also *Platoon*, Oliver Stone's gutsy 1986 work. While it appears to be quickly disappearing from pop culture radar, this lovely, over the top (what Stone does so very well) exploration of the would-be duality of the human (essentialized, universalized American) spirit largely sidesteps issues related to the frontier western. To the extent that it fits at all, it is better viewed as a traditional western. In 1987, as discussed at length earlier, Stanley Kubrick released the brilliant in-your-face post-colonial frontier western, *Full Metal Jacket*.

The fourth important Vietnam War film actually came first, in 1968. In fact, it is the only one of consequence to be released while the conflict still raged. Partly, in this way, it became the mother of all Vietnam and post-Vietnam Vietnam War films. It is, of course, John

Wayne's breathtakingly overcooked *Green Berets*, a frontier corker to the bloody core. It is not a good film by any standard, yet it endures. When Howard Hawks, who directed Wayne in *Red River*, was asked to comment on Wayne's direction, he responded simply and accurately: "Pretty bad."[6]

It may also be the last great simple frontier western, another reason it deserves close scrutiny. What I mean by this is that the western genre till the 1960s was overwhelmingly the most popular in American history. However, while Pauline Kael would have had it killed off by 1974, of course it has since rebounded somewhat (see *Dances with Wolves* or *Unforgiven*). That said, the post-sixties frontier westerns of substance are typically complex and primarily revisionist (or fascinatingly botched revisions, like *Dances with Wolves*) or provide canvases, say, to raise questions about America's love affair with gratuitous violence (see the richly ironic *Unforgiven*).

The Vietnam War changed the genre as surely as it changed America.[7] The conflict, a frontier engagement if ever there was one, set against and alongside the push for civil and equal rights in the 1960s, simply cut to the bone to expose America's neo-colonial cultural project in southeast Asia. It is as if Hollywood, intuiting America's mood, suddenly woke and thought, well, you know, these damn cowboy-killing-Indian movies are just plain stupid, maybe even offensive.

The result, though, was not that the western genre disappeared as such, anymore than mainstream America suddenly dropped its racialism, ethno-centralism, misanthropy, and classism. Not by a long shot, though it is true that the western certainly fell into decline and that social relations in the United States improved marginally into the 1970s (where they remain stalled). The western morphed like a caterpillar and took wing as something apparently, yet not substantively, different. In stolidly Freudian fashion it simply found other places to express itself and to hide from, to quote Charles Bukowski, obviousness. In short, on the whole the frontier western got sophisticated. Wayne's *Berets*, so implausible, so impossible, so execrable, only made it more imperative that the cover-up hurry up. Only the most brain dead among us could ever have taken it seriously. Its effect roared like scared silence. Almost a decade lapsed before another genuine cinematic attempt to capture the conflict took place. Meanwhile, what with America's defeat in the war and Nixon's criminal presidency, the country had clearly lost its way (as surely as it seemed to have regained it temporarily after September 11), stumbled, by the mid-seventies.

If box office returns are a reliable indicator, audiences liked *The Green Berets*, which turned a tidy profit.[8] Its particular attractions were several. First, the film starred (and was directed by) John Wayne, the most popular and enduring movie star in film history.[9] Second, Wayne wins this version of the conflict that America would in reality ultimately go on to lose. So the movie expresses a sort of pre-Rambo-esque machismo of the highest order.

Remember, too, that as late as 1968—the year of the Tet offensive (which signaled a turn away from conceivable U.S. victory) and My Lai (the infamous slaughter of innocents by American troops, as yet unknown)—a simple majority of Americans supported U.S. aggressions in southeast Asia. Third, and crucially, the film is a not very cleverly disguised frontier western, so it appealed to hard-core Americana, the Al Bundys and Homer Simpsons bleaching the landscape and voting for Nixon. Forget about the vocal and sometimes violent demonstrations against the Vietnam War, the conflict that the film unambiguously glorifies, I am talking about the silent majority that embraced America's most potent national myth (and voted for Nixon—twice; so much for the decade of sex, drugs, and rock and roll). So the popularity of *Berets*, in other words, was well founded, even if critics did not like it at all.

Across the board reviewers hated it. One appraisal in the *New York Times* called it "unspeakable, so stupid, so rotten and false in every detail...It is vile and insane."[10] Another *Times* review recorded: "An exasperated old Sergeant once told some troops who were being careless about their lives, 'There are two ways to anything—the right way and the John Wayne way.' *The Green Berets* was filmed the John Wayne way."[11] The important literary historian Richard Slotkin termed the film "tendentious, overblown and bogus."[12] Even *Variety*, known for its kid-gloves approach to film evaluation, lambasted the flick as "cliché cluttered" and rife with "wooden performances" and "pedestrian direction."

Variety also hinted that the film was enjoyable, at least in part because Wayne "still remains a most likeable screen personality."[13] Put another way by a different reviewer: "This is a very bad film. It also happens to be enjoyable."[14]

Agreed. My students abhor it yet thoroughly enjoy it at the same time.

So what gives? Audiences liked it, critics did not, though some recognized an inescapable appeal in the work. What is there to hate? What is there to like?

To begin with, the lousy reviews are well deserved and possibly understated. The story is entirely improbable, even ridiculous. A clearly aging Wayne plays Colonel Mike Kirby, off to save the day at a besieged army outpost—crazily yet significantly named Dodge City—in the generic jungle somewhere beyond Da Nang. Flitting unevenly and unfunnily between war drama, manly action, and campy humor, the movie has Wayne gather a predictably idiosyncratic yet toughened and talented rat-packish bunch of Marines to turn the tide against the dastardly Vietcong savages, otherwise dimming the bright lights of civilization. In essence, the film is a siege story, Americana hunkering-down to stand tall and victorious against yellow commie peril. Everyone knows (or used to) that Wayne does not give in.

Meanwhile, the direction of the film is extraordinarily, pathetically clunky. Indeed, it is so bad that much of the humor is unintentional. For example, as one reviewer noted, "The shooting down of colonel Kirby's helicopter must rank as the most amateurish special effect of all time: a plastic model of a helicopter, dangling on a length of fishing line, has its nose set alight with a match."[15] It is a real scream, all right. Apparently, even some former Marines found the unrealism hilarious in parts.[16]

Apart from the wonky mechanical shortcomings, the critics especially disliked the film's bald pro-war propaganda messages. Wayne never made any bones about his political sympathies, either. In fact, he wrote to President Lyndon Johnson in 1965 requesting the government's support for the picture, and he got it. While Wayne secured Pentagon cooperation, in return he also was required to re-write the script at one point to satisfy Pentagon nabobs. Wayne penned:

> Some day a motion picture will be made about Vietnam. Let's make sure it is the kind of picture that will help our cause throughout the world...We want to do it in a manner that will inspire a patriotic attitude—a feeling that we have always had in this country in the past during times of stress and trouble."[17]

As is well known, Wayne's politics were ultra neo-conservative, just this side of American fascism. It is as if, after all the westerns he played in, he came to embrace the frontier myth in its nearest political incarnation in the mid-twentieth century. To be fair, though, so did many Americans if we are to accept the proposition that in a democracy foreign policy reflects the will of the folks who elected the policymakers in the first place. Yep, it is the mythical frontier once again. Some reviewers edged close to the abyss, all at least noting the western contours of *Berets*, if not precisely plumbing its depths.

First, you have got Wayne, who by 1968 was closely identified with Turnerian political ideals. Then there is the inane yarn. A looming desk job threatens Colonel Mike Kirby's very energetic masculinity, but the Army will have none of it. Kirby is a fighting man, a highly trained special forces officer eager get back into the thick of things (what Kubrick more appropriately had called "the shit") in Vietnam, despite the obviousness of his support girdle and near senior-citizen status.

First, however, we are taken on a premise-establishing diversion to Wayne country. The setting is Fort Bragg, North Carolina, a public relations demonstration of equipment and training facilities for public and press. David Janssen plays the doubting liberal reporter, George Beckworth, challenging the soldiers to explain and justify U.S. involvement in Vietnam. He is scolded: "Foreign policy decisions are not made by the military. A soldier goes where he's told to go and fights whoever he's told to fight."

Beckworth grimaces, shifts uncomfortably in his seat just a bit, drags at a cigarette, looks downcast and cynical. He remains unconvinced. So he is told:

> As soldiers we can understand the killing of the military. But the extermination of a civilian leadership, intentional murder and torture of innocent women and children...If this same thing happened here in the United States every mayor in every city would be murdered, every teacher that you'd ever known would be torture and killed...

It is too bad Beckworth evinces little knowledge of American history or he might have pointed out that this had already happened on American soil—to Indians (and Wayne starred in that movie, too) and had he been a prophet he might have pointed to secret future U.S. prisons and the jail at Guantanamo Bay in the early twenty-first century. Plus, it also happened in Vietnam with the express support of the United States, only on the other side of the conflict. I wonder, for example, if Wayne understood the nature of CIA actions in killing off democratically elected officials in Vietnam. Let's be serious, the United States has aided this sort of behavior all over the planet. This is not even disputable.

Back to the lecturing of Beckworth: "...But in spite of this there's always some little fellow out there to stand up and take the place of those who've been decimated. They need us. And they want us."

Take that, Beckworth!

Yeah, those *little* yellow fellows are really something, played by Chinese actors in this film and universally identified by reviewers as "red Indian" stand-ins. That is the John Wayne way, too.

Meanwhile, though, Beckworth will not cave. "It's their war. Let's let them handle it," he suggests.

Sergeant Muldoon ("Muldoon"—and you can picture him perfectly with a name like that) cannot quite believe his Irish ears. "What's involved here," he explains with carefully controlled patience, "is communist domination of the world."

Ta dum!

Then we are led to the base itself where Kirby, a man of redoubtable reputation and a crack shot to boot, gathers up his loveable sidekicks. Then they are off to Da Nang, and then to Camp 107, aka Dodge City. But it is no city of course, this is frontier country and what unfolds is a sort of rearguard mythical tale. In this case the United States is not fighting to occupy a territory as it had when killing Indians and Mexicans but is instead combating a threat posed by ignorant savages under the sway of evil masters (yellow pinkos?) to its own right to dominate the planet. Dodge City is then a fort cut into the last edge of what separates (the) U.S. from them: civilization, decency, democracy, Christianity, capitalism, rugged initiative, and so on. Everywhere Kirby struts here he is caressing his phallic rifle, elevated Vietnamese officers sport neo-cowboy hats (do not look now, but it is Sulu from the original *Star Trek* television series!), and we learn how the Vietcong take fiendish delight in torturing Christians.

Preparing for an imminent Charlie assault Kirby assesses the camp's perimeter as Vietnamese residents serve as background fodder in their silence, their lurking Orientalist hats, tending fires and shuffling weakly. The attack is typically Indian, too, taking place amid treachery (with the Vietcong shamefully not playing by Wayne's rules about how war should be conducted when one invades another country) and at night (you know, when you cannot see clearly; the Indians love night fighting, too, don't they, when its easier to lurk sneakily). The siege is basically a circle-the-wagons shoot-up that might have been drawn from *Red River* or countless other westerns.

Reporter George Beckworth undergoes fundamental change as one consequence of the battle. He is stripped down as the result of his experiences on the imagined frontier. The new Beckworth is ready to get on board and fight the sturdy American imperialist war. For example, when Beckworth objects to the rough handling of a spy captured in camp, Kirby explains, stealing a line from *Liberty Valance*, "Out here due process is a bullet." Beckworth nods knowingly. As if that were not enough, the spy is fingered circumstantially as having beheaded and mutilated a decent citizen and good soldier.

Make me stop. We know from the minute Kirby arrives at Dodge City that Charlie can shell it at will. Why, then, the assault at all? The only apparent reason, as far as I can tell, is exactly for the sheer propaganda value (the critics were right), the pleasure of winning on film what could not be taken in the real world. When Rambo asked, "Do we get to win this time?" Damn right you do, in Wayne's world.

Then it gets worse. In what amounts to another stupider movie altogether, Kirby leads his unit behind enemy lines in order to capture a North Vietnamese general. It is beyond ridiculous and beneath contempt. At any rate, it also loses its mythical focus. The good news is that Beckworth ultimately is reborn, decides to stay on and learn (and perhaps fight, too).

Wayne's world is a cantankerous, mildly paranoid place because not only does it promote and reward violence, it also denigrates women, blacks, Mexicans, Indians, Vietnamese, Germans, Russians, Chinese, whatever you got that is not white, male, Christian, and tough as old leather. It is all about becoming American the imagined frontier way. It is as if once Wayne has thoroughly internalized Turnerian ideals he carries the frontier on his very broad shoulders, never complaining, always pressing forward, swatting away all comers like so many insects.

No-Name Brand

The nearest rival for Wayne's mantel in recent decades has been Clint Eastwood, widely embraced as a no-holds barred tough guy who also came to fame as a western star. Whereas Eastwood's politics are right of center, he is a talented director and thespian (though his Spartan acting style is not to all tastes). Like Wayne in 1968, in 1986 Eastwood directed and starred in a film about America's most recent, contemporary military adventure of the day, this time in Grenada. The two films are instructive and even fun to compare, then, for several reasons.

First, to some extent, at least in the public mind, Eastwood carries on the Wayne—strong and silent, knock-em/sock-em—tradition.[18] Second, Eastwood's film *Heartbreak Ridge* uses the first significant overt U.S. military aggression of the post-Vietnam era as an arena for frontier action, the invasion of the tiny Caribbean island of Grenada in 1984 to free American university students from the clutches of a Cuban takeover. Third, *Ridge* is another potent frontier B-flick, just an adult version. Finally, *Ridge*'s protagonist is a Vietnam vet who carries a lot of sixties' baggage. In this way, his character serves as a vehicle to comment widely on U.S. foreign policy, Americana, and the frontier myth. Further, it hints strongly that the Vietnam baggage has been America's bane since the war. Further, and importantly (and as is especially evident in *The Big Lebowski*), "Vietnam [is] seen not as a specific and unique war, but as part of a continuum of warfare stretching back certainly to Korea, implicitly to World War II, and forward into the contemporary plot of th[is] film."[19] Yet, at the same time, in order that the myth survive attempts to lay it bare publicly for all to see, strategies of mythical containment and smoke and mirrors became necessary. For example, films like *Dances with Wolves* have served as failed apologies for the historical frontier. As if a single movie could take on the role of foiling 80 years of Hollywood tradition. Not only that, but its revisionism stinks to high heaven and only reinforces that which it claims to subvert and convert (i.e., the frontier myth). Less ambitious but equally predictable films such as *Raiders of the Lost Ark* mark a clear (and popular) attempt to escape from the uncomfortable realities of the Jimmy Carter malaise, which set in so nastily after the U.S. retreat from Vietnam and the deeply disturbing menace of Richard Nixon's disgraceful and criminal presidency. The genius of *Raiders* lies in its hyper action, an exuberant flight of alienated fancy. It is like a frontier western on LSD.

Go Ahead, Make My War

Heartbreak Ridge also provided a welcome palette cleanser to the rank obviousness of *Berets'* melodic moronity. As a central theme *Ridge* invokes the dreamy frontier homoeroticism of *Jacket* and *Red River*. And them some. While it is not especially subtle (in fact, it is downright funny in its blatancy), Eastwood clearly knows that his core audience needs in-your-face treatment, as Ebert noted in his review of the movie.[20] Typically muscular-armed and laconically virile, Eastwood's character, Tom (a handle carrying the denotation of male animal) "Gunny" (a ready phallic moniker) Highway, both abhors yet longs for his feminine side. The abhorrence compels and propels his devotion to brute force; the longing is partly practical—he wants to win his ex-wife back (he had been such a non-existent prick while married, literally and figuratively), and it also reflects the conditioning of his life with grown boys, good soldiers. The latter point being that his obsession with masculinity both has fostered and in turn reflects a deeper attraction to other males. He punishes them and himself with brutality. The result is an enticingly rangy, brooding film stewed in angry barroom juices and foul language.

We meet Gunny in the tank where he is drying out after a night of disorderly conduct. Fiddling on a well-chewed stogie—and while sometimes a cigar is just a cigar, here it is not—he is regaling the other inmates with tales of his aggressive youth. But then he is challenged, labeled a faggot by a big fleshy brute who does not like Marines, "jarheads," as he calls them. Gunny just beats the shit out of him.

Of course he does. In this sense he really is our modern John Wayne.

If the cigar *qua* cock setup is not clear enough in this scene, it becomes so when Gunny gets to the base the next day. "Whyn't you suck on one of these," tempts a corrupted NCO who wants to solicit Gunny to look the other way from illegal trade at the base. Still, apart from the homoerotic stuff, Gunny's by the book. All the way. "You get that contraband stogie out of my face or I'll shove it so far up your ass you'll have to set fire to your nose to light it." It is a gorgeous come-on and a delightfully brutal and comically ironic rebuff: you get that cock out of my face or I'll stick it in your ass. What kind of rejection is that?

Gunny is gung-ho and he likes it that way. The flipside is that it has taken him over the edge. His not infrequent lapses in judgment, when he gets drunk and fights, might hint that he is so emblematic of the violence the military embodies that he occasionally implodes by exploding. Is he weak or is he overly strong? Eastwood's aim seems to be more complex, suggesting that the military itself, primed to fight for the sake of fighting (as we know from *Berets* and *Jacket*), in its unnatural obsession with order *and* violence has gone beyond homosocial camaraderie and triggered old-fashioned homosexuality (a scarily clichéd fusion, no question about it, not that Eastwood is the first to make it).

Gunny, on the edge of retirement, wants a transfer back to where he started, the 2nd Marine Reconnaissance Platoon, "now commanded by a bunch of military school sissies and ROTC nerds," as one reviewer has jibed.[21] His CO does not want to grant it—but it has all been decided upstairs somewhere. In a farewell warning he cautions Gunny about the irregular behavior. Gunny, always his own worst enemy, admits that he has had some problems with, what else, "limp dicks"—though he might be referring to his own as much as another's as his former wife, played by a washed-out Marsha Mason, later comments that he had been a bad lover.

Gunny's repressed scratch-the-surface violent gaiety bubbles incessantly in this film. For example, when he arrives back at Recon, he is embraced banteringly by an old friend. Gunny says, "If I was half as ugly as you I'd be a poster-boy for a prophylactic." Then as they hug, "Take it easy now," he says. "Everybody's gonna think I'm spoken for." In another case he mocks the recruits in his charge with wanting to shower together and tells them that their asses are his. His for what? Again, when he confronts the owner of the Palace (played by Ray Jenkins), the bar where his ex works, for taunting some of his soldiers, he is told, "I chew on jarheads and spit 'em out." Gunny responds with resolute Eastwood glee, "Oh, you do? Why don't I just bend you over that table and nail you in the keester?" And on and on throughout the film.

In due course Gunny's heart of gold is revealed, he wins back his ex, he triumphs over his new CO (who had dissed Gunny as an "anachronism...You should be sealed in a glass case that reads: break only in case of war"), and whips his boys into prime fighting shape. That said, what is there to fight?

Grenada, a spit of an island in America's colonial backyard, that is what. While the island held no economic value for the U.S., importantly the movie is set in 1984. Remember, these were the peak Reagan years, a time when U.S. foreign policy, till then so recently in retreat after the loss in Vietnam, was kick-started to a near neolithic conception of geo-politics. Remember Ronald Reagan, the president who waxed about the perils of the Evil Empire, prophesying that if Nicaragua was allowed to fall to communism then it was only a matter of time before Mexico fell (surely among the least likely prognostications ever stated publicly), and joked the bombing of the Soviet Union would begin in "five minutes?"

At any rate, Grenada symbolized for the Reagan White House the alleged dangers presented to the U.S. by Cuba and the Soviet Union. In other words, tiny Grenada *was* important symbolically and, as a result, given Ronald Reagan, geo-politically. So when an apparent Cuban-supported takeover of the island developed the U.S. sent Marines to thwart it—under the guise of rescuing American medical students (appropriately, as Rita Kempley pointed out in her review of the movie, they were "Americans who couldn't get into med school back home"[22]). Gunny gets the call. In *Ridge* Gunny and his troops carry the day, defeat the Cubans and rescue the Yanks. It is a frontier engagement all the way.

It is also interesting to note, by the way, that the film initially won support from the Department of Defense (DOD) but then summarily lost it because of "an excess amount of profanity," as if to suggest that real soldiers do not approve of or engage in cussing. Of course, it is also likely that the DOD did not approve of the homoerotic humor. Further, the script first called for Gunny to be re-routed to Grenada "while on [his] way to Beirut to replace Marines killed during the terrorist bombing in 1983." Eastwood agreed to re-work the script, dropping the Lebanon bit, because the DOD did not want to grant the embarrassing lapse in military security any more publicity than it had already received.[23]

With regard to the mythical frontier, to begin with, we know that Gunny is stripped down. In this sense Eastwood serves him up as symptomatic of the role that the military *must* play in America—

plying an aggressive, malevolent, win at all costs nativism. Echoing *Jacket*, it is savagery put to work in the service of civilization, defending as it cleanses. Eastwood further observes that, as in Gunny's case, taken to its logical extreme this lends to deviant behavior (Kubrick's point, too), which in turn ultimately fashions a sort of existential-Freudian dilemma: we need the violence to renew and protect civilization, as Freud argued that madness was civilization's inevitable reward for curbing instinctual desires, but in so doing we must necessarily suffer one plague of obsessiveness (homosexuality). The trouble is that to curb it would be to undue civilization in the first case.[24]

So Gunny fights. He fights because America needs him. But predictably, even methodically, he disobeys orders, takes the hill prematurely, behaves intrepidly and brilliantly in defense of Americana but also, importantly (and this likely speaks to Eastwood's personal politics) the egoism of the individual (that is, archetypically mythical Americana). It is a beautiful thing after the assault to see him resting easy, grinning gaily, chomping victoriously on a big fat stogie. He is a handsome and rugged sight to behold. This is a real man taking a moment to smell the roses. When his enraged CO arrives and threatens to court-martial him for the disobedience, Gunny rasps, as only the insouciant Clint Eastwood can deliver, "With all due respect, sir, you're beginning to bore the Hell out of me." And then a general shows up at the perfect moment and lauds Gunny for his daring and initiative and chews out the CO. He proudly notes that Gunny had "kicked ass." Right, kicked Cuban movie ass while kissing Turnerian butt.

At the Academy Awards show several years ago Clint Eastwood joked that he might have been Arnold Schwarzenegger's father. The audience understood the reference clearly; and John Wayne might have said the same thing about Eastwood. Though Schwarzenegger does not victimize Indians, Arabs have served similar purposes in his *oeuvre* (an appallingly inflammatory body of work). Two apparently very different movies—*Dances with Wolves* and *Raiders of the Lost Ark*—make this point eloquently. Just think about it. It is ever more the obvious thing in post-9-11 country. Arabs are only another mediated tribe of movie Indians, after all; *Raiders'* Nazis stand in for gassed-up eastern frontier corruption while tarnished and idiotic federal government agents in both films serve as garden variety frontier ninnies against whom the frontiersmen play off; and then the American pretty boy neo-frontiersman also "kick ass" all the way around. In this way, *Dances* and *Raiders* are basically the same film about becoming mythical frontier Americana.

Different Drummer, Same Tom Toms

Both *Dances'* Lieutenant John Dunbar, played (and directed) by Kevin Costner, and *Raiders'* Dr. Henry "Indiana" Jones, played by Harrison Ford (and directed by Steven Spielberg), engage in frontier quests torn straight from the pages of the mythical narrative. The parallels are startling—despite shiny exterior differences. Both characters (and the respective performances) are deeply narcissistic in an archetypically Turnerian vein, their heroic quests similar in a common search for personal bullion and the righteous rewards of necessary and just conquest, their tactics markedly similar in the improbable and yet inevitable crushing of all Other comers. Ostensibly revisionist, *Dances* fully fetishizes the Other as Noble Savage (the Sioux) while at the same time dissing the aboriginal Other the John Wayne way (the splendidly vicious, rigorously colorful, and predictably sinister Pawnee).[25] Likewise, *Raiders*, dazzling and breathless action filmmaking, champions the Noble Arab/red Indian slob (one man in a cast, as they say, of thousands) while braining untold numbers of Middle Eastern Muslims and dandified Nazis.

Dances is the more insidious, I suppose, because it whines loudly that it is something that is not—an upright and reasonable depiction of American Indians (that is, in contraposition to the John Wayne way, which was downright wrong and unreasonable). *Raiders* makes no such attempts at decency in its relentless devotion to championing Indy *qua* frontiersman. Do not be fooled by the ironic handle—"Indiana"—Ford's character is about as Indian as Colonel Kirby (John Wayne) in *Berets*, only in nearer hackneyed savagery. Both Dunbar and Indy are so preposterously formidable that all else, all other characters pale before their intense white auras.

In clever but predictable mythical frontier fashion Dunbar is born again early on. He is an accidental hero—a soldier maimed during the Civil War to the point that he chooses death over life. But he does not die (Confederate Rebs cannot shoot straight, though large numbers try from a close distance). Instead, his attempted suicide backfires: Union troops mistake his death wish for bravery and are reinvigorated to the point that they win an important victory; and the attending general is so impressed by Dunbar's apparently impassioned actions that he dispatches his personal doctor to patch him up. This provides the major undertow for the film: special treatment for the special. The fair-haired boy is just plain lucky. More practically, by winning the general's favor Dunbar secures re-posting anywhere in the blossoming American empire. Dunbar chooses the frontier. "I've always wanted to see the frontier...before it's gone," he says simply and anachronistically.

This crafty opening ostensibly sets Dunbar up as an anti-hero/frontiersman. Close, but not quite. On the one hand he is, after all, alive and thriving quite by accident. True to the frontier western, Dunbar is, after a fashion, stripped and rebuilt. He arrives on the frontier in a uniform that is slowly peeled away. His hair grows wild. He adopts Indian-style clothing, literally Turner's own buckskins. He befriends a wolf, an association which lends him an Indian name and a tropey connection with and to nature. In this manner he is more fully reborn in the magically mythical way: into decency, honesty, bravery, commitment to community and family and fair dealing. However, this process in this film also belies Turnerian illogic—Dunbar is not reborn on the frontier. Further, he is only stripped metaphorically. In reality, he is revealed (rather than reborn) for what he always was but just never, perhaps, knew it. He says as much.

On the other hand, the opening likewise frames him, more to the point, as the boy-darling of the feature. While star-making is an integral element of Hollywood filmmaking (see any Julia Roberts movie), Dunbar's luminous beacon shines so dazzlingly that by the time Indians come on the scene no attempt at full humanization can ever be possible for them. Everything is subordinated to Dunbar, pretty boy American hero, giver of temporary life to dying Indians (a benchmark of their Noble Savagery) and meter of justice to better-dead-than-red Injuns (the terrible Pawnee).

The only thing possibly bigger than Dunbar—because ultimately his dreams suffer disappointment—is the flow of American history, white conquest. But, then, he wanted to die in the first place. As it turns out, moreover, if he is not greater than history he is at least equal to it because in his martyrdom still he prevails for having fought the better fight. But, wait, come on! It is the same fight—Costner only attempts to sanitize it for the benefit of his displaced megalomania, which he confuses (naturally) with beneficence. Sioux writer Vine Deloria wisely put it this way:

> It is singularly instructive that the reviews of *Dances with Wolves* were mostly critical, and strong objections were raised by conservative columnists who took great pride in pointing out the brutality of Indian warfare...This evidence is cited to justify dispossession of the Indians. If you balance *Dances with Wolves* against the hundreds of films which distort the image of Indians, create stereotypes of brutality and incoherence, and justify a fictional western history, it is not difficult to see that the trend of the conservative movement is simply to deny any criticism of the old comfortable fictions.[26]

On the other hand, never one to stray far from the surface, Roger Ebert was overwhelmed by Costner's sensitivity, claiming that the movie "makes amends, sort of, for hundreds of racist and small-minded westerns that went before it."[27] Still, Dunbar's story *is* frontier Americana all the way, Indians be damned (or given the backhanded treatment offered them here). Costner's victory is colonialism's victory.

We are meant to like Dunbar because he makes us feel good at the same time as we take comfort knowing that we still won. It is classic warmed-over post-LBJ liberalism, and it worked for Ebert. In his self-assured rock-star beauty, Wayne-like witlessness, Costner assuages potential recriminations and hard feelings away by the redirection of his anger toward the Pawnee and his disgust for over-civilization in the east (made manifest by ovine traders and sodden military officers, those "I-just-pissed-in-my-pants-and-nobody-can-do-anything-about-it" types). In other words, it is a first-rate frontier shell game. The point is that whites won and the Indians lost. Thanks for making it all so easy to swallow, Lieutenant John Dunbar.

Keeping up with the Joneses

With Indiana Jones conquest is not only easier, it is more fun, too. I mean, if ever a movie was a three dressed up as a nine it is *Raiders of the Lost Ark*. One reviewer put it this way:

> I'd give you a plot summary, but is there really any need? Is there one movie lover who doesn't know that Jones is an archaeology professor/treasure hunter who's hired by the American army to go after the lost ark which, legend has it, contains the broken stone tables [sic] of the Ten Commandments, before Hitler's Nazis find it and use its power for evil? You probably remember it all...[28]

Who cannot remember it? The execution is nearly flawless, the action stupendous, the speed nearly incalculable. Spielberg, now a director known also for his thoughtfulness because of *Schindler's List*,[29] carries this off so well that the hard-core frontier tale and its attendant racism have gone basically undetected by critics and reviewers.

Pauline Kael labeled the movie "impersonal," a slight that Roger Ebert seemed to take personally. Yet Kael has a point. Adult human beings are sometimes hard to find in Spielberg's mawkish *oeuvre*. Kael's comments also would seem to have compelled Ebert, normally a pushover for subterfuge of any sophistication, to turn an uncharacteristically critical eye toward the film, calling it, "like an anthology of the best parts from all the Saturday matinee serials ever made." However, he also termed it "primarily a technical exercise" with "personalities so shallow."

Still, Ebert nearly wet himself about it. His take is that Spielberg is sticking it to the Nazis. And he is. And why not? Nazis deserve it. But why also pick on Indians and Arabs? Not to worry, the reigning king of reviewers counsels, "The movie is just plain fun...It's done with a kind of heedless joy." In other words, do not worry about it, do not think about it. Screw the Nazis and the Indians and the Arabs. Spielberg may have said more than he intended when he told an interviewer, "Raiders owes a lot to the Tarzan books."[30]

In *Raiders* we begin with Indy. It is always Indy. All Indy, mythical American frontiersman. Leather jacket (leather stocking?), crack bullwhip (which he knows how to use and is not afraid to), athletic, smart, savvy, self-adoring, pistol-packing, signature neo-cowboy hat (though equally the chapeau of a Great White Hunter), and so on. He really is a hero styling in Saturday matinee cowboy duds, hat, buckskins and whatnot.

John Dunbar (Kevin Costner) in *Dances with Wolves* after his stripping down and mythical rebirth into a higher state of grace.

The setting is the jungle somewhere, apparently anywhere, in South America, as if all land south of the Rio Grande is one big, undifferentiated mass. A mess. Exotica. Strange monkey sounds and shrilling birdcalls. Dark-skinned natives. Scantily clad savages—yet characteristically easily frightened. Blow darts (the local take on bows and arrows) shot into the trees so that any good tracker can identify them as Indian in origin and untrustworthy Latinos of unknown provenience (that is, yikes, watch out, them's halfbreeds!). While one might suggest that Spielberg employs the mythical frontier tropes ironically or for the sake of pure entertainment, to do so would be like saying that casting Jews as grasping, evil, smelly moneygrubbers might be, well, somehow hilarious. It is not. So what is so funny about these nincompoop South Americans?

Nothing and yet everything.

They move the story along, are conveniently disposable, and allow Indy to be revealed in all his splendor. They are as easy to overlook as circle-the-wagon Indians because that is basically just what they are.

As virtually all filmgoers know, at one level the basic tale in *Raiders* is about the race to locate, uncover, and steal the Ark of the Covenant: Indy vs. the Nazis, with a lot of Indy vs. Arabs thrown in for excitement. Turns out that Adolph Hitler is crazy for the biblical artifact because it allegedly will bestow upon its claimant "the power of God," Indy explains to American federal agent goofballs (the lighter side of mythical eastern bashing).

Indy's victory represents no more than one has come to expect of the frontiersman, his actions symbolizing American virtue and winningness; but also no less, for Indy has enemies in the form of—who else?—Others, here cast as Indians, Arabs, and Nazis. That Indy ultimately prevails reinforces nothing more than the basic truism of Manifest Destiny: God's own will. That is, God likes Americans best. He helps them out in a detached sort of non intrusive benevolent way, providing that—just to be sure that we're talking about American capitalist Calvinism here—they help themselves at the same time. Ark of the Covenant in Nazi hands? Forget about it! This biblical treasure belongs to America.

This racist cartoon-brought-to-life encompasses every schlocky frontier movie trick in the book. First, Indy has to rekindle the fires of passion in order to locate a medallion to help him unlock the secrets of the Ark's hiding place in Egypt. She is his former love, Marion Ravenwood. She is no maid, but a thoroughgoing, whiskey swilling, in-your-face waif tending bar in the Himalayas, given to ontological outbursts such as, "You can't do this to me. I'm an American." She and Indy team up partly because she wants to be sure to obtain her monetary reward (she does not trust Indy, he broke her heart once before), partly because they're thrown in together, and partly because, well, he is a real man, though on the self-absorbed side.

Plus, there are Nazis hot in pursuit. The most vile and pinched-faced, dressed in Flash Gordon black, is the Donald Rumsfield look-a-like whose mug melts so famously at the film's end. He'll stop at nothing; painful torture is his particular, fiendish delight. But he is thwarted in Nepal, amid the lusciously filmed, dark and steamy sequences, crisply edited, that leave Marion's bar in ashes. The tavern itself, meanwhile, closely and significantly resembles any cantina from a spaghetti western.

Duck, Duck, Goose

Marion is a loser. Oh, she is cute enough and scrappy, too. But she is only ever a match for Arabs (though, to be fair, she does not get a chance to fight Indians), as she bops one over the head with a frying pan—and, oops, almost forgot, she also shot one Nepalese native in the back. Further, Indy regards her, in the manner of Tom Doniphon in *Liberty Valance* or Gary Cooper in *High Noon*, in the first case as taking a back seat to his life's work. Indy's avocation, of course, is conquering savages and stealing exotic booty so that it might be put on display in American museums, actions which not only reify white mastery but signal the emasculation and objectification of the male Other (the female variety of which does not exist for Indy unless you want to count his untoward sexual relationship with a teenaged Marion, his mentor's own daughter, sort of analogous to how the U.S. has fucked over colonies it gathered from past imperial powers, in particular, in Latin America).

Indy has one Arab friend—the cardboard clown Sallah (acted by John Rhys-Davies). While he is a full-fledged jolly sidekick, at least this is better than the lurking, contemptible one-eyed man, an Arab smeared to the level of animal in his filth and association with the bad little spider monkey who inveigles against our hero and his girl (he is the cretin that Marion smacks with the frying pan).

Dances' John Dunbar, meanwhile, has Indian friends, too—Kicking Bird (played with disaffected charm and wit by Graham Greene), Wind in His Hair (played by Rodney Grant), and Ten Bears (acted suavely by Floyd 'Red Crow' Westerman). Though the film has many indigenous actors only one major player is actually Lakota Sioux (Westerman). This detail led at least one reviewer to ponder, "Perhaps the filmmakers believe that, unlike Europeans, all native Americans look alike."[31]

Dunbar's woman, far more human than Marion Ravenwood, is the adopted white Indian female, Stands with a Fist (actor Mary McDonnell). While Costner is never less than clear but that they exist for Dunbar's pleasure, these are fuller human beings than you get in *Raiders*. The performances too, at least, are authentic. The attempted, though derailed, empathetic direction also surpasses Spielberg *qua* whiz kid.

It is hard to imagine that anything could be less genuine than *Raiders*, a mean-spirited imperial romp passed off as rip-tootin' harmless mind candy. As an artisan Spielberg navigates the flow of the myth to near perfection. For instance, notice how Indy is always honed for skirmishing, for another improbable escape/victory/conquest. After he wins his way out of the sealed tomb/snake's den, against all odds, he is loaded for bear to nab that Ark. "I'm going after the truck," he sputters with boyish rancor and the indignant confidence of the master race.

"How?" Sallah asks incredulous yet reasonably.

"I don't know. I'm making this up as I go," Indy offers, as if throwing him a bone, to sheer audience delight (at least when I saw it in theatres on two occasions; and remember, the film earned $242 million in 1981, a huge sum).

But it is a fabrication as big as the movie itself, for in the exquisitely composed scenes that follow nothing is left to chance. The eventual success of Indy's non-stop thrill ride is never in actual doubt, it is the manner in which the thing is won (i.e., it is the ancient Greek play all over again, attendant with the moral conviction of the Spanish *reconquista*) that we applaud. Spielberg has certainly done his homework on that count.

As with Indy, though less obviously, Dunbar is on a mission from God to do the necessary work of Manifest Destiny. Yet Dunbar's sympathy stands in stark contrast to Indy's patronizing, colonial dementia. While self love glues both characters together, Costner earnestly and awkwardly goes through the motions of reaching for a kinder, gentler tone. He really wants to help the Indians, to feel their pain. Whereas for Indy they are, variously, mere props, largely inanimate objects, projected inverted mirrors.

But then the Sioux serve mostly as curiosities to Dunbar's penetrating, questioning mind, anyway. The Pawnee, Sioux enemies, are every bit as savage as any Injuns the Duke ever tangled with—and colorful, to boot, in their costuming. Besides, Costner's camera loves Dunbar, pitilessly framing him as the fount of all *doing*, whereas the Sioux are really good at *being*. The former acts while the latter are acted upon.

Dances offers up a sanitized Manifest Destiny by sugar-coating it and pretending that it is something else (what, say, a movie star's shimmering oblation to himself?). The trick, in fact, the knack of the film, is in its unswerving understanding of audience complicity. American filmgoers, wooed by Costner's hunky locks and passive aggressivity and ironic, endearing clumsiness (neato! just like Indy, a nerdier frontiersman for Baby Boomer sensibilities), are invited to embrace guiltlessness, as if John Dunbar in his perpetual rebirthing has washed *them* clean. He is the Jesus Christ of the frontier, equally fanciful and equally willing to suffer martyrdom for the sins of white America.

If Dunbar is Christ, then Indy must be Moses, delivering us to the promised land (in a kind of frontierish onanism, again and again and again). Through Indy, director Spielberg dishes up what surely ranks as one of the most astonishingly triumphalist expressions of imperialist frontierism since *The Green Berets*. That it is a substantive work of art, have no doubt—the execution is a considerable treat to behold—but it is equally a throaty descent and deeply disturbing hyper-ramble into imperial racism and conquest in the name of God's work, Manifest Destiny. It is another lapse into all-too predictable, what John Dewey referred to as Americana's near obsession with "pernicious dualisms," a classically American black/and/white approach to cultural history. This vision observes neither red nor yellow nor brown, let alone grey. No color at all. In a sense it is the absence of color because it is all about white light, sparkling and blistering white heat. After all, it is a work done for yet another of His chosen people where all those not chosen, Othered—Indians, Arabs, and such—are essentially conflated configurations serving to not so unobviously expose American exceptionalism. Just a movie, after all. Right, it is the John Wayne way, but with bells and whistles.

Cracking the whip as any mythical frontiersman might, Indiana Jones (Harrison Ford) wards off dangerous Arabs in *Raiders of the Lost Ark*.

Sly Gentility

The blare and the glare of *Raiders* feathered a new nesting spot for the mythical frontier tale. The movie's clatter and fireworks serve to obscure the ugly Turnerianisms at work not far beneath its scaly surface. Given Nixon, Vietnam, and a sputtering U.S. economy in the 1970s, *Raiders* was the perfect movie for its time, the ideal escape from an unpleasant American reality. *Dances*, too, hit the right chord in the early 1990s. One of the lasting effects of the dynamism of the 1960s was that long-standing social injustices were called out and challenged. Since much of mainstream America's deepest prejudice has long been lovingly coddled and safely harbored in the frontier narrative (that is, the frontier western), something had to give. And it did. First, as I will argue in the next chapter, science fiction and action films picked up the frontier trail and have taken it in new directions (importantly, without substantively altering the mythical meta-narrative). Meanwhile, *Dances*, in the spirit of the new gilded post-Reagan age, attempts an awkward, washed out, banal and ultimately insincere, "Oops, look at me. I'm kinda sorry." However, it is not in fact a *mea culpa* or any other sort of apology; the emphasis is on the "I." The focus is more that "I" am speaking than it is on what "I" (importantly) have to say (nothing). In this sense, one might also read these films as dying gasps of modernism in an increasingly postmodern world.

Skinning a Cat

The Big Lebowski, a sprawling and riotous pillory of the frontier myth addresses some of these very issues. It's premised upon the observation that the Vietnam War cleaved the American frontier male archetype, the results flavoring (amusingly, for the Coen brothers, makers of the film) the garden salad postmodernism of contemporary America. That is, while postmodernism (the idea that ultimate truth is unknowable and that things are best understood in historical and cultural context) has mostly swept away the old modernist certainties in American life, nothing in the updated model American male has been untouched by frontier-modernist imperialism. It's as if postmodern Americana suffers from a modernist hangover (but hilariously and without the headache).

Traditionally, of course, the myth has reflected modernist sensibilities; what the Coens are asking here is what happens to the myth and to its archetypes in an increasingly postmodern United States after, and as a result of, Nam? Combine this with the observation that American foreign policy has remained doggedly modernist in conception while, in practice, spewing postmodern progeny (again, here in this film with funny results), and the outcomes are, well, overlapping and multi-layered.

Briefly, the tale begins with a case of mistaken identity, one Lebowski wrongly substituted for the other. The former, known as the Dude, a mild 40-something hazed-over dropout, played with exquisite non-chalant intensity and hectic vibrancy by Jeff Bridges, is surprised by thugs who come looking for payment of debts to a porn filmmaker run up by the other Lebowski's teenaged wife. Before the toughs discover their error (wrong Lebowski), one urinates on the Dude's rug, and with this the extraordinary Coen anti-frontier flick/postmodern frontier western is off and galloping.

When the Dude, counseled by his tentatively explosive and rancorously indiscreet pal and sensitive bowling partner, Walter (a role inhabited deeply and gorgeously by John Goodman), seeks restitution for the rug from Mr. Lebowski, the Dude and Walter (and Donny, their quiet, cannot get-a-word-in-edgewise sidekick, played by Steve Buscemi) are dragged into a tale of mystery and intrigue. To begin with, Mr. Lebowski (acted by a jazzed up David Huddleston in a wheelchair) contracts the Dude to hand over a $1 million ransom in return for his suddenly kidnapped wife. The Dude, in the course of events, concludes that she has kidnapped herself just to get the cash. Then it turns out that there was no cash at all. Mr. Lebowski, we learn from his daughter Maude—who also mates with the Dude in order to have a baby—is broke, and is mostly a pathetic stentorian fraud, passing himself off as an achiever while in reality he is a business failure.

So, it turns out that Mr. Lebowski has set the Dude up—debtors think he has the million dollars so, Mr. Lebowski calculates, they will turn to the Dude to collect the wife's debt (somehow leaving her off the hook). They do. So do the German nihilists contracted by Mr. Lebowski to recover the (non-existent) cash from the fraudulent kidnap payoff. When it turns out that Mrs. Lebowski has simply taken off for a few days to visit friends, the big lie is revealed to the Dude and Walter. But the film has one major act to go.

The key sub-plot revolves around the three friends' preparations for league bowling playoffs. Much of the film is shot with grace, sensuous verve, and bundled poetic energy in the bowling alley. Before the Dude, Walter, and Donny can return to concentrating on their next match, they first face down the nihilists in the bowling alley parking lot. While they prevail, Donny dies of a heart attack. The

Dude and Walter cremate the remains, which they sort of dump into the Pacific Ocean. Then they go bowling. End of story, of that story.

Penetrating Camels

Step by step, shot by shot, *Big* is a fallout tale of the havoc wrought upon the United States by Vietnam and similar frontier engagements. It is a postmodern reflection viewed at the crosshairs of the soft underbelly of the consequences of America's imperial expansionism. It is an existential throwing up of the hands in favor of laughter over the hand wringing and shrill liberal outrage that might as easily have been portrayed. The film, and almost without exception the performances of its cast, is virtuoso in nearly ever respect. And the frontier narrative drip, drip, drips from its every frame. This is made more than clear in the opening two minutes alone. Let me explain.

In the beginning the camera pans a desert landscape, tracking the path of a rolling tumbleweed. The music, hauntingly and cornball western, croons all about a tumbleweed and pledging one's love to the ground. Then there is the sappy western twanged voice-over of the Stranger (Sam Elliott, who appears twice as a cowboy later in the film) setting up the viewer. The voice is deep and rough edged:

> Way out west there's this fella. Fella I wanna tell ya about...name of Jeff Lebowski. At least that's the handle his loving parents gave him. He called himself the Dude. Dude, that's a name no one would self apply where I come from.

The voice-over then pauses and the camera simply follows the tumbleweed—up over a ridge to reveal the lights of an evening in southern California. You can almost smell the night. The camera takes us across a bridge over Interstate 405, rolling down a street past a Mexican restaurant and a carwash, over a manhole cover (where the camera hesitates for an instant) and then the tumbleweed blows on to the beach and arrives at the Pacific Ocean.

What we have witnessed is a near perfect opening frontier western gambit. I mean, it is pretty obvious—the tumbleweed, the music, the voice-over, the western desert, and the west-est of everything geographically American, the California beach. You'll note as well that the Stranger takes partial exception to the Dude's name—"that's a name no one would self-apply where I come from." Right. But where is he from? Normally, western allusions such as this point us back to the prince of the genre—John Ford. Viewed from this vantage point the name suggests much. First, it evokes—especially for those not old enough to fully remember John Wayne's obnoxious and belligerent politics—the Duke. The Dude. The Duke. Similar sounding. You may well recall that in *Liberty Valance* the character of Liberty Valance belittles Ransom Stoddard by calling him "dude," a word substituting for, say, sissy-pants, geek, fairy, weakling—connotations the word no longer carries, in the main, but that continue to be recalled by the Stranger. The Dude then is the man for his times as surely as the Duke was for his. That neither is empirically real and that both ring culturally true is the Stranger's basic observation. Further, by invoking the many western signifiers the Coens seek clearly to establish a link between this tale and the frontier narrative. This is provided importantly at one level by the background noise, frontier jingoism—in this case, the Gulf War.

Then we meet the Dude—and we are still within the first two minutes of the film—later in the evening at Ralph's, the upscale California supermarket. He is clad in baggy shorts, worn t-shirt, dark sunglasses, dressing robe and cheap plastic sandals. He walks indolently, flip-flopping, pauses to purchase a quart of milk—which he opens and sniffs first. Then he writes a check for it, 69 cents. The Dude has fantastic locks, thick and lustrous hair that does not stop.

Meanwhile, in the film, the v.o. has resumed, reminding us that this tale is set at:

> ...just about the time of our conflict with Saddam and the Iraqis. I only mention it cause sometimes there's a man. I won't say a hero. Cause what's a hero? But sometimes there's a man, and I'm talkin' about the Dude here. Sometimes there's a man, well, he's the man for his time and place. He fits right in there...But sometimes there's a man. Sometimes there's a man.

Before we leave the scene and move to the Dude's apartment, where the bullies/rug pissers await, the camera picks up a newscast above the till, and there is George Bush Sr. famously uttering threats against Iraq and Saddam Hussein, "This will not stand," he sputters famously to reporters. "This will not stand. Uh, this aggression will not stand."

Of course it did not stand, did it? And the United States led the charge to free Kuwait in the name of, according to Bush, freedom and democracy. However, Kuwait is about as democratic as fifteenth-century Spain, about as free and upwardly mobile as late nineteenth-century Mississippi. Thus, for this film and for any sensible reading of the frontier myth, the Gulf War was a frontier conflict. One more example of the United States flexing its expansionary muscles and will on the international stage.

Symbolically, Saddam *qua* everyman-Arab posed a challenge to American frontier masculinity, Turnerian hegemony; more practically, Iraq threatened U.S. oil interests, and by extension capitalism itself. Culturally, you may note, by the early 1990s Arabs had long been portrayed as American Others, from centuries of Anglo orientalizing (that is, the cultural project in which western culture has internalized and promotes notions of alleged Arab inferiority[32]) to the action films of Arnold Schwarzenegger. While this observation may have deeper resonance viewed from post-9-11 country, it is important to remember that Arabs presented a culturally significant target *before* fanatics blew up the World Trade Center twin towers.

Like American Indians, in mythical terms Saddam invited sturdy and violent corrective reaction. In this way, it would have been impolite not to have attacked him. Besides, America needs Iraq's most precious natural resource, oil that keeps America's economy moving, fuels its transportation system. After all, what is oil to Arabs? A basic frontier trope would have you believe that they are basically (still) flying around on magic carpets (or copulating with dromedaries, "camel-fuckers," as Walter puts it). Well, let's face it, like the thugs who showed up at the Dude's home that evening, metaphorically in 1991 Saddam Hussein had more or less soiled America's rug, not so metaphorically threatening to hinder U.S. mobility by endangering its access to oil. That constitutes the running frontier gag tying the movie together, precisely how, as the Dude explains, the soiled rug had tied his room together. The allusion is made explicit in one of the dream sequences in which magic carpets are employed.

Then when the Dude confronts Mr. Lebowksi demanding payment for the soiled rug, the elder Lebowski dismisses him, "If you don't mind, sir!"

The Dude about loses his composure altogether, "Well, I do mind. The Dude minds!" he complains, his voice rising, aping George

Bush's very words. "This will not stand. You know. This aggression will not stand!"

Mr. Lebowski responds by blowing his cool, accusing the Dude of sheer laziness and cry-babyishness. "I didn't blame anyone for the loss of my legs. Some Chinamen took them from me in Korea. But I went out and achieved anyway. I cannot solve your problems, sir. Only you can."

The Dude sees he will get nowhere now. He slips his sunglasses back up his nose. "Oh, fuck it," he says, getting up.

"Yes, fuck it...That's your answer to everything," Mr. Lebowski shouts as the Dude wanders out of the huge office. "Your revolution is over, Mr. Lebowski," he hollers. "Condolences! The bums lost!"

Turns out, though, that Mr. Lebowski is a complete business fraud. His being physically crippled stands in neatly for his moral cravenness and the deceitful premises upon which American fiduciary comfort has been constructed. Further, you'll notice that Mr. Lebowski invokes yet another U.S. mythico-imperial dalliance, the Korean War. Again, in Korea as with Indians and Vietnamese and Saddam, the U.S. faced a real military threat—but one which it sought to understand fully only through Turnerian lenses, which in turn justified the initial aggression (couched as necessary and justifiable reaction). When the United States fights these wars for freedom and democracy and capitalism, why, after the conflicts conclude, does the United States not engage in policies of helping to rebuild? Simply defeating an enemy does not promote or build or provide sustenance to its paper ideals of freedom and democracy and equal opportunity—unless the ideals only apply to a domestic, mainstream, white audience. I mean, if defensive altruism was at the root of U.S. actions, where is the evidence? If it is simply a matter of the bottom line and phallic politics, then why not come clean? But this is silly. Of course, the answer lies in none of these places. U.S. expansionism and its battles to maintain/fine tune its empire have their own circular, morally grounded frontier logic.

Dull Roar

Big, right from the get go, reminds us that the world is more complicated (yet humorously no less absurd) than the frontier tale would have it, but the myth remains strong enough to continue to inveigle its modernist ways into an increasingly postmodern world. One result is that the flick is busy, even cluttered—a Coen trademark—but also in deference to the Dude's own story: decidedly anti-frontier, sketched necessarily then with knotty brush strokes.

Again, while the canvas is postmodern, at least one of the colors, that of U.S. foreign policy, is mythically modern all the way. If reviewers did not get it—you might ask, when do they ever? If the film's frontier angles went unnoticed by reviewers—you might ask, when have they ever noticed the frontier except from positions inside the box? Never.

The film received grandly mixed assessments, all noting *Big*'s enthusiastic and appropriate confusedness, its cussed determination to squeeze humor out of every pore, and its homage to many landmark American films (especially the traditional western genre). However, there was nary a word about the frontier. A review in *Variety* captured the mood, that the movie "nonetheless adds up to considerably more than *Big*'s often scintillating parts, simply because the film doesn't seem to be about anything other than its own cleverness."[33] This "cleverness" is neither identified nor explained.

Writing in *The New Republic* Stanley Kaufman offered a backhanded appraisal, noting that "Once again the Coen brothers are the brightest boys in film school," but the film ultimately "slips into pointless showing off." The film, Kaufman uncharitably avers, is about a lot of nothing. He espies "Not one moment of entertainment." The Dude's radical past amounts to "window dressing on a dummy." And Goodman, "who is sometimes funny and fat, is only fat here."[34] Even a review that scored *Big* above other critically applauded Coen efforts such as *Fargo* and *Miller's Crossing*[35] said it adds up to "a wonderful celebration of doing nothing."[36]

Never one to miss echoing the crowd, Ebert termed it a "genial, shambling, comedy...[but] persons attempting to find a plot in it will be shot."[37] Ebert noted the Gulf War setting but, echoing Kenneth Turan in the *Los Angeles Times*, identified no significance in it.[38] Similarly, Susan Stark, writing in the *Detroit News*, termed it a modern western, but then dropped the idea altogether. Grading the picture a "B," Richard Schickel commented in *Time* magazine, "there is always something fascinating about following the Coens' rapt gaze as they peer into the American nut bowl."[39] Alas, he never explains what is so interesting about it.

The Dude and Walter are casualties of Vietnam—the former because he waged war on the culture in which the conflict was germinated and the latter because he actually fought in southeast Asia. The Dude was a sixties radical, co-author of the "original" Port Huron Statement (not the watered down "compromise" version that most of us know) and member of radical political organizations promoting peace, pacifism, and such. Fast forward to the time of the first Gulf War 30 years later and he is burned out, hazy, sluggish, having smoked too many reefers and imbibed too many White Russians/Caucasians (Caucasians/White Russians? Yes, yet another over-the-head reference to an imperial global conflict, the results from which the United States engineered its Manifest Destiny/Monroe Doctrine/cold war frontier policy triumvirate of the twentieth century).

Walter fought in Nam. In fact, so conditioned was he by the experience that it remade his personality and dominates his every failing move. He is angry in the pursuit of relaxation, he is aggressive while championing his right to relax, and he is obsessive about others playing by the rules. He never misses an opportunity when under stress to note that his buddies "died face down in the muck," so he would not have to bear (any) such ignominy (for example, a waitress at the International House of Pancakes asking him to keep his loud cussing voice down in the family restaurant—he refuses angrily and loudly). Everything he touches turns to mud—a not unobvious comment on the merits of a U.S. foreign policy driven by the non-reality of the waking frontier dream.

The Dude and Walter are unlikely friends insofar as they radiate energy from either side of a substantive cultural divide (that is, what to make of Vietnam, on the one hand; and, more basically, the role and appropriateness of the use of violence as a means to settle disputes). Yet they embrace each other in part because of their shared American pedigree, symbolized neatly by their mutual affection for bowling, an everyman's pastime.

Walter is the living, nearly schizophrenic embodiment of the frontiersman: big, strong, independent, resourceful, energetic, violent, clever, and so on. Yet he is a disaster waiting to happen. For example, the film's first "chinaman" (prior to Mr. Lebowski's reference to how he lost his legs in Korea) was the thug who peed on the Dude's rug. When the Dude tells Walter about it, Walter boils over with a craving for vengeance, always tipping his hand to the seductive undertow of the background frontier noise, the direct issue being in this case: "I'm talking about drawing a line in the sand," he bellows. What sand? And where?

Later, when he catches a rival bowler (allegedly) stepping over the fault line, Walter challenges him, telling the Dude to mark the score a zero. When the bowler, Smokey, an easy-going garden variety American Indian complains, Walter pulls a pistol from his bowling bag and aims it at Smokey's head. "Smokey," he says, "this is not Nam. There are rules." Again, the simple action—stepping over a line, in the context of the frontier western resonates as a symbolic dispute between Indians and the United States over treaty rights and land claims (and the way historically the United States has dealt with Indians—with a gun in hand). Smokey says he never stepped over the line. Walter disagrees and menaces him. "Smokey, you're entering a world of pain," he presses, as much describing the results of his own Nam experience as throwing it up at Smokey.

Afterwards, in the parking lot, the Dude confronts Walter about the aggressive behavior. "Will you just take it easy, man!" he pleads, both of them oblivious to the police cars and flashing lights behind them (presumably called to the scene because of Walter's pistol waggling). Walter responds characteristically, "You know, that's your answer for everything, Dude. And let me point out something. Pacifism is not." Suddenly he is tongue-tied, turning on a dime, flipping switches brilliantly in Goodman's portrayal. "Look at our current situation with that camel fucker in Iraq. Pacifism is not something to hide behind."

"Just take it easy, man," the Dude implores him.

"I'm perfectly calm."

"Yeah," the Dude nearly screams, "waving the fucking gun around!"

Walter is zenlike now. "I'm calmer than you are."

"Will you just take it easy!" More shouting.

"Calmer than you are." A whisper.

If Walter is the fried-over result as well as the embodiment of U.S. frontiering, it is odd that he does not take exception to the Dude's quoting Lenin. This scene is remarkable. They are at the bowling alley. The Dude is seated on the left, Walter to the right, Donny as always framed between them. In fact, Donny, until moments before his death is always cast as the quintessential Eisenhower American sort of stunned Joe Average—quiet, unassuming, a stalwart friend, likes bowling, kind of dumb, cannot get a word in because of the racket from the left and the right. The Dude says, trying to reason out the real story to Bunny's kidnapping, "It's like Lenin said, you look for the person who'll benefit, uh," he grapples for words, "you know."

Donny mistakes Vladimir Lenin for Beatle John Lennon. "I am the walrus?" he offers, quoting the Beatles tune (and thereby cleverly foreshadowing his own death).

Dude, exasperated but muddled: "You know what I'm trying to say." He is talking to Walter.

Donny, questioning, helpful: "I am the walrus?"

Walter, taken aback, ignoring Donny: "That fucking bitch!"

Donny, innocent, querulous: "I am the walrus?"

Walter, angrily: "Shut the fuck up, Donny! V.I. Lenin...Those rich fucks. I did not watch my buddies die face down in the muck so that this fucking strumpet, this fucking whore could waltz around..."

Dude, ironically: "I don't see any connection with Vietnam."

This dialogue is meant to be spoken, of course, and indeed it fairly crackles in these actors' hands. My point is to cite it only in an attempt to demonstrate how firmly and far the Coens take us into frontier country and, further, how compelling and difficult are the questions they raise. America's empire building has been the formative experience of life both for the Dude and Walter (and Mr. Lebowski and probably Smokey, too). Now in middle age they are merely playing out the hands they have been dealt.

The Coens posit Donny as more authentically middle Americana than either the Dude or Walter. However, while he is not invisible, he is largely ignored by his pals. Walter is the eternal mythical past/present—and he admits as much to the Dude: "You're goddmaned right I'm living in the fucking past." The Dude is one incarnation of the popularly conceived postmodern relativist, I'm-okay/you're okay gang, dominating the present. Donny is mythically "real" America, the sort of normal guy who is sacrificed in the folly generated by the postmodern, post-Vietnam, always-the-frontier maelstrom. No wonder Jack Kroll calls the Coens "the two-headed monster of postmodern film."[40]

Let's be clear. The film lays America's troubles, its post-structural angst, at the doors of wars with Korea (Mr. Lebowski's madness and infirmity), Vietnam (the Dude's very dudeness and Walter's Sybil-like detachment from reality), even World War Two (the German nihilists whom Walter reinvents as "fucking Nazis"), and of course the Gulf War (as Walter explains, "Me and Charlie, eyeball to eyeball. Now that's fucking combat...whereas what we have here [with Iraq], a bunch of fag eaters wearing towels on their heads...this is not a worthy adversary"). Like the Stranger said, sometimes there's a man. Well, sometimes there's two.

The price of the Gulf War is Donny's life, another clichéd cinematic death of innocence. What Donny represents—heartlandishly American, again reified by bowling, an activity that is at once middle America yet also a throwback to a time when Donny might have had a voice—fades like a western sunset. He has reached the end of the line—literally. He suffers a heart attack and dies at the end of a parking line that separates cars on the lot outside the lanes. Yes, Donny goes down. It is a heart attack. Poignantly, Walter tells Dude to call the "medics." He comforts Donny by telling him that help is being "choppered" in. Nam, Nam, always Nam.

The Cat Came Back

Donny dies and Walter wins. Moved from the central framing between his two buddies just before his death, he is realigned at Walter's side. To add insult to injury, when they attempt to scatter his ashes the wind gathers them and throws them back in the Dude's face. Walter releases them into the Dude's face, albeit accidentally and with the best of intentions. So Mr. Lebowski was right, the Dude loses. Doubly so. Pacifism lost Vietnam and now it is losing the frontiersman (Walter). The Turnerian Walter won the Gulf War because he wins every war for the United States (except Vietnam—which partly explains, first, why he is so very messed up; and, second, why the Gulf War was so desperately necessary and successful in partially repairing, and at long last too, the damage done by Vietnam to the mythical frontier psyche). He wins simply because he is what he is, essential and projectively eternal, hard-core; and so American expansionism carries on. The Coens query, then, what is this thing called postmodernism in practice if the frontier myth (that is, modernism) in your face, while slightly tattered at its edges, remains essentially intact? Their response seems to be that it is just there, out there, that it is us. Perhaps this is what George W. Bush understood when he explained to former Canadian Prime Minister Jean Chretien that in his post-9-11 military actions he was careful to mind the "blood lust" of America.[41]

Leftovers

Finally, I want to draw attention to two aspects of the film widely commented upon by reviewers—John Turturro's hilarious super-charged cameo as the Latino bowler Jesus Quintana and the matter of bowling itself. Jesus (and his partner Leon—lion, in Spanish), whom the friends are scheduled to play, confronts them after hearing about the incident in which Walter pulled the gun on Smokey. This Jesus conjures up a clear image of the vengeful deity of Manifest Destiny who takes no prisoners, not the warm and fuzzy son of God so often portrayed by late twentieth-century Christians. He tells them that if they try any such shenanigans against him, he is gonna take the gun away and shove it up Walter's ass and pull the trigger "till it goes click." The three are modestly stunned by Jesus.

"Jesus!" the Dude gasps.

"You said it, man. Nobody fucks with the Jesus," Jesus responds cockily. At least nobody fucks with this Jesus—as generations of Indians, Mexican, Arabs, and Vietnamese Others well know.

Bowling figures prominently and importantly in this film, despite reviewers' assertions that it serves no useful purpose. Yet it seems to me that the Coens register a compelling case that, in the context of the late twentieth century, bowling offers a persuasive domestic metaphor for frontierism. Professional football has been identified as reflecting mainstream American values—the barely controlled violence, the rewarding of naked aggression, the symbolic seizing of others' territory to earn rewards (points), the defensive strategies taken against predictable attacks, the dominance of whites (quarterbacks and coaches) in positions of authority and dominance, team uniforms (like the military, we are all in this together), time management and such. The Coens suggest evocatively that bowling, far more an everyman's activity than pro football, which is reserved for testosterone-pumped mutant boy-heroes, reflects mainstream frontierism. Think about it. You get the controlled and repetitive violence, clear and predictable rules of engagement, a never-ending knocking-down-but-getting-back-on-your-horses-ism. It is simpler, dumber, and more democratic. It requires little skill—whereas football is complicated and requires great skill. It is a form of managed, gutless, victimless hostility that anybody can play. You are supposed to knock the pins down, that is what they are there for. Uniforms are not necessary. Anybody can play. Now that is a garden salad.

Chapter Six

Back to the Future: Frontier Westerns and the Final Frontier

> Culture is not a power, something to which social events, behaviors, institutions, or processes can be causally attributed; it is a context, something within which they can be intelligibly—that is, thickly—described.
>
> —Clifford Geertz[1]

> He had come to America as so many before him to receive the benison of being Ellis Islanded, of starting over. Give me a name, America, make of me a Buzz or Chip or Spike. Bathe me in amnesia and clothe me in your powerful unknowing. Enlist me in your J. Crew and hand me my mouse ears! No longer a historian but a man without histories let me be. I'll rip my lying tongue out of my throat and speak your broken English instead. Scan me, digitize me, beam me up. If the past is the sick old Earth, then, America, be my flying saucer. Fly me to the rim of space. The moon's not far enough.
>
> —Salman Rushdie[2]

> We may quite interestingly speculate that not only might cinema have permitted Americans to situate themselves within sweeping global expansion, it may also have promoted the fantasy that the entire world was available for the taking.
>
> —Diane Negra[3]

The frontier myth has been challenged and prodded and taken to task by filmmakers on a variety of occasions—among other things reminding us that the myth, while central to the American experience, is neither monolithic nor immutable. That said, the examples herein explored—such as *Full Metal Jacket*, *Heartbreak Ridge*, and *The Big Lebowski*—represent creative efforts emanating from the cultural core of Americana. One result has been the creation of rich and contemplative counter-frontier westerns. In these films our (anti-)heroes rent at the fabric of the myth from privileged white male positions. The existence in the United States of a powerful cultural centripetal regression toward the core—put simply, a dumbing-down conformism fueling and fueled by capitalism in search of expanding markets—only makes these kinds of works all the more remarkable, especially the surprising case of the work of Clint Eastwood.

That said, American capitalism and society have tended toward increasing openness and tolerance, most obviously, since the 1960s, despite the continuity of the longer threads of American cultural history so steeped in Manifest Destiny. Whether this improvement reflects the rational pursuit of greater profits (that is, Henry Ford's argument for better worker's wages so that they might be able to afford to purchase what they built, applied with increasing equality to women, blacks, Indians, and Latinos), or whether it mirrors the fuller homogenization of American culture via consumerist cooptation and other hegemonic apparatuses remains to be seen. At the very least, probably it is a little bit of both. Either way, at this point it is anybody's guess how the momentum of this slow-to-gather transformation survives the post-9-11 purge, look-back-in-anger mood so prevalent in the Bush White House.

The more open atmosphere of recent decades has accurately suggested and reflected the presence of other significant American voices. Certainly, for instance, academia has become super charged with competing noises—postmodernism, poststructuralism, feminism, ethnic studies, postfeminisim, black studies, postcolonialism, Latin American studies, the revenge of the positivists (while they may not carry the day in many university faculties, they keep winning U.S. presidential elections) and such. So, too, has multicultural change gone to Hollywood. Partly, here again market forces may have effected greater diversity. For example, the emergence of black movies, Latino films, gay and lesbian pictures, and so on feed on the thirst in the first cases of their own sizable target (and growing) audiences, thus this constitutes more than American-style *glasnost*. There is money to be made! What could be more American?

In any event, in short, change has come. It has clearly come to stay, too, despite the fitful progress of moving it forward and occasional apparent lapses backward (the exaggerations and preoccupations of the War on Terrorism come to mind). Of course, it is certainly not perfect. I mean, can you name one living aboriginal actor? Further, don't the overwhelming majority of Hollywood flicks put white men at the center of the civilizing action? Still, things are better than they used to be when Hollywood's black roles seemed automatically to go either to Sidney Portier (drama) or the late (but great) Richard

Pryor (comedy). Then in 2002 two African-Americans earned best actor awards at the Oscars—Denzel Washington and Halle Barry. As we have seen, too, at the same time, the frontier myth endures—(that is, Manifest Destiny has no more gone away than has its promotion in film taken a leave of absence; yet, too, the myth has been poked and prodded in what you might characterize, in fits and starts, as a more tolerant, more liberal America.

The question is how all this change has affected the frontier western? If change for the better has indeed occurred in the way that Hollywood has become marginally more multicultural, should there not be evidence of it in film? The short answer is yes. So how have nonhegemonic voices—promoting the margins, the Other—weighed in on the frontier western? In short, what about, say, frontier westerns shot, if this is even possible, from Other points of view? What about black frontier westerns? What about female frontier westerns? What about genre bending—for example, sci-fi frontier westerns? Further still, how do these speak to issues of Manifest Destiny? For example, is it conceivable that black frontier westerns, if they can be said to exist at all, might promote a cultural mantra specifically employed historically to keep blacks down? It might be tempting to conclude that frontier westerns that promote little more than greater inclusiveness and racial tolerance—for example, the black version that merely substitutes black frontiersmen for white—reflect the central cultural depravity and vacuity of a nation deeply given over to consumerist capitalism. For example, when the United States mourned the tragedy of 9-11 its citizens were admonished to do so by their president by going shopping, the mall apparently having become a suitable modern-day place of worship in the mind of the leader of the free world. In other words, does the idea and very possibility of a black frontier western (after all, movies are neither easy nor inexpensive to make) suggest that blacks are finally getting their place at the table or should it give us pause to lament that the behavior required of blacks in order to have secured an invitation to dine at that table has been one of compromise (or practicality)?

These are not questions that I hope to answer in this chapter. In fact, not only do they belong to another book, but it strikes me that it is probably too early to address them effectively with much certainty. To begin with, alternative "Other" readings of the myth are simply too infrequent at this point to suggest: a) that the table has been fully joined; and/or b) that Other filmmakers find it worth joining. What this chapter considers, however, is three frontier westerns shot from Other points of view, Mario Van Peebles's *Posse*, Maggie Greenwald's *Ballad of Little Jo*, and Ridley Scott's *Alien*.

Space Case

Anybody who has ever watched television understands that space presents the final frontier. But what does this mean? As everybody knows, Captain James T. Kirk, commander and chief womanizer of the Starship Enterprise, got right to the point in every episode of the original *Star Trek* series, reminding us that the final frontier is that place, that arena of mythical action where white male agents "boldly" go where no real man, no other frontiersmen, has gone before. Pretty obviously, that is what *Star Trek* was all about, Kirk and his ragtag bunch of misfit subordinates conquering the galaxies in the name of incorruptible mainstream white Americana. When not taken seriously, I suppose, the show can be a lot of fun. Still, the transparent inclusiveness that the program and its various bland spin-offs attempted to promote should have fooled no one. Captain Kirk was little better than a house-broken interplanetary General George Armstrong Custer, though to be fair he preferred hectoring over slaughter.

But is all sci-fi space like that?

It certainly tends to be. In short, you will not find the frontier myth confounded in the main by science fiction flicks. Think about them. Surely, the first *Star Wars* released back in 1977 was an unsubtle frontier western? You know, Luke Skywalker raised without "real" parents on a planet looking a lot like the deserted yet dangerous old west. Han Solo emerging as a gunslinger and reluctant (anti-) hero contributing to the re-fighting and winning of the American war for independence. In other words, it is sort of a frontier western overlaid on science fiction based on a "true story," the heavily mythologized American Revolution.

Essentially, though, the *Star Wars* films are boy movies, aimed not at the middle-schooler in us but at his ten-year-old little brother, the one who still derives pleasure from play with action figures and fiddling with toy cars. By far the most original and provocative frontier sci-fi western was released in 1979, Ridley Scott's *Alien* (not to be confused with the trashy ripoffs made by less talented directors that followed, *Aliens*,[4] *Alien 3*,[5] and *Alien: Resurrection*[6]).

Scott's *Alien* broke altogether new ground in genre expanding. It took the intelligent frontier western to space. Well, that much had been done before—notably in the original *Star Trek* television series. But here is the twist. As is well known, *Alien*'s protagonist is female, played with statuesque athleticism by Sigourney Weaver. The enemy faced on this celestial mythscape, too, is female, the titular alien. However, director Scott uses the film as a vehicle to suggest far more, that the Other—in this case, a monstrous killing-machine of a stupendously ugly bitch alien life form—in fact is a metaphor for another alien, the seed of the Other, that, as it happens, resides in us all. The nominal alien of the film is the projection of what we loathe and fear inside ourselves. Like the Other, this alien then both absolves our transgressions—it is her, the bitch or the greaser or the nigger, not me!—while at the same time threatening to eat us all from within.

When Did You Know It?

Any film buff knows the story of *Alien*. A mostly blue-collar crew of seven on a commercial space freighter are awakened prematurely from suspended animation while lugging a load of ore back to Earth. The ship's computer, Mother, has picked up what appears to be distress signal emanating from a nearby planet. Predictably, the crew is required to investigate. Turns out that the signal was actually a warning—but it comes too late, as the nominal alien attacks one of the crew, Kane, and attaches itself to his face. When he is taken back aboard the rescue ship, and then the mother ship, all hell breaks loose as the creature systematically polishes off the squad, leaving only Ripley (a fairly radiant Sigourney Weaver) to fight it to the death.

Several things made the film an instant hit. First, it came hot on the heels of the popular *Star Wars* (1977), and *Close Encounters*[7] (1977). In other words, sci-fi seemed all the rage for a moment there and everything related to it on screen seemed primed to succeed at the box office, especially a product fashioned by the hands of a most capable filmmaker like Ridley Scott. However, far more than that, the work presents a visual thrill ride, the mysteries of sci-fi stung with near-

Gothic horror burrowed deeply into frontier western country. Though it borrows heavily from genre conventions and periodically pays homage to past masters, it was at the same time thoroughly original. The creepy and stylish tag line, "In space no one can hear you scream," is served up effectively by the tale.

Its frontier western pedigree, though unnoticed by reviewers, stands out clearly. To begin with, it is set on the final frontier, and in case this is not obvious in the eloquent introductory shots of deep, murky, and empty space we are reminded of such at both ends of the film. Lambert, the second female, in trying to assess precisely where they are in space after the premature wakeup, says, "We haven't reached the outer rim yet." Driving the point home, as she signs off two hours of film later, Ripley records, "I should reach the frontier in about six weeks."

Given the location—the film pits the crew against an alien at or even beyond the frontier—we slide easily here into frontier western territory. Well, that is the essence of Turner, too. That is, like Turner, *Alien* offers us the good, cleansing, redemptive battle waged against alien life—Indian, Vietnamese, whatever—in this case, an actual other-worldly life-form. That said, notice how this alien's characteristics stack up against the classic frontier Other.

First, you have got the habitat—the scantily occupied nether regions of non-civilization set chronologically in the magical eternal present (also sometimes known as suspended disbelief). The effects, by the way, hold up well here from 1979. I mean, there is nothing so dated as the costuming of the original *Star Wars* released only two years prior. Second, the alien is female—a classic means via which, in a patriarchal and paternalistic society, to reduce and debase it. She is a ruthless, remorseless bitch with, literally, highly corrosive acid for blood. She is a real ball buster. Third, she evinces unmitigated and unprovoked hostility. In fact, her aggressiveness is apparently pathological. She is a distilled savage Other, in this respect. Fourth, she is immoral in the extreme. Has not a scruple to go by. Exists seemingly for the sole purpose of attacking decent people on their way, as if, to grandma's house or the office. Fifth, she is greedy, insatiable in appetite. Sixth, she obviously cannot be trusted. Seventh, she seeks to destroy civilization as we know it. As a result, she invites violence upon herself. I could go on but there is little need to do so. You get the point. She is a bad, bad, bad alien. What she deserves and what she gets is the wrath of a frontiersman as payback. As Ripley tells Parker, employing the old art of foreboding, "You'll get what's coming to you."

Ironically, and here is the first of the ways in which the film is special, Ripley, the frontiersman is female. Scott, no stranger to making good films with strong female leads (see *Thelma and Louise*[8]), seems to query simply: why not a female in this role? In fact, he teases us in getting her there. By refusing to privilege one character among the crew a viewer might naturally, that is, by conditioning, assume that the ship's captain, Dallas (played by a savvy Tom Skerritt), a leader, brave and smart and all, will seize the mantle of the last one standing. But he does not. Ripley does.

Does Ripley pass through a Turnerian trial by fire? Sure she does. To begin with, she comes loaded with the basic ingredients for the role—she is tough, capable, angry, intuitive, not reluctant to buck authority, believes in fair play, she is lucky, individualistic, rugged enough, athletic, physically attractive, brave, sexy, inventive, and so on. Yet neither the camera nor the narrative singles her out as such in the early going. She is just third in command (of seven). No, she earns her authority through her deeds. One result, apart from her emerging ultimately as the only survivor, is that she is stripped down, metaphorically illustrated by the putting up of her hair near the end of the film and, more to the point, her disrobing. In this way the mythical frontier has built her down.

The mythical frontier here is imagined differently here than in, say, the old west, though. It is not only about a change in location. The normal Turnerian western finds the Other on the dreamed frontier and systematically engages in a cleansing operation, that is, of Manifest Destiny. In *Alien* the Other is portrayed in exaggerated form; it is a horror show too, after all. However, this Other casts a shadow back upon the frontier western's representation of the alien, of the one who does not fit and must be vanquished, because here the alien inveigles itself literally into your body then bursts out, suggesting that, in fact, inside of you is where the alien finds its home, that the alien we fear is in fact within us and only becomes a danger when it gets out. This is not to ignore the actual alien out there on the planet's surface; but that creature exists as the personification of our deepest fears, horror...and that is what makes it horror. Scott has cleverly blended horror and the frontier western because of their shared quarter of overlap—both project what terrifies us about ourselves back against us, despite the usual differences as presented in the genre conventions. Scott seems to intuit that in real, not necessarily reel, history, we push the alien out inasmuch as the Other represents a projection of those traits we fear about and in ourselves.

Mothers of the World Unite!

Scott also takes careful aim at capitalism in this flick, a common Turnerian bugaboo portrayed frequently in film as dudes, eastern sharpees, land hustlers, bankers, railroad men, business corporations, and the like. They stand in for eastern and, by extension, European corruption. These entities threaten most everything the frontiersman symbolizes—individual freedom and unfettered range of social mobility in particular.

Eastern-style corporationism menaces the crew in *Alien*. They are all working aboard a commercial ship, to begin with. At least two crew members are agitating for a greater share in the profits earned by the voyage, hinting that the company was not treating them fairly. The worst, by far, absolutely the lowest, scummiest behavior is the company's utter disregard for the crew's very existence. To her considerable outrage, Ripley discovers from Mother, the ship's computer, that the company is so enamored with the financial potential inherent in the discovery of a new life form (the alien) that it instructs the science officer, Ash (a "fucking robot," Parker labels him), to reprioritize the mission: preservation of the life-form first and at all costs, rendering the crew "expendable."

Suddenly we are reminded of another element in the earlier gradual construction of Ripley's frontiersman credentials. She never liked Ash, did not and does not trust him. Of course, she was right not to. Ash, we learn, has all the while been acting in strict accordance with the ship's newly redefined mission. Ripley, with life-saving backup from Parker, prevails and Ash, now nearly headless after the melee, is reduced to playing the role of a sort of helpful, talking computer.

"How do we kill it?" Ripley asks him/it.

"You can't."

"Bullshit!" bellows Parker.

"You still don't understand what you're dealing with here, do you? A perfect organism. Its structural perfection is matched only by its hostility."

"You admire it," Ripley says in disbelief.

"I admire its purity," Ash explains, shilling for anything-for-a-buck style capitalism. "Unclouded by delusions of morality."

Yeah, morality can be a real problem. In fact, it is one of the central issues on the mythical frontier, isn't it? Devoid of morality and biologically mutated more or less sum up the alien and its softer, less durable filmic counterpart Other. In this sense, Ripley is doing nothing more than what John Wayne and Governor Arnold have done countless times before her.

Get Bent

The strength of *Alien*, apart from its elegant blending of genres—sci-fi, horror, and western—lies in its reshaping of the frontier western. It is not that Scott has dispensed with stereotypes and conventions. Not at all. His contributions derive, first, from the insertion of a female into the frontiersman role. This quite simply broke new ground.

The second significant disruption proffered by the film is in the novel way it casts the Other. The Other here is not human and therefore not identifiably the member of a non-white visible minority. But it is not merely an inoffensive monster, either. Scott has deliberately genderized it. This secondary playing against type both tickles our susceptibilities to one of the genre's great soft spots—its portrayal of females; yet in so doing ironically fuels the pithy motivations of the beast, the heart of "the bitch." We know her already.

This female componentry and its residence within us all, as I have suggested, supports Kubrick's notion in *Full Metal Jacket*, as mouthed by Joker, about the duality of humankind. Scott is not promoting a flavor of the week postmodern, fuzzy-liberal, I'm-okay/you're-okay idea that there is no real difference between men and women anyway pop drivel. Without much elaboration, the film suggests that the way we categorize male and female, especially in the frontier western—but also in sci-fi and in horror—and also, by extension in American life generally—is at the very least ridiculous and counter productive;

but, more than that, it does lasting damage to the duality within us all that the female is expected to dance just so on a public stage. That Scott employs these quiet social monikers ironically to fashion a scarefest does him credit as a filmmaker.

Black and White and Red All Over

One premise of Mario Van Peebles's *Posse* rests upon the assertion that black cowboys have been forgotten and ignored in US culture, history, and film. Van Peebles is correct on this point. Moreover, while blacks have not figured prominently in westerns, or in Hollywood at all until recently, the western has clearly operated as a barometer of race relations in the United States, interactions that have typically been perceived as basically black/white and mostly based on the one-drop rule. So Van Peebles had at least a couple of good reasons to make this film. Plus, keep in mind that while American racial issues have been cast as black/white in a public discourse that has all too predictably ignored the much greater complexity of the matter, the western contributed to the marginalization of blacks by refusing to notice them—or, when it did, by portraying them with demeaning, cardboard characterizations. *Posse* serves as an attempt to offer up a frontier black western, an alternative take on the frontier narrative.

But wait. Is it possible to conceive of a black frontier western? I have argued that the form has relegated Others to stereotyped colonial conditions while promoting Manifest Destiny with nearly every breath. Yet Van Peebles would have it otherwise. He appears to locate a potentiality for black empowerment in the frontier myth. What he presses for in this film is not an undoing of the frontier western as genre; rather, he is advocating its reshaping. He is saying, on the one hand, and in a tinny and, I am afraid, pubertal voice, that the U.S. needs a healthy dose of liberal tolerance. He actually has one of his characters, the barber in Freemanville ape Rodney King's unforgettable mourn, "Can't we all just get along?"

The result is that *Posse* pulls us in two incompatible directions, which suggests strongly that the director never reasoned his way through the myth. So, yes, Van Peebles reproaches us, we must learn to get along. Let us erase prejudice and discrimination based on perceived racial characteristics. Great idea. Inexplicably, though, then Van Peebles demands the right of the black man to claim the mantle of the frontiersman and all that it entails, which thoroughly spoils—or, at least, works at cross purposes to—his major theme. Unfortunately, this is not done ironically, as in, say, Clint Eastwood's *Unforgiven*. Instead, Van Peebles clearly relishes the popular concept of payback and at every opportunity frames his black protagonist as a straight-up western hero of the most swaggering, serene proportions. The results for the film border on schizophrenic.

Black Is Black?

Unfortunately, the very idea of a black Turnerian frontiersman, we can quickly surmise in this film, makes no sense at all. In fact, he is every bit as aggressively colonial—especially as a gender bigot—as the white frontiersman ever was. So what is the point. It would be one thing to aver that violence in the name of freedom and versus tyranny is justifiable. Under certain circumstances that seems reasonable. For example, everyone hates the Nazis. Good. And who would fairly argue that Others do not have the right to fight back? Unfortunately, Van Peebles is not half that clever. Instead, what we get in this movie is a vehicle championing, albeit inconsistently and awkwardly, black retributive justice delivered by a black wannabe frontiersman. The result is a simultaneously challenging, stimulating, and obtuse film.

In the former case, the flick opens with an aged and laconic narrator (played by Woody Strode—no less than Tom Doniphon's sidekick from *Liberty Valance*) who, in real time, introduces the story and its central ideas. He drawls out:

> A Colt .45. Single shot. You had to cock it every time you shot. It's called a peace maker but I haven't seen much peace that it brought. No…History's a funny thing. They got us believing that Columbus discovered America and the Indians were already here. That's like me telling you, and you're sitting in your car, that I discovered your car. Then they want to call them evil red savages because they don't give up the car soon enough. There's one thing about time. No matter how much or how little passes, it changes. People forget their past and they forget the truth.

This is fair though, right? In this way, Van Peebles seems to be setting us up for an anti-frontier western, what with the black-centered story and the radical idea (for a western) that the wholesale historical white seizure of Indian land constituted aggressive, racially primed theft. In other words, Van Peebles seems straight away to identify the darker reaches of Manifest Destiny inherent in the frontier myth.

The film then moves to, and we meet the core of what will become the eponymous posse in, Cuba, 1898. This diachronic positioning, too, makes a certain amount of strategic sense because the conflict there raging, in which the group's members take part (more or less unwillingly, and any decent history primer will tell you that black American soldiers in the Philippines during the same conflict began to empathize with the plight of colonialized Philippine blacks[9]), was for the remnants of Spain's once-sprawling empire. The United States took Cuba for its own in that conflict and, by most conventional historical accounts, became an unwitting imperial power (that is likely the version you got in university, that the U.S. did not actively seek out an empire but more or less stumbled inadvertently into one?[10]). Of course, the empire-building had begun long before this and was anything but accidental. Van Peebles appears to choose this setting deliberately, then, reasonably, perhaps even wisely to make a statement about America: it was racist, aggressive, and land hungry. Again, all true.

The incipient posse is then compelled upon pain of death into capturing, in plain clothes, Spanish bullion from behind enemy lines for which its members will, as it turns out, be summarily shot as deserters. Meanwhile, the booty will go to the evil white Colonel Graham (actor Billy Zane) and his corrupt underlings. But Jessie Lee, our hero, played by a well-muscled Van Peebles himself, is quickly onto this game. He leads the black soldiers in a fight for their lives, in which several white soldiers die and where the colonel is shot in the eye by Jessie. Then the nascent posse escapes in coffins to New Orleans. Moreover, huzzah, they have got the gold, too!

Inverted Alchemy

Now the complications start. In order to spend or convert the precious cargo it first must be melted down. Jessie, meanwhile, has plans of his own for heading west to avenge a personal life trauma that we are given glimpses of sporadically in the form of annoying flashbacks.

We learn, for example, that his father, King David, a black pastor had been lynched for preaching the gospels of peace, tolerance, love, freedom, and education in the town he had helped build, Freemanville, somewhere in a myopic Turnerian west. Jessie's ragtag bunch—oops, I mean his manly posse—follow him westward because: a) Jessie, as magnetic frontiersman, inspires disciples; and b) they're all on the run from the demonic colonel, appearing now as a sort of pirate, with an eye patch and cape and a band of cutthroats, who wants the gold. So the posse rides west. And if this sounds ridiculous, believe me, it is, but it gets worse.

Once in Freemanville, the posse is compelled to take on the sinister white Sheriff of nearby Cutterstown, who was directly responsible for the death of King David and also heads up the local KKK. The film culminates, not artfully, in a series of poorly rendered, melodramatic encounters between Jessie and the white sheriff, Jessie and the colonel, and Jessie and his own black erstwhile friend-gone-bad/rival, Carver.

Let me back up. Regrettably, just as quickly as the film promises to engage the frontier western meaningfully it bifurcates clumsily and pointlessly. One track grudgingly and without subtlety beats us into submission with precisely that Other message. You know the one: Manifest Destiny was bad. Just awful! A second track establishes Van Peebles as the quintessential black frontiersman, in this case out for bloody vengeance, dominating all that he surveys in a poor imitation of Eastwood's Man With No Name signature western performances, themselves stylized on the work of Gary Cooper.

Well, it is clear that Manifest Destiny has blemished and continues to tarnish the United States. There is no particular need here to rehash the obvious. The question you might ask is what insights Van Peebles has to offer. In fact, plenty. Indeed, this is the strength and value of the movie. Not only does the flick argue that blacks have been unfairly marginalized but also that the black experience has much in common with that of the American Indian. On the surface, this might appear to be a stretch—blacks came kidnapped from Africa and endured centuries of legally sanctioned slavery in the United States, whereas Indians were here already, largely failed as slaves, and only later became the principal subjects (objects) of abuse under the rose-colored aegis Americans once proudly called Manifest Destiny. The similarities between the groups, as Van Peebles sees it, outweigh the apparent points of divergence. Both groups were Othered in remarkably similar ways and for basically the same reasons—not because they were the same (they obviously were not, in fact, great cultural diversity existed within early American Indian groups and within African slave populations, let alone between them), but because they were different from whites in the same way—not white, and perceived as different in a variety of similar ways—not civilized, not strong, not well-mannered, not effectively Christian, not non-promiscuous, not clever, and on and on. In practice, this meant nearly criminally non-white by definition.

Mario Van Peebles as African American frontiersman in *Posse*.

Van Peebles has his characters remind us of this, too. For example, here is Father Time, the black dude gambler, played enthusiastically but with maximum hip hop energy by rapper Big Daddy Kane, waxing to the posse's token mangy white hustler, Jimmy J. "Little J" Teeters, acted with idiotic aplomb by Stephen Baldwin:

> Red man ain't got not problem with the Black man. As for you, white boy, ha, ha, that's a whole different story. I mean, first you enslave the Black man, just flog the yellow man, and then kill off the red man so you can snatch his land for railroads and such. Can I get witness?

Little J retorts, "I ain't never personally enslaved nobody."

To his credit, Van Peebles attempts to demystify race relations. To begin with, he throws in Little J as a sort of token white. At heart this character is a thoughtful, if lovingly stock-violent, fuzzy, snaggle-toothed liberal. He tells Time, "Seems to me that the only problem a white man has with a colored is that he is afraid. You know how people are always afraid of what they don't know or what they don't understand."

The film also offers up a standard western conniving, rotten sheriff—but this one, Carver, is black (and Jessie's rival). Turns out that Van Peebles's mentor was a black man who married an Indian woman. Their Indian Princess of a daughter once was and again becomes Van Peebles's love interest, arrayed in buckskins and flowing ebony hair. In short, Van Peebles resists the temptation to portray race relations as two-toned yet he simultaneously exercises poor judgment in peopling his film with ridiculous stock characters.

Unfortunately, the rest of the film does not register such lofty ambitions. In fact, in many ways the strengths of the film are undone or become lost in a morass of silly stereotyping. The most obvious case is that of the womenfolk. With two exceptions—a dirty-faced little blonde girl (to whom Jessie says with such astonishing absurdity that you can only shake your head in amazement: "You tell the sheriff that Father Time and the outlaw posse is in a killing mood") and Jessie's girl, they're all whores. Every last one.

In fact, even Jessie's girl serves as little more than an object for his sexual and masculine gratification. I mean, there is neither chemistry between the characters nor a meaningful narrative strand tying them together. We only know that she prefers him to the corrupt black lawman, the dude-like Carver, whom she had otherwise agreed to marry. Papa Joe, her father and Jessie's martial mentor, sketches the contours (and the vital source) of her (and the movie's) limitations. "She's my daughter, but she's a woman first," he explains to Jessie, as if this should make it obvious to us. She is a woman! Get it? Nuff sed.

When Jessie makes plain that he wants to have sex with the daughter, Papa Joe does not bat an eye but simply asks if Jessie can spare him some cash to go play cards at the bar while they screw. He does and they do. The love making scene constitutes her moment to shine as a mantelpiece ornament; afterward she fares less well, serving as a sign prophesying the inevitable victory of his Turnerian, albeit black, phallus, but little more.

Blazing Saddle Sores

Another difficulty with the film stems from its hackneyed frontier western love affair with violence as a legitimate means of settling disputes. While it seems unfair to criticize Van Peebles for playing the genre straight up, you might ask, what is the point of having a black frontiersman merely ape the white frontiersman? Is it a matter of them striving against and conquering a common enough enemy—the archetypal Turnerian corrupted eastern white guy? Apparently, that is the simple way in which Van Peebles interprets the mythical frontier. Yet simultaneously he harries us, and fairly, with the (for him) news that the history of the west and, indeed, of America generally, has been one of utterly contemptuous, even murderous, behavior towards Others—blacks and Indians being the subjects of this film. But you cannot have it both ways, you know, preach peace through violence. Not without a good deal of irony, at least.

Van Peebles's disastrously played attempt at "truth" and historical accuracy is further undone by his apparent ignorance of American geography. As the posse rides west it chooses to pass, without event, through potentially hostile Sioux country—yeah, but it is set in Monument Valley, about at least a thousand miles away. On the one hand, you can hardly blame Van Pebbles for borrowing from John Ford's beloved mesa scapes, but on the other, if you take Van Peebles at his word, you might fairly question such geographic inaccuracy.

The result, finally, is that Van Peebles's film, in the name of, let's see, fuzzy liberalism and adolescent-style revenge, creates a work streaked with Uncle Tom-like highlights. First, he crafts Jessie by styling on the classic western model—strong, violent, quiet, clever, indispensable, a leader, handsome, rugged, inventive, and all that. To be fair, Van Peebles is not half bad in this role (but he is not half good, either), though he is physically slight in the way that Alan Ladd was in *Shane*. Bodily, he is certainly no Wayne or Eastwood. But that is okay; he does not need to be. He delivers the appropriate lines with relished, if bland, detachment: "You all wanna ride with me, that's okay. Don't ask no questions that need answering. And don't get in my way," he blabbers. Jessie is a rebel, after all, having improbably survived a failed attempt at desertion in Manila, assaulting an officer in Nicaragua, and three escape attempts in Cuba. The camera frames Jessie in ways that invoke Sergio Leone's spaghetti westerns, lots of shots of (less than) burning eye close-ups.

The problem with this is that it hardly promotes an alternative to frontier-style Manifest Destiny. To begin with, Jessie employs similar retributive violence sanctioned for similar reasons. He tells his woman, "The only way you all's gonna keep this land is stand up and fight for it." Again, fair enough. However, how does this distinguish the black frontiersman from the white? In practice, at least in this film, it does not. We already know that the director's point of view reflects unbridled misogyny. The model characteristics of the black frontiersman, in fact, as portrayed in this film, are identical to that of the frontier western white. So where is the improvement? Jessie is only out to kill a slightly different variety of scum—he has added racist to the stock of evil characters lurking on Turner's imagined frontier. But you know it is an uneasy fit because the frontiersmen has been a lightning rod around which historical processes and a cultural project coalesce to promote American-style imperialism. Put simply, the west is not big enough for Jessie Lee and Manifest Destiny. Worse yet, Van Peebles does not even know it. Even worse than that, Van Peebles seems to have conflated historical black cowboys with the Turnerian frontiersman.

Second, and in other respects, Van Peebles's historical sense and knowledge is woeful. Setting the film during the Spanish-American-Cuban War may be a good idea, as noted. However, then depicting subsequent action as contributing to the closing of the frontier suggests that Van Peebles's reading of U.S. history is spotty, at best. For example, while he knows that lots of black cowboys roamed the plains and Southwest, he appears not to know that the settling of the kind portrayed in this film happened typically decades earlier than he illustrates. So much for the assertion that historical accuracy is, in fact and after all, important. Yet worse, his dandified rival Carver tells him, "So the west is going to be settled. Ain't gonna be no more frontier or frontiersmen." But this had already happened.

Further, the disenfranchisement of Indians from their traditional lands was long over by the turn of the twentieth century (the Dawes Act notwithstanding). Same goes with the rough treatment of Chinese "coolies" working the railroads, whom Van Peebles shows being pushed around by heavy, jauntily armed railway goons. While it is important to remember that the western is built upon fanciful history, Van Peebles asserts directly that a precise problem with America has been that it does not know its own "true" history. And he is going to correct it, at least insofar as the western and black cowboys are concerned.

But all he manages to effectively promote is that blacks were cowboys, too. Otherwise, this film's historical accuracy is probably worse, on balance, than most traditional westerns—and that is saying a lot. Certainly we should be able to expect more of a film released in 1993 than this. Roger Ebert summed it up neatly:

> I guess this sloganeering is an attempt to provide the film with a meaning that its story fails to deliver. If Van Peebles had cared a little more about his closing messages, he might have made a movie about them, instead of this self-indulgent exercise in overheated style.[11]

Reviewer Hal Hinson of the *Washington Post* was equally, and fairly, disappointed. "*Posse* is a great idea for a movie," he writes, "but rarely has such a solid idea been exploited with greater indifference or lack of imagination."[12] Finally, a review in the *Austin Chronicle* chimed in with, "The beginning is both starling and exciting...Unfortunately, there's the rest of the film."[13]

A Man's World

If the possibility of a black frontier western presents potentially fascinating and ironic opportunities for a filmmaker—ambitiously, if tenuously, staked out, but disappointingly rendered by Mario Van Peebles in *Posse*—what about a female frontier western? A flick set on the mythical frontier that privileges a female? Is this possible?

Is it ever.

Director Maggie Greenwald takes up the challenge in the formidably original film, *The Ballad of Little Jo*. Josephine Monaghan, protagonist and would-be frontiersman-with-a-twist was tossed out of her prosperous eastern family as a common "whore," as her father phrases it, after giving birth to an illegitimate child (she did it with a portrait photographer). She seeks refuge and a future on a rugged frontier, set mostly in or near the mountainous Ruby City (in Idaho or Montana) in the later nineteenth century. The west is no place for a decent single woman, though, and Josephine, in order to eschew kidnapping, gang rape, and other hinted-at depredations, is compelled to don the identity of a man. She cuts her hair, lowers her voice, scars her face with a razor, and dresses as a fellah. Hence Josephine becomes Jo.

The movie is her compelling saga. It is not tragic inasmuch as Little Jo, played with somber playfulness by Suzy Amis,[14] proves able to endure, to prosper even, yes, and to find love. But her gains are ironic, essentially solitary, hard-won, usually bitter, and offer up a stinging indictment of the aggressive frontier western culture that aids and abets an American imperialism awash in patriarchy and paternalism.

Director Greenwald's initial, powerful, and lasting observation, one that helps string the movie together, is simple and direct: white men had—and disproportionately continue to maintain, in case anybody had not noticed—a social mobility as well as occupational opportunities simply unavailable to women. White men made and make the frequently arbitrary and inane rules and enforced them, frequently with extreme prejudice, on the dreamed frontier, as elsewhere (the place called reality). The opening scene hints openly at some of the difficulties facing Jo, and by extension all American females, which plague the imperial western. The camera pans in on Josephine, clad in tight fitting, cumbersome fancy women's clothing, employing a parasol in one hand and toting a heavy suitcase in the other. She is weighed down by womanhood and she is trudging along—but we do not know where (and neither does she, as we soon enough discover).

Come as you may, men pass by on horseback or in horse-drawn buggies, providing a contrast that instantly reifies the viewer's sense of Josephine's relative immobility. Literally, she is burdened with the baggage of womanhood—and it not only slows her down but, given the temper of the film (the wild west), renders her an easy sexual mark.

Shortly she is picked up by a creepy but jocular traveling salesman. He is heading west and offers her a lift in return for assistance in his roadside selling. And she is all the proper gal, too, demure, polite in her manner, clean and classy in deportment. Not so the salesman. He sells her secretly to two thugs on horseback, one of whom kills the salesman, and both of whom fail in an attempt to capture and rape her. She makes her escape by dashing into a river under the cover of darkness.

Soaked through and through, freed of her luggage, wrap, and umbrella, the next morning she discovers that she simply cannot purchase fresh women's clothing ready to wear. Further, the thugs remain on the prowl, lusting after her. Cornered and presumably frightened, Josephine seizes her best option. Because being a single, ostensibly free, unencumbered woman threatens her very survival, she chooses to disguise herself as a man, despite the warning from a grouchy storekeeper, "It's agin the law to dress improper to your sex." But what other choice does she have? To freshen the effect of the artifice she slices an ugly scar into her face with a razor. And just like that, all at once, she is a new man.

What we have thus far witnessed constitutes an intriguing rip-off of Turner: the easterner compelled to the mythical frontier, systematically stripped of cultural self, only to take on necessarily the identity of survival—the frontiersman. Whereas the immigrant, according to Turner, was stripped by his environment only to be reborn as a prototypical American, Josephine is stripped by the harsh environment to rebirth herself as a male (and it is not over yet, either, the film shows). Where Turner's agency of change is geographically deterministic and simultaneously magical, Jo's transformation is deliberate and conscious—though no less a reaction to a dangerous environment. Further, what writer/director Greenwald is suggesting, of course, and the rest of the film bears this out, is that the frontier was not as Turner would have it in yet another significant way. The West, she asserts, was not something altogether original and newfangled. Instead, the society of the mythical west was essentially the transplanted east, but with bad manners and dirtier underwear. She observes that the east-west bond was basically paternalistic, patriarchal, and macho. As such, a woman (and a man) damned well better know her (his) place in it—or else.

Or else what? Well, the possibilities are several. First, you have got social death, as in censured banishment. Interminable rape and enforced deprivation offer second options. Finally, there is physical death. These threats menace Little Jo; especially the last, something Little Jo clearly understands and jealously guards against.

The west is east in another basic way in this film. Go-getters and men of talent succeed, men such as Frank Badger, who hires Jo and seeks his friendship, but whom Jo also confounds and rebuffs at every turn, lest she be found out. Meanwhile, in the west, as in the east, uncouth underlings abound. In a crucial way, Greenwald expresses the popular idea that America is a remarkable place where, to paraphrase Susan Sontag, one always has the possibility of rebirth. It is a place where you can start over. However, this is not the same as issuing a blank check; thus in important ways, Greenwald's movie sketches some of the possibilities as well as some of the limitations of the possibilities of renewal.

Oh, Give Me a Home

So Jo, then, has taken steps toward rebirth, first, by giving up her essential public identity as a woman. The transformation also incurs metaphorical makeovers represented effectively, as noted, in the contrast between her clothing and baggage and men on horseback, the unwanted baptism in the river all set against a looming full moon.

As a male in Ruby City Jo defends her private identity by donning the mask of a cordial but gruff, polite but none too friendly loner. This serves her well and, because she works diligently, effectively, and responsibly, it earns her due respect—which, in turn helps dampen unsettling suspicions about her distinctly unsocial (they're all unsocial to a certain extent, and proud of it) mien.

In turn, Jo unsuccessfully attempts to mine for placer gold, works briefly as a stable hand, and spends five winters alone tending sheep in the mountains for Frank Badger. Then Jo purchases land adjacent to Badger's, along the river, on which to raise her own sheep. Her labors, and keep in mind there is a lot of life to cover in two short hours in this film, only further the process of stripping and rebirthing. To begin with, her manners, apart from politeness—she calls everyone "sir"—are discarded. Shortly after she arrives in Ruby City—is there a hidden jewel somewhere in these mountains?—she eats at what passes for a restaurant. She closely observes the men eating, the awkward-fisted handling of the cutlery, the grunting, the groaning, the burping, the farting, the shoveling of food. Jo needs to blend in and she does so, in part, by aping their eating habits.

In truer western form, she learns to gunsling. The sheep herd high in the peaks is ravaged frequently by wolves. Jo must learn to protect them. So in Greenwald's hands Jo's prowess as a pistol packer serves narrative ends but also adjusts the genre's compulsion to equate gunslinging with mythical manliness. For Jo it is a matter of survival, in the first instance. More, when Jo unholsters and shoots up a tin can in celebration of maid Mary's wedding to a Texan, the other fellows in town are delighted. Jo fits in; and the delight she/he experiences is palpable.

Live by the Sword

Actually, early on Jo wears her pistol tucked into her belt, in front, right above where her penis might otherwise hang. Greenwald reminds us of the shaky foothold Jo has gained, in spite of the emergent pistol savvy, in the very next scenes. Jo's would-be mentor, Percy, the local ex-pat Brit assay clerk, cut slightly above the local riffraff, has become wise to Jo's secret identity. A letter from Jo's sister, who cares for Jo's son in her absence, had arrived over the winter and Percy (played with methodical craft and wicked subtlety by Ian Mckellen) has read it.

He does not rat Jo out to the community. Instead he throws himself upon her sexually, insistently, tongue flailing every which way. This is attempted rape. But actual rape does not occur because Jo draws her pistol (how is that for ironic!), forcing Percy to back off. But Jo cannot pull the trigger and the compromise the two reach is that Percy will stay quiet and leave town for good in return for Jo's paying him off.

This is not to suggest, though, that Jo's advances by the gun in any way achieve mixed results. In fact, as things turn out she could no more have survived intact without them than could have *Red River*'s Dunson. So, without it, she would hardly be a real man. The gun is necessary and it serves her well. In the first case, against the wolves, she needs something for defense. Literally, the wolves are at her door, and she wants not to suffer the fate of just another sheep.

Things are different, of course, when Percy launches himself at her, insofar as she does not specifically need the weapons to defend her masculinity until she has them. Moreover, the picking up of the gun figures as another element of the stripping-down. It is not just the fact of the weapon's existence but a willingness and the ability to employ it. Further, her public identity and masculine currency is augmented by this martial improvement. The gun makes her hard and keeps her erect.

Percy, meanwhile, reminds us of the shopkeeper's admonition, "It's agin the law to dress improper to your sex." It is far more than that in this film. The improprieties taken at the expense of public roles menace and threaten to punish all transgressors. Percy also has something to hide and to guard. He is feminine. To begin with, he is overly civilized. He has better manners, a salaried job, English accent, knows how to cook (and wears an apron while doing so), smokes a pipe, and such. Despite all this, is he possibly a man beneath it? Well, of a certain variety. Before attacking Jo he had a go with a mute prostitute, who had ridden into town with a midget pimp to service the menfolk. Percy explained to Jo that he did not care for women, though he had been married for a time. No, he preferred a monthly tumble with a hooker. Far less trouble, he said, in a mentoring way. Then, though, falling-down drunk, he viciously slashed the prostitute with a knife and kept the men at bay with an awkwardly wielded pistol. Jo rescued him.

Consequences? Apparently few or none. Women, in this film, apart from Jo, are either portrayed as whores or lackies. For that matter, while portrayed as a female Jo, too, was a whore. In any case, they are subordinated to men. This is a man's story, after all—and are not all westerns about the centrality of men? Women serve men here—literally serve by waiting on them at table, staying out of sight while men conduct their business, and spreading their legs.

Sino Synecdoche

Five years pass and then one day Jo happens upon a scene that changes everything. Badger and some other town louts have strung up a Chinese man. He has got a rope around his neck. His arms are bound. Pilloried physically and taunted by the ruffians, his body swings at their amusement. On horseback passing by Jo pulls up short, fires her pistol into the air. "Let him go, Frank," she orders.

"Now, Jo," says the irrepressible Frank (acted with roguish charm by Bo Hopkins), "the fellow had the nerve to walk into Ruby City looking for work like a free white man."

In other words, the Chinaman had done precisely as she had done, *sans* disguise.

"We're sick of these slant-eyed sons of bitches stealing our jobs," a voice off-camera mouths a common-enough late nineteenth-century anxiety in the West.

"He's trying to eat," Jo asserts.

"He's not a man," Frank snorts, explaining, "He's a celestial heathen. They're all ravishers and opium smokers."

Frank is a bully, but a good-natured one. He agrees, at Jo's pistol-packing insistence to cut the man down. But then Frank uses the occasion to embarrass Jo into hiring the man, Tin Man Wong. Jo squirms but cannot refuse.

And so we get a conflicted gender stew. Tin Man Wong is a man but cooks for Jo and mends her clothes. Jo is a woman, of course, but carries on otherwise as a man as far as anybody can tell. Jo keeps Tin Man at arm's length, forcing him to sleep outside at night; but, then, in a rainstorm relents and offers to allow him to build on his own room to her log cabin. It takes Tin Man all of three days to uncover Jo's secret. Then, to top it off, they become lovers and, by the way, it is a love that carries each to the grave.

Greenwald uses Tin Man to explore the inner life of an Other not forgotten but altogether ignored in filmic representations of Turner's frontier. Like Jo, this Chinese American has been stripped of his public sexuality, his gender. In this sense, publicly, he is not a man at all because real men are, first, white. As a result, though he had labored for 15 years as a coolie on the railroads, here he is feminized, what with the cooking, mending, the long pony-tail hair, earning the overall subordinate status of feminized Other. Through such sketching Greenwald manages to achieve a poignancy altogether missed, though alluded to, by Mario Van Peebles in *Posse*.

The stripping down and the subsequent public piling on of frontiersman-like characteristics takes another and final turn as Jo's fortunes as a sheep rancher prosper. She has got 800 acres. Frank's got 5,000. But echoing a classic frontier western theme, these family establishments are menaced by burgeoning corporate America. The western Cattle Company, an eastern corporation, has begun gobbling up land for cattle stock. What it cannot stake or buy outright it takes by force, killing those unwilling to sell with hired guns. Jo witnesses the murder of a Russian immigrant family whom she had befriended years before. Yet she is powerless to stop the three masked riders.

Badger is deeply troubled by the corporate invaders. Jo comforts him by swearing her political support for his attempts to keep the cattle company at bay. Further, she reminds him that she will never sell out. Nevertheless, Jo changes her mind when she is menaced by the three killers. Intimidated, she agrees to sell.

Her collapse outrages Tin Man, but she is too frightened to remain. In one remarkable scene she sews a dress and dons it for Tin Man's pleasure, even going so far as to bake him a pie. Her actions simply disgust him.

"You have a flock to tend," he admonishes her.

But she has baked him a pie.

"I don't need a pie! I make very good pies!" he remonstrates.

"I've decided to sell. I can't live like this anymore. It's a chance for us to start over somewhere else." She is clearly unnerved.

"What kind of girl could you be someplace else?" he queries scornfully, clearly stung that she would give up so easily—an implication, she loses him too, that she has perhaps not considered. "What man would want you? You have no hair. Half your face is destroyed by that ugly scar. You can't even make a pie!" He thrusts his hand into the heart of the pastry and throws it on to the floor.

"Then you fight them," she responds angrily, thrusting a rifle into his hands.

Of course Little Jo does not sell out. She comes damn close, though. Here is what happens. The Badgers come over, Frank's wife is tending to a deathly ill Tin Man, when the Grays arrive. Mr. Gray runs operations for the cattle company. He is the man employing the killers, pushing good people off their land. He is here to have Jo sign over the papers for the sale of her land. Frank goes ballistic and punches Jo in the face. "Dirty, lying bastard," he shouts.

But Frank leaves. Inside, Mr. Gray then sits at a small table and sorts the papers that need signing. Through the window Jo observes

Mrs. Gray, the wife sitting up on the open carriage with their prepubescent son. The boy jumps down and runs all over but the wife sits rigidly, having already complained about the absence of culture "for a thousand miles." Greenwald has set us up effectively, for we reach the same conclusion that Jo must as she gazes out at that pathetic creature in her full-length dress and immobile composure. First, we understand that Jo is immeasurably better off as a public man, as it turns out. It is a question not of biology but of the opportunity to live with greater freedom. Men's autonomy was obviously not absolute but indisputably offered men a greater range of choices, enhanced mobility. Men were, in a word, freer; and Jo has come to cherish freedom. Greenwald's underlying point is much like what Stanley Kubrick says in *Full Metal Jacket*, nothing more profound than that gender roles are social constructions. This is hardly news—but it is news on the mythical frontier and for the frontier western and it is, further, a significant contribution shot from an Other point of view. Plus, Mr. Gray unwittingly removes the scales from Jo's eyes in a backhanded attempt to compliment her, "A person raised in the east, Mr. Monaghan, can never truly call this wild country home."

That is precisely what Jo has come to do, however. Her lingering tie—her son—has been cut loose, too, as a letter had informed her that her sister has told the boy that Jo (nee Josephine) has died. All that, and she sees over in the corner of the room that Tin Man is on his feet, pulled back from the brink of death by Mrs. Badger's unusual remedies (e.g., onions strapped to his feet).

Little Jo rejects Mr. Gray's offer.

Then she faces down the three killers with Frank. Frank shoots one. One wounds Frank. Then Little Jo kills the other two.

Years pass.

Jo survives Tin Man, and Frank survives Jo. The movie flashes far into the future. Upon Jo's death Frank orders that she be given the best funeral Ruby City has ever seen. Frank then sits in the bar buying drinks and waxing on about Jo's many virtues. This is funny now because we also know that the coroner, to whom the film cuts intermittently will shortly discover Jo's secret as he readies the body for burial.

He does. Comically the camera pans the drop-jawed crowd around the body. They're all men, save for Mrs. Badger, and she laughs and she laughs and she laughs. The meanest, cussedest frontiersman in the locale was a woman! Who knows what the men are thinking.

Ballad reminds us that Manifest Destiny and American imperialism begin at home. It is a home-grown colonizing process that has filtered its way up, naturally, into politics and into foreign policy. Further, in ways starker, more powerful, and of higher quality filmmaking, it picks up from *Far and Away* and *Man in the Wilderness* not simply to set the mood for empire but to plumb the workings of its cultural progenitors—regular American lives—from the inside out and from the Other side in. Or, to look at it another way, imagine projecting the sorts of prejudices and points of view occupied at the center of the frontier western onto foreign policymakers. What would that get you? My answer has been throughout this book: War in Vietnam, Wars against Mexico, the expropriation of Indian lands, neoimperialism draped inside the rhetoric of wars on drugs, unfreedom, terrorism, Iraq, and the lot.

Chapter Seven

Lying Line Laying: Remembering the Alamo

Since the beginning of time, men have been moving into empty spaces, and we in America were no different than those others, the Goths, the Mongols, the Indo-Aryans. We were but the last of the great migrations, and I wondered as I rode...how much choice did we really have? Plants move rapidly into areas for which they are best adapted, and human migrations seem to follow the same principles.

—Louis L'Amour[1]

A nation is defined as much by what it forgets as by what it remembers.

—Terry Eagleton[2]

'Oh, It'd be just my luck,' she exclaimed, disheartened as she kicked off her boots.

'What'd be?'

'To get stole by stampeders or scalped by redskins or drowned, or lose yu, just when I'd begun to be happy.'

'Wal, Reddie, don't give up. Hang on like a Texan. Remember the Alamo!'

—Zane Grey[3]

The drawing of lines in the sand is a practice common in metaphorical schoolyards and Hollywood action films. You know how it works, some kid or action hero draws a line in the dirt with his toe or with a piece of chalk on the blacktop and then dares you to cross it. Go ahead. Make my day! Or you may recall that famous Charles Atlas bodybuilder advertisement, pitched in the backs of comic books to young boys, where the skinny kid pumps iron, bulks up, then dares the bully who had earlier kicked sand in his face to step across such a line. In this way, the line serves much the same purpose as so-called fighting words or juvenile insults directed at one's mother (she wears army boots!): they provoke violence even as they simultaneously wash the perpetrator clean with guiltlessness for the aggressive actions to follow.

Such lines separate *us* from *them*. That is, the line not so subtly reminds us on this side of the line of our inherent rightness, often cloaked in images of our innocence (such as the scrawny kid at the beach not bothering anyone, or George W. Bush's discourse about innocently "expanding freedom"). We—us—are the peaceful player. You—them—have provoked us to this violence. So it is your fault, not ours, and now I am going to kick your ass for three good reasons. One, self-defense, from provocation to preemptive strike, may be justified in a civilized society. Rule number one of all life forms, countries included, is self-preservation. Two, striking at you is just recompense for your aggression or intention to commit aggression toward me. After all, you brought this upon yourself. And three, just maybe you'll learn something from this ass whooping. Do you some good. You know, us is no Neville Chamberlain. Failure to stand up, stand tall, and fight back and, next thing you know, every bully on the schoolyard will be after you.

Sadly, international relations, under the guise of non-binding club membership (e.g., the United Nations) operates *de facto* in much the same way as the schoolyard. The bullies rule. When there is no effective policing agency (the teacher is absent, or, the UN has no fangs anyway), the toughs run the playground. Moreover, they attempt to shape the would-be police in their own image via bribery (e.g., the International Monetary Fund has always been run by the United States) or police directly and claim legitimacy based on this or that (for example, George W. Bush's Coalition of the Willing). This is not surprising; it is just politics played realistically. You play to win, always operating on the assumption that you're right. No point in vacillating like Canadians. Of course, this is made easier when you aver that God is on your side—it increases the fervor and stops potential guilt in its track. This assessment resonates with American cultural norms today and, in fact, has since the birth of the republic because the premise for it was established when the thirteen colonies were first settled, as Richard Slotkin tells us in his book *Regeneration Through Violence*. Richard Flores agrees and avers that the "mythic tale of the Alamo" is synonymous not just with the birth of Texas but with the mythical birthing of the United States.[4]

All Things Past

Do you remember the Alamo, America's paradigmatic line-in-the-sand psycho event? Well, of course not, the historical siege that occurred at that Texas landmark took place in 1836. No doubt, though, you recall the phrase: Remember the Alamo! It has long been used as a patriotic American shibboleth, a palimpsest of a call to arms, a stern reminder to remain steadfast and dutiful in the various ways the white nation has had to protect itself from alien threat, invoking the treasured characteristics of the heroes who perished at the Alamo—Davy Crockett, Jim Bowie, and William Travis, so many frozen-in-time frontiersmen.

However, while you could not possibly remember the historical Alamo, one may take comfort that nearly every American generation since has endured its own personal Alamo and has generally responded in the same myopic, mythopoeic fashion to its own private Alamo as pop culture has (re)imagined the historical Alamo. In other words, different events, same mythically grounded interpretation. For example, in 1846, just ten years after the historical Alamo siege, the United States went to war with Mexico on trumped-up charges that Mexico had invaded the country. While the opposite was true—the United States had provoked and attacked Mexico—the call to arms was cast very much in a Remember-the-Alamo mood. In fact, at that point (1846)—just ten years distant—the events of the historical remained viscerally near in historical memory.

In reality, the U.S. invaded Mexico in 1846. So why then should Americans have fashioned a memory at all like the one that took root and that continues to flourish? The answers are deceptively simple. Americans had long held negative, pejorative views of espied Mexican inferiority, and they were not about to change them because of Texas. In fact, the converse held true. The idea that Mexicans were so many greasers, possibly even more debased than stereotyped Indians—lazy, criminally inclined, deceitful, ungodly, whorish, and so on—served to remind Americans that the Texas border dispute with Mexico presented an opportunity of the first order.

In this way, events conspired against Mexico rather seamlessly. First, U.S. politicians wanted to lay claim to Texas and the rest of what is today the American southwest, though all of it had been part of Mexico's colonial inheritance just as sure as New England or Virginia belonged to America's past. The U.S. wanted the land to grow itself and it wanted Pacific ports for expanded trade. Second, Americans had been flocking into Texas for 30 years. Initially Mexico had invited them in but then attempted to close the door when it became apparent that the Spanish-Catholic population was being overwhelmed by white slavers and other Protestant Anglos. In short, if American politicians wanted Texas, and they did, well, so did Americans already living in Texas.

Third, given that Americans had strongly negative views about the Mexican and Mexico as Other, framing the struggles as one of civilization versus barbarism was entirely sensible for Americans—because they believed it and because it was good politics to do so.[5] American soldiers, for example, saw their Mexican counterparts as racially and morally corrupted savage heathens, veritably begging to be attacked. In the end, the war with Mexico was cast as one pitting civilization against savagery, light against dark, Christian against heathen...us against them. The root cause of the conflict has been pitched inaccurately as Mexican aggression coupled with righteous American self-defense.[6]

Similarly, in 1876, after the homicidal blond-haired playboy of Manifest Destiny, General George Armstrong Custer, was killed as American natives waged a war of bonafide self-defense at the Battle of the Little Big Horn, Americans reacted collectively to the news as one big Remember-the-Alamo event. This, despite years of aggressive U.S. land grabbing of indigenous property. I mean, you think about it: whatever gave the United States the right to take Indian land in the first place? There would have been no fighting for it and no need to establish reservations had the land been empty, as the frontier myth avers. Besides, Americans cherish the right to self-defense, the right to fight for and defend private property, but would not acknowledge such a right for the continent's first inhabitants and owners. Possession is nine-tenths of the law, goes another popular axiom...but apparently not for Indians. All told, by the same logic today either Mexico or Canada might decide to invade the United States if they chose. What is the difference? Theft is theft. In international affairs such conduct is known by what it is, imperialism. And even today Mexico could register a reasonably strong claim to the American southwest (except that its Spanish forebears, too, built an empire with stolen Indian land).[7]

Nevertheless, upon Custer's death the outraged and somewhat frightened nation felt much self-pity and media-abetted fear. Again, the story ran as in the war with Mexico, guiltless Americans had been viciously attacked (while doing nothing more than expanding freedom via theft, murder, and pillage; burning homes; and killing women, old people, and children). So America wrapped itself in its frontier flag of Manifest Destiny and turned its energies to violently pacifying the actual owners of the American west, Indians. One need not feel empathy for the natives, for they had, in the popular view, invited their own destruction. That popular view does not note that the long war to crush Indian nations was basically an imperial exercise.[8] Remember, America's sense of self was forged in a war with imperial England, therefore the United States was comfortable in defining itself as anti-imperial. Period. This delusion was not only encouraging but also politically expedient.

Put another way, a key to the Remember-the-Alamo phenomenon rests upon the idea that the United States is a blameless victim of alien aggression and always has been. Plus, Texas agitated for its own independence, all the while ostensibly promoting American-style democracy and Protestantism. Little mention is ever made that these Texans were also deeply racist, embraced and endorsed and practiced slavery, granted franchise only to land-owning white males, and systematically dispossessed Mexican-Americans of legally held lands after independence was won. The preferred story is that Mexico attacked viciously and that American heroes fought valiantly to the death at the Alamo. The lesson? Well, that real Americans are heroic and embody the mythical characteristics of the heroes of the Alamo siege, which also happen to be mythical frontier values—self-reliance, bravery, toughness, and so on.

Same with Custer, and the list goes on.

For example, in 1898, a generation after Custer's debacle, the United States went to war with Spain over Cuba after Spain had done everything short of rape America's honor, the popular story ran. In reality Spain had done nothing directly to the United States. Not to worry, though, the war itself ended quickly, America won, dictatorship was vanquished, and freedom and democracy were granted to Cuba.[9]

Well, not quite.

Actually, democracy never came to Cuba, at least not as long as the U.S. was involved with the island (that is, until 1959).[10] Cuba is still waiting, though things have been more democratic since Fidel Castro introduced limited democracy, universal health care, free and unfettered access to quality schooling, and so on, after decades of U.S.-sanctioned dictatorship ended abruptly in 1959. To his great credit Castro swept out the pimps, American sugar monopolists, Mafiosi, as well as an authoritarian leader who served only at the whim of the United States.

Here again the enemy—in this case, Spain—was framed as a gang of debased, autocratic, criminal, Papist greasers. On the other hand, American. suzerainty of Cuba granted the islanders nothing better. As democracy blossomed in the U.S. and real wages sky rocketed, Cubans endured decades of rule by American-installed puppet dictators, Mafiosi, American sugar barons, and whoremongers. In this light, Fidel Castro, certainly no angel, represented a vast improvement.

And the list goes on.

The United States got involved in World War One after Germany sunk the ocean liner *Lusitania*. In the United States press the event, very much in keeping with anti-German propaganda fashioned from the White House, was framed as a case of evil, foul-smelling German "Hun" baby killers attacking defenseless American freedom-loving tourists. The reality, as is well known now (but rarely discussed), is that the United States and Germany had had good relations before the war but that the Woodrow Wilson administration in time had to choose where to cast its support—to England or to Germany as the war drew along. Wilson chose England for two basic reasons. First, England was culturally more like the United States. England, despite its flaws had actually given birth to the U.S. Second, and importantly, England owed more money to the U.S. than did Germany. Taken together, in this way financially and culturally the U.S. risked far more—too much, the calculation held—by a British defeat. This, however, is not the place to debate the war. The point is that the sinking of the *Lusitania* was cast in a Remember-the-Alamo frame, where Germany stood in where stereotyped Mexican or Indians or Spaniards had earlier served.

The list goes on.

Domestically in the United States, after decades of massive European immigration that began in the 1880s, at the end of World War One, Americans turned on their own newest residents. That many of these immigrants were of eastern or southern European extraction made the Othering, and the abuses thereby generated, almost predictable. The immigrants were disproportionately swarthy skinned, poorly educated, Catholic, and such. On paper, in this way, they resembled Indians or Mexicans. So not only did the United States close the door on immigration for such undesirables in the early 1920s, especially so on Asians who had contributed much of the labor necessary to construct the continental railroads stretching westward, but when workers tried to organize so as to demand decent working conditions and wages, the government and the mainstream struck back hard with the first of several so-called Red Scares, beginning in 1919, resurfacing in the 1930s, and culminating infamously with the McCarthy witchhunts of the 1950s. These Remember-the-Alamo events are possibly more reflective of the present mood in the United States where Americans of middle-eastern background are routinely discriminated against because of 9-11.

Still the list goes on. There was December 7, 1941. Yes, Japan attacked the United States but does anybody really believe it was necessary to lock up all Americans of Japanese origin? In the War of 1812 did anybody consider locking up all Americans of British origin? Again, I am not at all trying to assess blame for the events as such, so much as to demonstrate that successive American generations have constructed their own private Remember-the-Alamo events as responses to real-world events.

The Gulf of Tonkin resolution, which in 1964 afforded the U.S. presidency the legal right to wage undeclared war on Vietnam, provides another good example. Allegedly North Vietnam had attacked a U.S. patrol boat in international waters, but it had never happened. It was completely fabricated. However, like the lie that Mexico had invaded the United States in 1846, it served as sufficient cause for the United States to start and conduct war against a Third-World country on the other side of the planet for strategic, economic, and philosophical reasons. Significantly, it cost 58,000 American boys' lives in a losing effort, though incredibly the losing president (Nixon) declared victory even as the United States retreated.

Fast forward to the post-9-11 world. The mood today in the United States has been conditioned by the events (and the propaganda following the event) of September 11, 2001, when ideologues flew passenger jets into the World Trade Center towers in New York City. Religious fanatics killed roughly 3,000 innocents that day, a significant figure, in fact, nearly a fifth as many as those Americans who annually die in gun violence on U.S. city streets, yet, to be fair, immeasurably fewer than the policies of another religious ideologue, President Bush the younger, have killed in Afghanistan and Iraq.

But while Americans apparently do not have the right to defend themselves against homegrown violence in any better fashion than by arming themselves, the country does have the right and the duty to defend itself when aliens attack. Fair enough. It is not the first time, either. After all, Custer's demise—his "last stand" (how many had he formerly stood?)—was framed the same way—menacing foreigners in our midst attacking innocents without just cause.

The kneejerk comeback to this point is that 9-11 is different because it targeted innocents, including women and even children. True. But then so did Custer. So did military regimes the United States propped up in East Timor, Guatemala, Chile, Nicaragua, El Salvador, and so on. The fact is that Custer killed lots of women and children and he was only one among many, many American military leaders to engage in the wholesale slaughter of Indigenous Americans by Americans. Slavery, too, constituted and sanctioned massive violence and moral fraud, of biblical proportions, against a defenseless civilian population, including seniors and children. Similarly have Bush dynasty policies annihilated many thousands of innocent children in Iran and Iraq. Reagan policies led to the deaths of countless thousands of babies in Central America, the rape and torture of college students in Chile. George Bush the elder's policies helped fry hundreds of thousands of unarmed Iraqi soldiers in 1991. Ulysses S. Grant, Civil War hero, as president okayed policies that attempted to commit genocide against a domestic population, as did Adolph Hitler.

In sum, the United States has suffered many historical events that are framed and interpreted as Remember-the-Alamo psycho events: we have been attacked viciously by the dark forces of evil, let us strike back hard. In none of the cases were the attacks on the United States unprovoked. In each case, the United States had engaged in deliberate, purposeful policies that inevitably engendered counter-reaction—ironically, in the best American tradition: in the name of self-defense. While this does not justify them, because the idea of an eye for eye seems outdated, it at least partially explains them.

Your Own Personal Jesus

The mother of all Alamo psycho events, the historical Alamo, served up an American hero for all times—one Davy Crockett. As a mythical archetype Crockett expressed frontier tropes almost perfectly, for he was a frontiersman without peer, capable of anything (except lying) and everything (though he was famed for lying) all at once. In addition to the standard characteristics—bravery beyond compare, honesty honed to the point of discomfort, decency without equal, cleverness distilled to the essence of guile, and a childlike wonder that in its innocence forgave all transgressions with extreme prejudice—Davy took the mythical frontier downtown (or at least to the suburbs). By embracing politics, however unwillingly, this Jeffersonian icon tacitly endorsed Hamiltonianism or, at least, the inevitability of the Hamiltonian triumph in American politics and economics. He bridged the mythical past to the mythologized present. He righteously excused precisely as he politely conquered. Perhaps fittingly, then, he sacrificed himself for America. In short, he is Americana's Jesus—and he died to prove it. Remember the Alamo! Davy died for your sins there.

Speaking of icons, who better to don the crown of thorns in Hollywood's most lavish incarnation of the Alamo siege than John Wayne? As one might expect, and in keeping with the framework of Manifest Destiny, the 1960 film made no bones about the event's religious significance. The movie opens with a printed scroll, as if to suggest some biblical documentation:

> In the year of our Lord, 1836, Texas, which has known many flags, was then under the colors of Mexico. Though its inhabitants were made up of settlers from far countries and all parts of the United States, they were Mexican citizens all.

This statement is hopelessly misleading, even deceiving. In the first case, Texas had not known many flags. True, the land had been occupied and owned by natives for thousands of years prior to European invasion, but the reference to "many" was clearly an attempt to imply that no one really owned it fair and square. Therefore, it was ripe for the taking, especially if God wanted you to grab it. A review in the Motion Picture Guide called it "an inspiring history lesson" and stated further that "splendid research" had contributed to a "superb epic."[11]

The next sentence suggests another falsehood—that Anglos willingly submitted to Mexican rule. First, the settlers, many of whom were slave owners, sought land in Texas either to expand their operations from the south or, because their land had been overworked in the south, they now sought new lands on which to grow cotton. Even technically they were not really Mexican citizens because had they been so, they would have learned Spanish and adopted Roman Catholicism and Mexican culture, as they had promised to do when they opted to emigrate to Mexico. The passage also suggests a multicultural quality existed in Texas's population ("settlers from far countries") that historical reality will not support, unless it means to refer to Africans of many national backgrounds in chains in Texas cotton fields.

The movie scroll continues, becoming progressively less accurate, incredibly enough. It reads:

> Generalissimo Santa Anna was sweeping north across Mexico toward them, crushing all who opposed his tyrannical rule. They now faced the decision that all men in all times must face...the eternal choice of men...to endure oppression or to resist.

José Lopez de Santa Anna certainly was no saint. Although, to be fair, he also was not a slave owner, as the sitting U.S. President James Polk was. He also did not in historical reality sweep northward till the slave owners who had migrated to Texas had decided to break their agreement with Mexico and declare independence. Even more interesting, though, are the next lines that effectively universalize ("all men") and essentialize ("in all times") America's struggle to become itself politically by referencing the struggle to the American war for independence and the Paine-like propaganda employed to wage it ("endure oppression or to resist"). You are meant to understand, if you do not yet get it, that this means white men, not men of color or women of any variety.

The movie, which was directed without subtlety by Wayne himself, modestly attempts to show that, apart from the core requirements of frontier heroism, handsome and athletic white males, may take several forms. For example, the rigid Lt. Colonel William Travis struts about in a military uniform, is dogmatic, does not get drunk, and is rule-obsessed. He is just not likeable (played to a wooden tee by Lawrence Harvey). On the other hand, Jim Bowie (acted laconically enough by an earnest and ever pleasant Richard Widmark) is flexible, adaptable, whiskey-drinking, and happy. They are square-jawed and broad shouldered, one and all. And importantly, while Travis and Bowie do not like each other, they do trust one another because at some level they each respect the other's core values—in much the same way the election of 1960 pitted Nixon versus Kennedy.

But where is Crocket?

Our hero among heroes emerges from tall grasses, on horseback, leading a group of men toward the mission. He is exactly what you would hope for in a frontiersman. Buckskinned. He is reassuring. He is John Wayne. And so while it comes as no surprise, that is, the posture that Wayne raised to a manly artform, we are meant to sigh as if with relief that the avuncular Crockett, lord over all that he surveys, can drink whiskey and brawl with the best of them, yet also exacts respect and admiration from Travis.

Early in this laborious three-hour beast of a film, Travis further solidifies the frame for us, Crockett's and thereby America's everlasting dilemma, when he says to Crockett:

> Of the many and unendurable hardships the people have been subjected to under the tyrannical military dictator Santa Anna. We have no rights in the courts. No market for our produce. He has forbidden trade with the North.

Curiously, this sketch bears some considerable resemblance to the United States itself. First, Santa Anna, Mexico's greatest political figure of the mid-nineteenth century, parlayed his military career to significant political gain, much the same way as had George Washington or countless American war heroes (think of Andy Jackson, Ulysses Grant, Teddy Roosevelt, Dwight Eisenhower, John Kennedy, among others). So smearing Santa Anna by tagging him as a president carrying martial baggage is, well, two-faced.

Second, Texas itself engaged in legal prejudice against those Mexicans who decided to remain in Texas after independence was won, this despite promises to the contrary. In other words, Texans of Mexican ancestry were systematically discriminated against in Texas after independence—not just in courts but in trade, socially, religiously, linguistically, and so on. Such conduct typified anti-Latino thought and behavior in Texas long after, too, carrying well into the twentieth century when Texas had long since become part of the United States.

Third, Mexico did in fact seek to limit trade, as Travis says, but mostly because it fearfully anticipated exactly what came to occur—a push and fight for Texas's independence and eventual annexation by the United States. It is important to recall that much of the trade derived from a slave-based economy, so the charges against Mexico for tyranny and injustice may be accurate—Santa Anna was a *caudillo*—but they do not ring true because Texas and the United States sanctioned slavery for decades after Mexico had abolished it. Was Santa Anna more of a tyrant than your average slave master?

Independence, meanwhile, serves as its own tropey gambit, conjuring up dreams of heroism and plenty, of frontiersmen and God, of milk and honey. Here is Crocket/Wayne waxing about independence:

> Republic. I like the sound of the word. It means people can live free, talk free, go or come, buy or sell, be drunk or sober, however they choose. Some words give you a feeling. Republic is one of those words that makes me tight in the throat. The same tightness a man gets when his baby takes his first step or his first baby shaves or makes his first sound like a man. Some words can give you a feeling that makes your heart warm. Republic is one of those words.

It does not take Michel Foucault to understand that the Duke is comparing the need for Texas's independence to the glory of the U.S., where the notion of independence has achieved an inviolable status along narrowly defined lines. That is, for example, the word "independence" gives one pause to get tight in the throat about other related matters, too, because for the large majority of Americans it offered nothing of the sorts of things Crockett identifies. So independence may be great in theory, but in the United States it actually strengthened the hold of slavery on the country, offered nothing for Indians till the 1960s and even then it was only the paperbag right to vote) (whose land had been stolen in the first place, did not offer suffrage to women for well more than a century after independence.

Davy Crockett (John Wayne) styling in buckskins and coonskin cap in *The Alamo* (1960), which Wayne also directed

To back up his claims Crockett essentializes independence through a series of clumsy masculine metaphors about youths growing to manhood. Like in the other quoted passages, he invokes the spirit of capitalism at the same time as impugning Mexico, displacing it as Other, as a place where one cannot live free, talk free, go or come...and the like. This is nonsense because the comparison is invidious. Women were not free in Texas or the United States. Neither were blacks or Indians or Irish or socialists, for that matter. Are Muslims and Arabs free in the United States today?

Ironically, it really does not matter that the movie gets it all wrong historically because it gets it all right in core cultural terms. Where it is Crockett. Always Crockett. As our hero, as the agent of transformation, as the son of America who will gladly give his life in order that the land experience rebirth, Crockett frames himself as the American Christ (move over John Dunbar/Kevin Costner). He has sacrificed himself for us. At the very least we should be eternally grateful. As writer Richard Flores has noted, "The case of the Alamo demonstrates how events from the past serve to advance various plots in the present by endowing them with a sense of historicality and genuineness."[12]

In another scene, where Crockett makes metaphoric love to a Mexican damsel he has rescued from a domestic bully, from the un-American clutches of patriarchy and paternalism—as if! any adult American female might respond—we are again reminded of the biblical proportions of this epic narrative. Crockett and the dark and dignified Flaca pose beneath a great leafy tree by the edge of water at dusk. Crockett marvels at the tree in language that does Elmore Leonard justice. "This tree," he says, "must have been growed before man put his first dirty footprints on this prairie...Kind of a tree Adam and Eve must have met under," he offers, in what must be one of the corniest and simultaneously kitschily sublime come-ons in movie history.

She moves to lean against the tree, beguilingly.

He continues, explaining that he came to Texas in search of something he could not define, yet hints at a higher level of spirituality and commitment. It is his fate, as we already know, because we understand completely the setup to a Remember-the-Alamo event. It is his mythical fate that he is here awkwardly articulating and it is America's Manifest Destiny that he is invoking. "I'm not empty anymore," we are not surprised to hear him confide, now that he has her and the Alamo to scrap for. "There's right and there's wrong. You gotta do one or the other. You do the one and you're living. You do the other and you may be walking around but you're as dead as a beaver hat," he concludes, fusing his ardor with Americanized Christian binaries.

The fight itself is a dull affair, poorly lit, hokey, and choreographed without finesse. Basically, it is a poorly wrought circle-the-wagons affair. What else could it be? Hunkering down, wallowing in self-pity, quashing all dissent in times of trouble, that is central to any Remember-the-Alamo event. Our heroes defend from the inside as they are assaulted by treacherous, overdressed marauders outside.

Meanwhile, in the prelude to hostilities, the film busies itself with gawky patriotic frontier gesturing. For example, Jocko, one of many buckskinned Tennesseans on site (though by his own words the historical Crockett was one of only three from that state at the Alamo siege[13]), expresses his fervent devotion to Christianity. "I believe," he says with a dash of buckskinned eloquence, "in the Lord God Almighty, all knowing and all forgiving. And I believe that good shall be triumphant in the end and that evil shall be vanquished."

Consider a scene as baffling as it is morally repellent. Jim Bowie decides, once he knows that death is imminent and that the Alamo will fall to Santa Anna and hordes of treacherous Mexicanos, to emancipate Jethro, his own devoted black slave. It is a gesture that a grandiloquently ambiguous review in the *New York Times* termed "piercingly affected and visually overwhelming" in its authenticity.[14] But this is ridiculous because Jethro represents, like the other African Americans portrayed in this film, just another slow-witted cardboard clown.

Jethro struggles with the concept of freedom and does not consider that in America it is something one is supposed to own by virtue of being born a human being and not something that one has to be granted, as by the divine right of kings or the master race. And, besides, we as audience know something that the silly constructed Negro does not. Freedom is right and good and, with enough conjuring, even a black man can understand it. Yet Jethro gets it just fine. "If I'm gonna be free then I got a right to decide what I'm gonna do. Seems to me that's what you men are fighting for. So," he concludes, "I'll stay."

The logic is boggling. Jethro will stay and fight. This, despite the fact of a lifetime of slavery, premised on the twin towers of the implied threat of violence against him and his alleged black inferiority. He'll choose that over freedom from it? I mean, it is not as if Texas ended slavery after winning its independence; in fact, in many ways the war for Texas's independence was about preserving slavery. Mexico had outlawed the barbaric practice in the 1820s.

Even granted his freedom, it makes little sense for Jethro to declare in favor of "what you men are fighting for," when not only did it offer him nothing but more or less guaranteed him, even as a free black male, a life of abject poverty, aggressive discrimination, biting fear, and predictably early death. No, Jethro had nothing to fight for in this battle between colonialist powers.

And Then Along Came Davy

Once the battle ensues we find the Mexicans clad in red uniforms, to underscore the villainy of the enemy, like so many English redcoats, and the prototypical Yanks often shirtless, stripped down to the bare essence of frontier manliness. You know or can guess the rest. Crockett and his comrades hold out the longest—but fall this American Jesus must. He has to die so that the rest of us can learn a valuable lesson. And he does, pierced through the chest with a lance, which as easily might have been an Injun arrow, African spear, Vietnamese pungi stick, Soviet machine gun, or Muslim-steered jet plane.

But it ain't over.

It is never over. Remember it! How could you forget?

Remember it, we are enjoined in the hymn that leads us through the red, white, and blue sunset closing the frame and the movie. The film, as academic Richard Flores has noted, "serves as a key example of a master symbol of [American] modernity."[15] In the garish way it is presented in Wayne's world, the Alamo writ as frontier yarn becomes both an apology for and an expression of Manifest Destiny—fighting a take-no-prisoners zero-sum game for American-style democracy, American-style capitalism, and American-style religion, all framed in the cloak of a woeful victim's tale: we won't get fooled again. Thank you, Jesus.

Grin and Bear It

Consider a real man. A man "who don't know fear." The kind of a man who "killed a bar when he was three." Say, a "buckskin pioneer." He is the sort of man who can swagger humbly about while donning a coonskin cap. Such a man is of course a figment of the American imagination. Walt Disney's imagination, to be more precise; but also America's mythical imagination. Yes, bigger even than Disney could have imagined (or Uncle Walt would not have killed Davy off so quickly, after just three movie episodes) was Disney's adoring television audience in the 1950s, when this buckskin Jesus, this marketing icon, sold 10 million coonskin caps to a doting male American audience of boys and men aspiring to emulate, or at least posture like, Davy Crockett, the "king of the wild frontier." The theme song went straight to number one on the hit parade and stayed there for 13 weeks.

The 1950s are often portrayed in popular culture as an idyllic time of two chickens in every pot, two cars in every garage, a more sensible time before the advent of postmodernism and the arrival of hippies and racial politics and lesbians. Yes, a simpler, more pleasant, even harmonious time. But this is no more accurate than the mistaken idea that the 1960s—which saw the assassinations of Martin Luther King and Robert Kennedy, the U.S. bog down in Vietnam, and Richard Nixon emerge with a comfortable win in 1968—added up to nothing more than sex, drugs, and rock and roll. Despite the counter culture, the 1960s found America turning to the right politically. Meanwhile, the 1950s, more realistically, were the last decade before African Americans began a courageous and frequently dangerous struggle to gain fuller equality in a racist society. Likewise, women and Latinos would come to fight for their rightful place at the table, only to have reactionary forces set against them in the late sixties. In foreign policy the United States excelled in more of the same, confounding those who believed the rhetoric about promoting freedom and democracy, as the U.S. not so secretly waged wars on democracy in Guatemala and Cuba, to name just two examples in this hemisphere, not to mention the Korean War.

In short, tensions ran high beneath the superficial luster of the Eisenhower years. Beneath the surface a series of long-neglected sores were nearing the festering point—in particular race and gender relations stunk, continuing to privilege whites and especially white males. And then along came Davy.

Disney's Davy Crockett served to divert and assuage hegemonic white-male America, that sector of the population mostly responsible for the sorrowful state of race relations, gender imbalances, and ongoing frontier-style foreign policy. But where John Wayne served up a standardized Duke job of work, a stock Wayne character not just in coonskin, but also draped in maudlin preachiness and a near pathetic casting of Crockett as a passive aggressive victim of alien interloping, Disney brewed up something simpler, more basic and dead to rights, something playfully boyish to Wayne's truculent early adolescence, and Walt sugar coated Crockett as "Davy" (not Crockett and certainly not David), the idiot savant of the woods, the bear handler whose grin washed away the stains of history, whose buckskins cleansed violence by inverting it, in whose white teeth shone the promise of American virtue and uprightedness. In this way, if Wayne's Crockett is the American Jesus spreading the good word of imperialism, Disney's Fess Parker as Davy is more the Peter Pan of Manifest Destiny, the impish boy wonder of imperialism, enticed by delusions of grandeur and never-ending male bondage and gunplay to desert his family and never grow up.[16]

The standard frontier signifiers are embedded without the least sophistication and with absolutely no irony in Disney's greed fest. For example, opening credits are set against the backdrop of a musket, just one of Davy's chosen phallic weapons of death. The U.S. army, we learn quickly, is hopeless—incompetent, lazy, stupid. Davy, the archetype for the model male Republican, surpasses collective wisdom and group action any old time. Like Peter Pan, this overgrown boy—a boy! almost a toddler in his inability to articulate English like an adult—is too much a match for big government (which stands in for all government, the military), Indians (standing in for all people of color), women (and the wife that Davy forsakes in order that he fulfill his destiny on behalf of us all), blackguards (like so many Captain Hooks, pesky terrorist types, swatted away like flies). Yep, he is a veritable boy wonder.

He is the embodiment of an ever-youthful America.

Situating Davy as a boy was pure genius on Disney's part. First, ask yourself: how dangerous can a clean-cut white boy be? You know, the sort of a kid who helps little old ladies cross the street, delivers your paper in the morning, mows lawns to earn money to buy a new catcher's mitt. Not very dangerous at all, most of us are likely to conclude. The results, couched in this way, then pay huge dividends for the myth. For, on the one hand, by association (or is that projection?) U.S. foreign policy is being conducted symbolically by just a healthy normal boy, so it cannot be very bad because good boys are pure of heart, as we all know, and they do good things. Second, that a mere youngster could carry out such a policy only reinforces the level sense of the mythic plan. It is so stupid-simple that even a lad who cannot grasp the basics of the English language can master the fundamentals of it. Note, too, that it only takes a good-hearted lad to conquer those simplified dangers posed by the real world. So Davy grins down a bear in much the same way the United States went eyeball to eyeball with the Soviet Bear and, well, as the story goes the bear blinked (which begs the question, among others, of why Fidel Castro is still in office). Or you will notice how Davy actually claims to like Indians, at least the ones who play by his rules; he kills the other ones—but harmlessly, you will note, in much the same way that boys will be boys and that playing cowboy and Indian is, after all, just a game, not serious, right! Wrong. Davy is as deadly serious as he is deadly intent in engaging in a political game that dances to a mythical tune, not so different than George W. Bush's non-sequitur about the United States expanding freedom in and for Iraq. Only a child could absorb such sentiments at face value; but this is precisely what Disney asks of you. Moreover, it is exactly what the frontier myth has always promised, childlike freedom from the responsibility of one's actions. Real history is for grown-ups, whereas myth appeals most fundamentally to the child within.

When Davy and his sidekick George (Buddy Ebsen) face trouble for the first time in this flick, they master it quickly. The army cannot pacify aggressive Indians, despite its larger numbers. So Davy and George, just the two of them, whip the Indians into shape by pretending to be a regiment unto themselves. Naturally, the stupid redskins fall for the ruse and then more or less serve as target practice for the two frontiersmen. The rest run away screaming like the "varmints" and "cussed varmints" Davy declares them to be. As George gamely puts it, "I'm more scared of snakes and gators than I am of Injuns."

Maybe he should be because these Hollywood Indians are exactly what you would expect them to be—treacherous, sneaky, conniving, given to the pleasures of torture. But they are neither dangerous nor the slightest bit realistic.

Later Davy presents the voice of reason to the natives. He explains, "I ain't a soldier. I'm a settler. I'm a hunter, like you."

The chief responds: "Hunter? You hunt Indians."

The progenitor of the coonskin cap craze, Disney's Davy Crockett (Fess Parker) looks for signs in the forest.

Now, like it or not, historically we know that this much is true, that settlers promoted and pursued policies of aggression and genocide towards those Indians whose lands they coveted and took by force. Sharing those views, the U.S. government acted similarly. Remember, Andrew Jackson did not campaign his way to the White House in 1828 as being a formidable Indian killer for no reason.

So Davy lectures the chief, pointing out that he hunts Indians "only because you made war on us," when any fair assessment might begin with the observation that Europeans invaded the Americas, not the other way around. But never mind that. "Your chiefs, the smart ones," Davy continues in his folksy way, "have give up. They found out that war's no good." Translation: just give up or we will smite you.

The chief, though, is not prepared to roll over just like that. Instead he offers a sexist comeback to the king of the frontier. "You talk like woman," he says dismissively.

"I'm talking sense and you know it," Davy complains with sincere exasperation. "You're brave Redstick and your warriors is brave. But in the end they're all gonna die." No argument there. Maybe Davy was talking a little sense.

The trouble is that Redstick seems to harbor a stubborn notion that the land his people has owned for thousand of years actually belongs to him and his people. To decide the issue, as if once and for all, Davy challenges Redstick "according to Indian law," which means a tomahawk fight between the two men.

Sound crazy? Not to Davy or Walt Disney.

"Indian law no good for white man," roars Redstick in a feeble attempt to suborn the rules of engagement.

"Why not," Davy is nonplussed. "White man's law'd be good for Indians if you gave it half a chance. How about it?"

You know the rest. At first Davy tries to grin him down as he had done with the bear earlier. But the gag fails. Redstick growls in response. "Well, it worked on a bear," Davy jokes. Then they fight. Redstick cheats, Davy wins, spares his life. And the glory of redemptive, restorative violence, and America's virtue emerge spotlessly from this encounter.

Jesus Loves Me; This I Know

God plays a role in this, too. When Davy passes on the opportunity to sacrifice Redstick's life, the chief is baffled.

"Why you no kill me?" he says.

"Maybe because of another law. It ain't bad for red men or white men alike. Thou shalt not kill." Yet Davy and George have already happily slaughtered a score of Indians who were doing nothing more than exercising their right to defend themselves and their property. But never mind.

Now they're off again on Davy's adventurous life, as the lyrics remind us, "restless for places he'd wanted to see." Or, after snuggled for just one winter with his family, whom we never meet, he is "itchin to move away." So he abandons them. He is searching, perhaps elusively, for virgin land, "untouched...looking for paradise." That he deserts his wife and children seems the least he can do for our benefit, though it is increasingly more difficult to reconcile him as a hero after the abandonment.

Still, take him at his word we must, for more trouble looms on the horizon. This time it takes the form of a French-Canadian bully, one Bigfoot, who has been terrorizing some edenic hill country that Davy and George stumble across. Worse, Bigfoot has been beating up on Davy's passive new Indian neighbor and family, Charlie Two Shirts.

They fight. Davy bests him of course in hand to hand combat. But, true to form, after the dust has settled Bigfoot aims to shoot Davy in the back so, in a calculated preemptive strike, George shoots Bigfoot in the back.

Then Davy summarily cleans up the whole region in what seems nothing more than a few short hours. Presto, another problem solved, another building block of Americana erected. However, then there is always another complication with Davy. America was not built in a day, after all. First, Davy is asked to run for state legislature because, as everyone knows, politics could use an honest man. Plus, news comes that Polly, Mrs. Crockett, has died. Without a single shred of poignancy, Davy needs to be alone to get over his grief, which takes about 15 seconds of posing. Apparently, real men are more interested in their own games than in responsibilities to family (as he had already established in the abandonment). His children are sent to live with the in-laws, lest they crowd the king of the wild frontier with paternal duties.

Eventually, as is well known, Davy ends up in Congress. But he goes only reluctantly, in order to please those whom he represents. He notes, ruefully, "This job's twice as tough as fighting Injuns and ain't half as fun."

There in Washington his political mentor, the hero of the Battle of New Orleans, noted Indian killer, and future President Andrew Jackson, counsels the frontier king. "We're bursting [in America] at the seams. We need room to grow. Expansion. That's what I'm thinking of. Expansion. And by the eternal I'm not letting anything stand in way of that." That "that" is of course Manifest Destiny (conveniently endorsed by the eternal), which Davy too endorses with his every boyish move. For example, he later waxes on in Congress that "we got a responsibility to this strapping, fun-loving, britches-bustin young bar cub of a country. We got a responsibility to help it grow into the kind of nation the good Lord meant it to be."

Ta da! With the applause in Congress still thundering in our ears off goes Davy back to the frontier where he really belongs. But this time, now that he is unemployed, a widower, and a dead-beat dad, he is going to Texas to help the slave owners.

Even George cannot figure this out. He complains, "Texas! We got the whole entire nation to choose from and you gotta pick—why there is nothing there but a mess of trouble," alluding to the fact that Texas had by then broken away from Mexico and declared its independence.

"Americans in trouble," Davy explains in the somberest mood of an eight-year-old who has his history backwards.

"Yeah, a bunch of crazy fools trying to take on a whole army," George counters. "And so far away from the rest of the country they ain't going to get no help. Bunch of rock-headed idiots that won't quit because they think they're right! How soon you reckon we'll be headed out that way?"

The logic in this passage smells of Zane Grey or countless mindless Indian westerns where it is not so much an argument as it is a pose. This occurs in part because the truth is less kind than the pretense. The truth is that Texas was a breakaway republic with dreams of fulfilling a dream of unencumbered slavery. It is much the same dream as the Confederacy's thwarted dream to break away. Yet the difference is that in 1836 slavery was more politically acceptable than it was in 1860. In other words, in 1836 the United States as a whole was willing enough to go out on limb for slavery, something only roughly half of it was willing to do 25 years later. Besides, were they Americans in Texas or Mexicans? Davy's own logic suggests that those Texicans were traitors to the land that gave them next to free land, and lots of it. Of course, this makes more sense once the film reminds one how debased and unworthy the half-breed nation of Mexico to the south really was.

Davy is predictably determined, as always, to hold the tide at the Alamo. That they are able to hold as long as they do before dying tragically yet heroically, we can chalk up to Betsy, Davy's rifle (which conjures up milk and cookie imitations of *Full Metal Jacket*'s Mary Jane Rotten Crotch), and "the hand of providence." God, of course, might, had he really been on the side of the United States, spared all the death and destruction...but this idea remains unexplored.

And though he dies valiantly, we expect Davy to carry the day emotionally and spiritually. He does. It begins on the eve of the final and thirteenth day with a virtuoso guitar and vocal number by Fess Parker, who in real life sought to crossover as a modestly successful recording artist. And to be sure Davy goes down strumming, the last man standing. The king is dead. Long live the king. And the king will live long, we are reminded, as long as, you know, Americans "remember the Alamo."

Disney's *Alamo* reminds us of the centrality of the basic elements of American imperialism. First, there is the sense of an exclusive right to define and occupy and rule in and from the center. Long live the king! Second, violence is licensed, even encouraged. Play at killing, make it fun, Davy stresses in his utterations and deeds. Injun killing ain't hardly work; it is a pleasure for Davy. Third, God is on America's side. Like any frontiersman worth his salt, Davy is humble, after all, yet he is also our hero. He recognizes that his story is all about fulfilling God's vision for His chosen frontier people. In this way Davy serves as an American Christ. Fourth, despite his repulsion for politics, Davy Crockett was an honest (pardon the anachronism) Abe, not just the man for his times but the man for all times. As a result, he is a necessary politician, for as much as mythical Americana distrusts bureaucracy and government, it is a job that needs to be done. And any job that needs to be done needs to be clean, needs a cleaner, hence

Congressman Crockett. Finally, Davy reminds us of the sanctity of capitalism and its fixation with property rights based on ownership of, in the first case, the land. Apart from a happy-go-lucky willingness to kill to get and secure the land, Davy asks nothing more than that Indians and other Others obey the law as he sees it. If, as Garry Wills put it, John Wayne was Manifest Destiny on horseback, Hollywood's Davy Crocket was hegemony in Jesus boots, some imperial Peter Pan.

Return of the King

Maybe it is easy to dismiss the early filmic Davy incarnations as the product of a simpler, even simplistic time (at least in Hollywood), to chuckle them away as musty baggage of the Cold War era or the last vestiges of an age when people might distantly have remembered the actual historical frontier. All of this rings partially true. I mean, the films are at the very least quaint and sometimes outrageously funny when viewed today, even as they were deadly serious, earnest, very public teaching tools 40 years ago. Further, Crockett tales, especially Remember-the-Alamo psycho events, are like Sunday school narratives, situating biblical sorts of American characters (e.g., frontiersmen such as Davy, Jim Bowie, Daniel Boone, Shane, Tom Doniphon, John Dunbar, the Man in the Wilderness, and others) in mythical harm's way. These hallowed morality tales, in which our hero is required to choose from a series of conventional signifiers to do right on our behalf, reify the moral goodness of America at the same time as rebirth it. In other words, Davy tales both teach us how to be good *a la* the mythical frontier as mother of all myths at the same time as remind us, onanistically in the repetitiveness of it all, of the natural wonder of American origins. Further, normally these matinees grant our frontiersman license to employ violence, so as to lead by example. It is not quite that he is necessarily a guy wearing a white hat riding on a white horse squared off against a black hatted, black horse guy, but then it is not far from this either.

But this is too quaint. Can you imagine such a film being made today? Certainly neither Wayne's Crocket nor Disney's Davy could cut a deal in Hollywood today, except possibly as animated characters (and why not? they're cartoonish in many ways). While I have argued that it is not especially difficult to unpack imperial baggage from a host of frontier films, generally the task is a whole lot more complicated than what John Wayne's *Alamo* and Disney's king present us with. So it is likely that today not even Disney could pull it off for an audience older than about 11 years. Yet, all that said, the Alamo—where Texas plays the frontier card and the psycho event (re)births America—recently staged a comeback in Hollywood in 2004.[17]

This took *cojones* on the part of the filmmakers, given that the Alamo has achieved canonical status in Americana; given 9-11 and the possibility that the film might stray, even if unintentionally, on to the consecrated turf staked out for that tragic psycho event and thereby besmirch it; given postmodernism and the more cynical quality of Americans today versus those of two generations ago. In short, who could or would do Davy Crockett and the Alamo story justice today? Is such an endeavor either possible, let alone desirable (the latter of which should be understood, probably, as whether it would make money)? While these caveats have not kept the frontier narrative at bay elsewhere in Hollywood film, there clearly has been a trend away from traditional westerns, as noted much earlier in this book. But the Alamo? That has got to be quicksand for the filmmaker of the twenty-first century.

Maybe not, though. One way to end run around the potential difficulties is to revision the story in keeping with a more contemporary sensibility. But what does this entail? Playing against the hand of filmmakers is the fact that the Alamo story fundamentally lacks fireworks and the need for groovy special effects, so you cannot simply dazzle your way past an audience. Remember the Alamo! Well, people do remember it as a psycho event and as such it carries certain delimiting expectations. Eminem cannot play Davy Crockett. Further, the narrative is, frankly, somewhat bland: it is a hunkering down to fight to the death kind of story. It is a self-righteous, circle the wagons martyr's tale. The inducement derives from its similarity to Christ's self-sacrifice. That is the payoff: everlasting life via martyrdom for our star(s). So how much can you do with it? Or, to put it another way, is that not enough? Shouldn't it be enough? Possibly, but maybe all it needs is an update, where the stars strike more contemporary poses. Maybe we just need Brad Pitt or Tom Cruise or Jim Carrey.

On the other hand, the story offers in spades what drives and has always driven Hollywood (and Christianity)—white guy heroes. The

Alamo tale is a natural star vehicle. It was for John Wayne and it was for Fess Parker.

Billy Bob Hurtin

This time, however, in 2004, Hollywood really blew it. For not only was the role feebly cast, dismally acted by Billy Bob Thornton as one David (he prefers David to Davy) Crockett, and written confusedly, ambiguously, and without distinction, this Crockett is no hero at all. Neither, for that matter, are any of the Alamo characters. The result is that the new Alamo will strike you first as a movie with no heart. Like it or not, heroicism and self-sacrifice and regeneration through violence are the whole point. Without this you have got nothing, at least nothing American.

In much the same way Manifest Destiny in Hollywood film has worked, in some sense, because it coughs up archetypal heroes for us to emulate, adore, swoon, and occasionally even cry over, this film fails to deliver. To its credit this work attempts to make up for the lack of heroism, however awkwardly, not by decentering the film so much as by adopting a foreign policy strategy gambit not unknown to the frontier myth. For that matter it is central to the Bush dynasty: payback. But revisioning the Alamo as mere payback is ultimately unfulfilling because it abstracts the cause of American-style imperialism, which has been placed squarely on the shoulders of the frontiersman. Sure, payback may be comforting, but it works better—or possibly it works only—when it is carried out by characters whom we have been taught to admire. A Remember-the-Alamo event cannot be equated with Charles Bronson's revenge tale, *Death Wish*.[18]

Like the 1960 version, this film first presents us with a condensed screed:

> The Alamo was established as a Spanish mission in 1718. For more than a century armed conflict deprived it of its sacred purpose. The church became a makeshift fortification against marauding Indians, rebels, and as a succession of conquering armies.

Next page: "Location, proximity to settlements and perhaps even fate made the Alamo a crossroads for siege and battle." So we are presented, then, with a setting framed for conflict and ripe with possibility. We know that those who are likely to attack are on the same plain as "marauding Indians," that they do not respect the "sacred purpose" of the site, and that it has always been up for grabs—in other words, it was never really a part of Mexico.

Then we meet the Enya-like woodwinds that deliver us soothingly yet triumphantly to the heart of the story: those heroes held out for 13 days against impossible odds. We know, we know. Enough already.

We encounter Sam Houston, praying fervently and angrily before a candle as the news is shouted by a rider that the Alamo has fallen. What, have we missed it? Nope. We jumpcut flashback suddenly to one year earlier. To a fancy ball held in Washington, D.C. And there is Sam—Uncle Sam?—drinking heavily, for that is one thing that American heroes like to do, shows us that they're human too, even though better than the rest of us (the us who tend not to be drunkards).

Sam is waxing to Congressman David Crockett about the virtues of Texas. "You come to Texas," he says in a growly attempt at baritone that actor Dennis Quaid matches impressively with a pouty grimace for the next two hours, "timber, water, game, cattle, more land than you can possibly imagine...you will receive 640 acres of your choosing."

David, meanwhile, is already a star here, entertaining folks, in a contradiction that only makes sense in myth, with his tall tales, yet he is renowned simultaneously for his truth-telling.

However, at this point the film is still only setting up the plot. Now it flashes to a heated discussion of Texas's would-be founders. They are edgy, angst-ridden, these Texicans, because of the behavior of Mexico's former president and now military commander General José Antonio Lopez de Santa Anna. "I, for one," we hear loud and clear from an angry democrat, "ain't swearing allegiance to no son of a bitch dictator!" The room erupts in cheers and applause.

So suddenly we have the setup established. Americans are going to fight for democracy and the potential for riches and land ownership. The contradiction between American avowals of love of freedom and the enduring practice and expansion of slavery to Texas is not addressed. Nor is the reality that the land's first owners—Indians, those "marauders"—had the most legitimate claim to the land. I mean, if Mexicans were not fit to own Texas then why not fight to give it back to the Indians? In a sense, this is not a serious question because the very idea of Indian ownership is not possible in Hollywood's frontier discourse. The logic operates this way: if Mexicans could not behave properly, there is no way Indians could. Besides, we have already been introduced to the concept that this a "sacred" setting, sacred in a Protestant sense, not pagan. Remember the Alamo and forget the Indians.

Shortly, we meet the rest of the Alamo's metaphorical posse: Jim Bowie, he of the famed big cocked knife, so big in fact that it rivals a small sword; Lt. Colonel William Travis, again cast as a "two-bit dandy" (Bowie's words), unreasonably obsessed with pomp and ceremony, though at heart a good man willing to die for the cause.

These characters are flawed. Bowie is intemperate, drinks too much, is undisciplined. Travis, his nemesis, is too disciplined, has deserted his wife and children, and is obsessed with regulations and rules. Houston is inflexible, a drunk, intolerant, and egocentric. In short, he is a tyrant. David Crockett is understated, at least in comparison to his earlier filmic representations. He is quieter, abundantly tranquil in his humble and fearless addiction to the ideals of equality. In rendering our ostensible heroes with all too human characteristics one might hope and expect that the director aims to humanize them. But if this was his goal—and it is not at clear that it was—it backfires badly. Instead, because we are never fed any reasonable grounds upon which it might have been reasonable to fight to the death here, the film strongly makes the case that we should simply overlook, say, child abandonment or alcoholism, when it is committed in the act of following a higher cause. But since the higher cause is never clearly articulated, the message is one that would disgust many Americans. What, after all, was the creation of the American nation about — mythically or in reality—if not the championing of family, democratic virtue, decency, tolerance, and so on? This is a sordid film.

Meanwhile, in keeping with the mythical narrative, the enemy is debased in the vilest terms. Mexican soldiers are simultaneously ill shod yet overdressed in excessively ornate uniforms, eager to fight yet simultaneously cowardly, their leader a well schooled general yet an overfed pompous maniac. The officer corps are so many sissypants posing sycophants, sucking off Santa Anna, a deliciously well-acted villain (portrayed by Emilio Echeverría). Santa Anna is pure Other. He is ugly, obstinate, vain, sexually lecherous (raping a pretty young Mexican gal), sips champagne from fancy glasses with his pinkie extended, rash, cruel, elitist, and more or less personifies everything that David Crockett is not. He is a megalomaniac to boot. Crockett calls him a "peacock."

Throughout the movie we get studied obviousness writ large. "As goes the Alamo, so goes Texas," one says here, where another adds that self-sacrifice is all that stands between good citizenry and Santa Anna's armies, between democracy and tyranny. Mythical America forever! As says Sam Houston, this is an exercise that "will birth" a nation in the image of the mythical frontier, buffered by God and by the geography of the "sacred" place, so oft defiled by pagan Indians and Papist hordes of Mexicans.

Race also surfaces uneasily in the film. Apart from all Mexicans being given the John Wayne treatment—they cannot shoot, they explode more readily, follow rather than lead, blindly tag along behind Santa Anna—Mexican Texans are split. Even families are divided, some throwing their lot in with Santa Anna and some with the American Texans. But why, you might ask, would anyone, given Santa Anna on screen, throw in with Mexico? The film offers no hint, except perhaps in the way that Mexican soldiers bumble, follow senselessly, and die conveniently and without protest—perhaps, indeed, "fate" is on America's side.

African Americans are a different matter. Here the film seeks to establish a clearly revisionist frame vis-à-vis Wayne's 1960 mess. In the 1960 *Alamo*, Richard Widmark as Jim Bowie frees his slave, Jethro, who then improbably elects to stay and fight for the freedom he suddenly cherishes (yet will never experience, even if he had survived). In 2004 this is just not on, the updated film soundly reasons. Here, in small scenes that have an added-on quality, not so much subversive as politically correct, through the dialogue between two slaves we dance around the issue of slavery. An elder slave counsels a younger one to quickly announce his status as slave once the Mexican hordes take the site; for, it would seem, the savage Mexican multitudes had inexplicably for some decades abhorred slavery enough to banish it. A better film might have chosen to foreground this important historical and racial issue, not bury it; because, again, it is subsumed under the greater good—the birthing of Texas *qua* synecdoche for the symbolic rebirthing of the United States. In reality, both nations were born into and long embraced slavery.

What of David Crocket? The best part of his role in this film, because he does actually almost nothing of substance, is his fiddling. David fiddles. This buckskin pioneer plays the music that Texas and indeed all of America, can parlay to. Metaphorically, it is the imperial soundtrack of our lives. Fittingly, on the eve of destruction, the last night at the Alamo, David fiddles life yet into the American soul. For it is the rhythm and the soul of the frontiersman that separates America from its antithesis, say, Mexican or Indians or Vietnam or the former Soviet Union. David fiddles, and it is jazzy and improvised, as if to suggest that the sound of America birthing and growing is entirely natural and requires no predetermined patterning; this stands in sharp contrast to the marching tunes played on the "Other" side of the wall, where Mexican musicians march to the beat of a different drum. That is, literally, they march; David fiddles like some reverse Nero. He plays that fiddle.

With such ersatz heroes, martyrdom is not enough to sate an audience in 2004, and so we must rely on payback to fill the mythical void. Enter Sam Houston, obstinate, angry, defiant, unyielding, yet true in some way (we are not sure just how apart from the fact that he is pals with the principals) mythically American, unless one wants to argue that the ends justify the means. Houston answers only to God, he declares—and why not, when he is in command of an army, birthing a nation in the image that God Himself desires? Santa Anna, he declares, is a wannabe Napoleon of the West. So, like Wellington, Houston will wait for Santa Anna to meet his Waterloo. For as sure as Napoleon slipped, that sissy French aristocrat erred via hubris, Santa Anna is sure to do the same, ridiculous overreaching greaser; and when he does, Houston—and we are meant to understand this as the interjection of divine providence—will strike back hard.

He does. And as the moment at length presents itself Houston rears up on his white horse to enjoin the men to fight well and true. "You will remember this battle till the day that you die," he snarls. "But that is for tomorrow. For today, remember the Alamo!"

The Mexicans fall quickly. Rather than fighting like men, they turn tail and flee in retreat like, well, Hollywood Mexicans. Consistent with the retaliation motif, despite begging for mercy like blubbering childish miscreants, they are given no quarter. In this way, closure dawns for the viewer. It is all in-your-face, Homer Simpson-style payback trumping the martyrdom and self-sacrifice that may have played well for an earlier generation. Perhaps this is fitting in the post-9-11 world, where the mood in America seems to have shifted, perhaps returned, to more of an Old Testament understanding of the nature of Christian rights and responsibilities; or is it just modernism rearing its head in what we are told by the mass media is an increasingly post-modern world?

Houston, meanwhile, in a grandly civilizing gesture, will not settle for Santa Anna's blood. He is after a bigger fish here. "I want Texas," he says. He gets it. In exchange for Santa Anna's signing Texas over to American immigrants, the general secures his own freedom. But there is an important catch missed by all of the Crocket films here. While Houston in this film may gloat over his canny use of Santa Anna's body as a bargaining chip, the gesture was legally meaningless. Santa Anna no more had the authority to sign over Texas to independence than any American general would have to carve Texas away today and hand it over to a third party. Put simply, only a head of state can do so; and Santa Anna was not the head of state in Mexico. He had been and would again become—but he was not on that day.

Evidently, I am confusing actual historical events with myth. The reality of the frontier myth has its own logic. In this mythical universe, as shown in this and the earlier Crockett love poems on celluloid—"shimmering poetry" the *New York Times* would declare in 1954[19]—possession was ten-tenths of itself, layered in the icing of the many virtues of the frontiersmen. Texas's destiny was manifest, too. The film reminds us as it closes that "Nine years after the fall of the Alamo, Texas became the twentieth state of the United States." Of course it did.

Chapter Eight

Mirror, Mirror: Imperialism Is a Palindrome

> Do I contradict myself?
> Well then I contradict myself
> (I am large, I contain multitudes)
>
> —Walt Whitman[1]

> Thanks to advertising, everydayness has started singing.
>
> —Milan Kundera[2]

> All around me, white men were consulting other white men. My son lived with a consultor, or was it spelled differently? Did my son live with a consulter? The whole world could live in that space between that *o* and that *e*. My son lived in that space."
>
> — Sherman Alexie[3]

Many times I have had students tell me, as if struck by epiphany, that the mythical frontier seems to be active everywhere in present-day popular culture. Everywhere! Not simply in film but on television, they exhort me, in literature, advertising, presidential politics, music videos, billboards, magazines, you name it. I usually agree but caution them not to get carried away with it. The dreamed frontier looms nearly everywhere in American culture. That said, insofar as the romance operates as America's origin story, one should expect it to be at work not simply in political discourse (witness George W. Bush since 9-11, the self-styled cowboy riding high in the saddle) or Hollywood (the subject of this book) but in everyday life, in fact. And it is there, especially and blatantly, as noted, in advertising.

It comes as no surprise, then, that Hollywood's long-running love affair with the frontier myth has prospered financially and creatively into the twenty-first century. As much as ever today the myth weaves its way into the fabric of Americana as it is written on screen. Three films released since 2000 aptly and amply illustrate the mythic hold that the genre maintains—*About Schmidt*, *25th Hour*, and *Hidalgo*, though one might have chosen from many, many more (I must admit that some—for example, *Pearl Harbor*,[4] *Independence Day*,[5] *The Last Samurai*,[6] while potentially fitting, I simply could not bear to watch more than once, let alone the multiple occasions necessary).

All About U.S.

The first, a big box-office success, starring the redoubtable and sassy screen legend Jack Nicholson, playing cleverly against type, focuses on the life of an idyllic loser in his twilight years, "a life's third act," as a review in *USA Today* put it.[7] Nicholson plays the newly retired Warren Schmidt, a dreary, myopic, and hugely self-centered man. And Schmidt's life's work for the Woodmen of America—not woodsmen, for he is the anti-frontiersman in this effective black comedy, the first way the character plays against type—amounts to, well, nothing much. As Roger Ebert noted, "He has spent his entire life working at a job that could have been done by anybody or, apparently, nobody."[8] The accumulation of Schmidt's oeuvre is carted out in cardboard boxes and dumped into the trash more or less the moment he is out the door and officially retired.

Meanwhile, his home life is no better, where he has been henpecked for 42 years and reduced to the status of a spousal malingerer. Then his wife, a demanding old moss bag, who had been unfaithful to him with his best friend, a barber, looking every bit a one-dimensional senior, up and dies while vacuuming up a mess on the kitchen floor. Schmidt's life changes.

And Schmidt loses his way. In fact, he had always been lost—we know, after all, the director takes pains to tease out some of the nuances of his meaningless career in insurance and his life of safety-first, sheer drudgery. However, now that his wife is dead, suddenly he discovers it for himself. And it is sad and kind of funny, oddly. Of course, insofar as Schmidt is everyman Americana, as Charles Taylor noted in a review penned for Salon.com,[9] in the same way that Homer Simpson is or Al Bundy was a generation ago, Schmidt also remains truer to life than what Hollywood normally dishes out as protagonist(s). The result creates a certain discomfort for the viewer (an uneasiness that did not sit well with critics, for example, at *Rolling Stone*[10] or *Slate*[11]), but also makes the film click. In this second way, then, the film, like Nicholson, the godfather of on-screen edginess, plays against type.

The film also, importantly, plays against the frontier myth. This generates part of the black humor and the unsettling and subtle irony. At one level you get Jack Nicholson, superstar of the explosive characterization, buried in failed character and thereby assisting in registering a telling comment about the nature of Hollywood and the quality of celebrity-based culture, as the film takes a broad and substantive swipe at the myth and its central lack of touch with empirical reality. What Roger Ebert mistakes as "tragic," the film more accurately posits as pathetic, albeit comically so.

Especially interesting is the decision to put anti-frontiersman Schmidt on the road and give him an inverted mythical frontier makeover of limited measure. The signs emerge tentatively then become humorous in their obviousness. For example, Schmidt sets out to visit his daughter, who for good reason shuns him. The man is a pill, a real headache, a cheap bastard who built a career and a life out of petty bean counting and their attendant sphincter shrinking rules. His daughter lives in Denver, and so he drives west to see her.

He charges along in his motor home, a Winnebago "Adventurer," the company named after the indigenous group that formerly inhabited the Midwest. This vehicle effectively delivers him to near idiotic self-awareness as an ironic delivery vehicle of the myth. This is a woodman on the move, not a woodsman. This is key, for as critic Charles Taylor noted, Schmidt has "no identity outside his work."[12] Taylor is not promoting dialectical materialism here (philosophically, that is, you are what you do) so much as noting precisely what the film wants you to note: I knew a woodsman; the woodsman was a friend of mine; you are no woodsman. Whereas the frontiersman embodies and expresses mythical American traits such as strength, youth, energy, risk-taking, bravery, and such, Schmidt personifies the opposite characteristics. Remember, this is a man who has wasted his life effectively managing down risk to its most acceptable level. An insurance man. A man who sits down to pee because his wife told him to.

About Schmidt works because it plays effectively against audience expectations. It might be funnier, however, if it were not also simultaneously unnerving. For the film implies that everyman who, while he might mythically style himself on the frontier archetype, in reality is much like Schmidt. In short, Joe American is considerably nearer a loser than he is to the imagined frontier archetype. It is not that Schmidt's life and work are unrepresentative that renders him a loser, it is that our expectations that he be something more that generates the black, ironic humor. He is a normal, run-of-the-mill American senior citizen. Warren Schmidt: woodman, American, immortalized on celluloid, stands as a testament to the depth of reach of the myth. That his life has been one of quiet desperation and careful, ultra-cautious planning, is to say, well, nothing more than welcome to America.

The most obvious example, among many, of the film's mythical intentions occurs in a scene where Schmidt, on his way to Denver but temporarily spurned by his daughter Jeanie, parks his recreational vehicle next to a river late one evening. He had earlier been forced out of a regular campground after making unwarranted and clumsy sexual advances toward the wife of a cloyingly friendly motor home aficionado (he had been unable to read the signs properly; remember, he is no scout). So Schmidt finds himself sleeping on the roof of the Adventurer, and what a night it turns out to be, there under the stars wrapped up in a sleeping bag. "This morning," he narrates jauntily in a voice over, "I awoke from my night in the wilderness completely transformed. I'm like a new man." Accept that he is not. Nothing changes behaviorally, though he does act with renewed misguided purpose.

The film also speaks ironically, blackly, and slyly, to the frontier myth as an agency of imperialism. This emerges through the ongoing relationship Schmidt develops with a Tanzanian foster child whom he adopts after his wife Helen dies. They're not exactly pen pals, 66-year old Warren Schmidt and six-year old Ndugu, because all we ever hear are Schmidt's letters read aloud as voice overs; the Tanzanian boy, in all likelihood, is illiterate (the one return letter Schmidt does receive was penned by a Catholic sister at the orphanage where Ndugu lives). It is here in the letters, again with Schmidt framed as everyman Americana, the inverted woodsman *qua* woodman, that we encounter the sinister domestic shadows of Manifest Destiny and the myth's complicity in casting it. For the relationship between them is literally all "about Schmidt" in much the same way that the domestic support thrown to U.S. imperialism in Iraq is not so much about "expanding freedom," as President George W. Bush puts it, but all about addressing American domestic insecurities (themselves fueled by Bush's policies and neuroses[13]). It epitomizes a classic case of projection. And cutely, where the traditional American colonialist tack has been to treat adult Others as if they were children (an operational premise of Manifest Destiny), Schmidt does just the opposite and treats the Other (Ndugu, a child) as if he were an adult (but still an Other). This doubly-bound mistaken identity makes the letters funnier than they should be in the same way that *Pulp Fiction*[14] made you laugh about things that maybe are not really funny at all.

This noir-ish element operates on two tracks in the film: at the same time as Schmidt heads west to reclaim something he never had in the first place because the having of it was never more than his slice of a sacred imperial dream, so too his relationship with Ndugu mirrors a similar disinclination on everyman's part to engage the real issues engendering Ndugu's plight. As everyman, Schmidt's dream world is also America's dreamscape, simultaneously of its own making yet meanwhile denying its very existence as dream. It is a world where the consequences of one's actions remain actively unhinged from responsibility, both by willful ignorance—and this is as pure Schmidt as it is authentically American, witness the public anger generated by the suggestion that perhaps American behavior played a part in encouraging terrorists to attack the United States in 2001—and arrogance, that it is all about me, that Iraqi behavior is all about us, all about America. The results fuse indifference, ignorance, national ego, and intolerance with anger and subsequently breed and sanction Manifest Destiny. Meanwhile Schmidt drives blithely onward, tuning his radio to that place where Rush Limbaugh tosses orts from the head table at the core of the empire.

A Second Chance

Writing in the *Washington Post*, critic Ann Hornaday called Spike Lee's *25th Hour* a "rarity in filmmaking: a movie we need, right now."[15] Others, including me, agree that it is a formidable piece of work. The *Philadelphia Inquirer* said that it "resonates with power and poetry."[16] The *Miami Herald* wrote that it "hums with vibrant energy."[17] *Slate* called it a "melancholy tone poem."[18] Roger Ebert viewed it as "unique" and "extraordinary."[19]

The basic story revolves around Monty Brogan, acted by an emotionally charged Edward Norton, a jejune twenty-something former drug dealer who is being sent to the hoosegow for possession. The film narrates his final 24 hours of freedom, before his dad drives him off to prison. It is a curious kind of freedom, too, and the title of the film prompts us to ask, well, what next? What happens in that 25th hour? The narrative tension derives from whether or not Monty will go willingly to jail. While the film neither apologizes for Monty, nor fashions Monty as a very likeable character, still as audience we ask, will he stay or will he go? As trained movie goers we have long been primed for this, and director Spike Lee knows it and works with it.

Staying means enduring a long term in an overcrowded prison, which rightfully frightens the physically slight Monty, especially the virtual certainty of anal rape. In a way, too, and here is where we can begin to identify with him, dealing dope is nearly a victimless crime. I mean, Monty never forced anybody to do drugs. Plus, he is an entrepreneur, right? He is resourceful, clever, brave, loyal, forthright, nonviolent, decent, even honest, despite the illegality of the profession. These are admirable American qualities. Further, he has made a decision to go straight, to give up his life of crime. Everyone deserves a second chance—in America. And he is in love with a good and beautiful Puerto Rican woman, Naturel. Taken together, then, we root for Monty in spite of Norton's canny and insouciant distancing of the character from the audience. But we're never given any sense that he will run for it. Running is not in him, it would seem. He is loyal.

The second source of tension is supplied by director Lee, who frames the story not just set against New York, but post-9-11 New York. So we get lots of flashing lights, red, white, and blue, shots of ground zero, and so on, establishing for us that Monty's story is also America's story. Does this mean that where Monty went wrong, perhaps America also went wrong? Conceivably. America has long acted as an international foreign policy pimp, serving to screw over others and laughing all the way to the bank, arguably like a two-bit drug dealer. Easy money and a smug self-righteousness tinged with callous indifference would seem to have supplied the principal seduction for both.

Despite all this, more hopefully, and echoing Sean Penn's contribution to the brilliant collaborative film *11'09"01-September 11,*[20] Spike Lee frames 9-11 as a potential watershed for America, symbolized by Monty's desire to go straight and get his life right, back on track, to fulfill the promise of his early years. I mean, Monty was basically a good kid, he played basketball in high school, had nice friends, his dad was a firefighter. How much more American can you get?

You cannot. And that is the point. Yet he went bad nonetheless, at least temporarily. Sometimes bad things happen to good people. Monty fucked up just as America has fucked up. But America is also a land for second chances. It is mythical frontier country, after all. By granting Monty this chance for redemption—if he runs for it, ironically, because he will not survive intact if he stays and goes to prison—Lee argues that America likewise can still get it right. It is all about making smart decisions, the right choices. Choosing a new path. You look at yourself in the looking glass and you choose a new path.

Thus, as Monty is learning to be a better man maybe America might, too, learn from its errant ways. Probably the best enduring scene in the film, where Monty rants at a mirror about anything and everything that is New York and how he hates it, is simultaneously, gorgeously, an ode of love. The list is long. But "fuck everybody," is how it concludes, spitting angry. "Fuck the whole city and everybody in it." It is an exquisite rendering of the phenomenon of projection. What he really loathes is what he has become. Truth be told, he loves New York, presented here by Spike Lee as dark, lush, dangerous, full of possibility, multiethnic, Hobbesian, and vibrantly alive. Monty Brogan, Irish-American lad, deeply loves what makes New York (and America) great: its bursting diversity and the promise of a second chance. Everything he claims to deplore in fact is what contributes to making the city and the country remarkable. And nearly everything that made it great speaks to and from the fundamental decency of a second act. Forgiveness and the opportunity for renewal are American hallmarks, Lee offers. They are worth cherishing. This may well be the best love story of 2003. But it is tough love because Lee is unflinching in his criticism, but never cynical; yet at the same time this is not a dark film, though it is often shot with minimal lighting. The real light, of course, is offered by the mythical frontier, which again saves the day.

Two things happen. First, Monty with difficulty is able to elicit a sound beating from his two best friends, a bloody dust up designed to make him look tough as well as undesirable when he arrives at prison. It also quickly proves to mete out atonement for letting them down (as they come to relish the pummeling), for disappointing his father, his city, his American dream, his America.

The scene is constructed with considerable nuance. First, by this late stage of the film we know that we are in a frontier dreamscape. The three friends are gathered under a bridge that looks more like a short tunnel, in Central Park, about as nature-ish a spot as you'll get in New York City. And here begins the ritual unclothing *cum* stripping down. They shed their garments and violence ensues. Monty is badly beaten, even potentially disfigured—but emerges reborn through this violence, from the tunnel which has acted properly as a sort of American birth canal functioning on Turnerian terms there in the park.

Second, then Monty's father picks him up for the drive to jail. But does Monty go to prison or does he reach for the second chance? The viewer must decide. For we are offered an alternative story here, one where Monty runs. It is narrated through the voice of Monty's father. In it, Monty goes west and never looks back. He gets an honest job and settles into a decent hard-won western, American life. He never returns, except to send word to Naturel. And then she comes west, too, and they make a life together. And they have children and grandchildren together. They grow old together. And they live the American dream, these easterners, one the Irish scion and the other a Puerto Rican beauty.

As this plays out our eyes are drawn to the American flag on the vehicle's antennae, as his father preaches, "Take that road...you find the silence out there, the peace. You can find God...So drive west...You make a new life. You forget your old life...This life came so close to never happening." So you take your pick; but be careful what you wish for.

Back in the Saddle

Pretty clearly, *25th Hour* conjures up Lee's best work since his terrific, *Do the Right Thing*, and has much to recommend it. Its sophistication and thoughtfulness contrast sharply with the loopy simplicity and studied childishness of *Hidalgo*, a throwback to the frontier adolescence of *Dances with Wolves* and *Raiders of the Lost Ark*, though without the skill behind the camera.

Hidalgo is an equine drama. The story centers around Frank Tompkins, played by Viggo Mortensen (of *Lord of the Rings*[21] pedigree), a champion long-distance horse racer at the end of the Indian Wars in the late nineteenth century. This Sioux/white half-breed is a message carrier by trade, though he has turned his back on his indigenous side.

So it comes as very bad luck when he delivers a message to the Seventh Cavalry at Wounded Knee, North Dakota, during the winter of 1892. The Sioux had been in the midst of a Ghost Dance, which unsettled jittery and trigger-happy army regulars (who also still pined, we are meant to understand, for avenging Custer's death sixteen years earlier). The message delivered instructs the Seventh to subdue the natives by any means necessary. A misunderstanding leads to a first shot being fired and, well, the rest is history. The ensuing slaughter of unarmed men, women, and children, of course, stands as just one among many such massacres directed by the United States against its aboriginal population in the nineteenth century.[22]

It strikes Tompkins hard and he quickly falls into despair and alcohol abuse. Suddenly we are witnessing a more familiar Hollywood story (that is, a down-on-his-luck drunkard with a heart of gold; you know where this is heading). Hence he rises; and winds up somewhere in the Middle East for a horse race of the most epic of proportions (3,000 miles long and 1,000 years old) offering a sizeable fortune of $100,000 to the winner. Actually, the race occurs in the more mythical west, featuring an alternatively unforgiving and magical desert, whores and virgins (though color is partially flipped here as the virginal beauty is locally indigenous and the whore is a Brit), Arabs (as in *Raiders of the Lost Ark* standing in for mythical Indian savages), and Tompkins himself as a half-breed (and his champion horse is likewise of unproven provenance—get the picture yet?), and so on. It is the mythical far west set, sort of, in the Middle East. Plus, it is preachily, uncleverly revisionist.

Okay, so it may be clunky, in part because it is not at all clear whether this sort of movie can be pulled off anymore. As a review in the *New York Times* complained, "The picture may be like having to finish an entire pot of broccoli to get a couple of jelly beans for dessert." In short, the film "may yet be declared cruel and unusual punishment for kids of all ages."[23] Roger Ebert disagreed, observing defensively that "Hidalgo is the kind of movie Hollywood has almost become too jaundiced to make anymore." He then goes on to champion its exuberance, "purity and simplicity."[24] In an attempt to settle this dispute I asked my daughters, at the time aged eleven and nine, to weigh in. My eleven-year-old loves nearly every Hollywood feature she sees; her favorite movie is *Far and Away*. My nine-year-old can take or leave television and movies, but adores Mr. Bean. I expected my kids to vote with Ebert (they usually do). To my surprise, they voted with the *Times* review, suggesting Ebert missed the boat on this one. They found the story contrived and, well, kind of dumb. "Not funny. Not interesting. Boring," I was instructed.

Yet the film prospered modestly at the box office, and I agree with Ebert that it pushes some buttons in a reasonably effective way. It certainly takes you back to the supposed values of an earlier, allegedly happier time, but it differs in an important way in that it, like *Dances* and *Raiders*, also unsubtly attempts to frame itself as a revisionist frontier flick. Like its two better brethren, it mostly fails, not solely because of its intellectual vacuity (though this is a problem) but equally because it is just not very well sewn together. That is, one may still appreciate the artistry of the colonialism rife in *Raiders* or *Dances*. But not here.

Part of the problem is confusion. For example, Frank goes to ride the long race in the burning hot, locust-plagued, sandstorm-whipping Middle East partly for personal vindication. But mostly he goes for money. Moping and drinking to excess, it would appear, were not enough to cure his guilt. However, lots of money will do nicely, thank you very much. That is not revisionist; it is just greed. Moreover, he is encouraged to do it by an elder/mentor Chief Eagle Horn (Floyd Red Crow Westerman, from *Dances*). "You have a chance to save yourself, Far Rider," he sagely counsels Frank. Hmmm, save yourself *and* cash in nicely. How novel.

The presentation of Muslim Arabs poses the more serious problem. In an effort to more fully humanize American Indians and to use them to imply that America itself is of mixed parentage, Arabs get the John Wayne treatment. The result is that they bear close resemblance to mythical Hollywood Indians. This picture delivers your Noble Savage, clownish Others, regular savages, and even an Indian Princess thrown in for good measure. What, you might wonder, do the Arabs do to deserve such treatment? Well, in this movie they actually literally invite it. Early on, a savage and a clown come in search of Tompkins because their master, a Noble Savage (a tired Omar Sharif), has sent them in search of the famous Tompkins.[25]

Once on site, director Joe Johnston gives the film the Indiana Jones treatment, though unlike Indy, Frank is quiet and respectful, yet still violent and lucky, as if God was on his side. Of course, God, the real God, Christianity's God, is on his side. Allah, the pale Muslim version is lampooned in this film as ineffective, arbitrary, and sort of witless. Not only are things generally preordained, expressed as the will of Allah, but through an obsession with maintaining honor Allah is diminished as hopelessly outdated. Yet Frank's Christian baggage and his inherent decency and the promise of his good intentions are precisely what Noam Chomsky writes of, that "it is important to recognize that profession of noble intent is predictable, and therefore carries no information, even in the technical sense of the term."[26]

In fact, this is the crux of *Hidalgo* and, indeed, of much frontier western iconography. We have become accustomed to view murderous behavior as harmless entertainment. We cannot see the imperial urges at work because the good intentions partially blind us and, as with Warren Schmidt, the stereotypes also shade us in our comfortable continental amnesia.

Make It Stop

Somebody observed that the reason why university politics is so frequently poisoned with rancor and prickled with petty malevolence is precisely because so little is at stake. As novelist Joseph Heller once put it, "While none of the work we do is important, it is important that we do a great deal of it." The frontier myth operates on much the same principle as the former, but reverses the equation. So much is at stake, yet it tickles us pink. Turner's vision, wrought faithfully, even lovingly by the likes of John Wayne and Ron Howard and Joe Johnston and countless more, has served and continues to serve as an imaginary mask, projecting inverted cultural truths—where imperialism, a real no-no, becomes recast as triumphal Manifest Destiny—as it contributes to disguising Others (say, the idea that the Indians or Iraqis veritably invited American expansionism; to have done less than conquer them would have been impolite; or that God favored Texicans over Mexicans). The result renders Turner's essay, a munificently glib patriotic elegy, as a series of shiny, happy imperial surfaces without sharp edges. The whiff of these delusions is the body odor of America—and it smells like empire.

Regrettably yet predictably, then, in the same way that academics, especially in the humanities, can take deep personal offence when reminded that what they do, in the larger world, does not count for much, so too mythical Americana suffers mightily at the suggestion that its principal narrative is built upon a collection of festering half-truths, wallowing expressively in preternaturally aggressive cock-fighting yarns. The story of America, to follow this sordid trail to its end, equates with imperialism of the highest, slickest, and stickiest order; very nearly the opposite of its own mythical self-perception—or itself, but embedded and by another name. It is so brilliantly packaged by Hollywood and rigorously hummed by audiences and all those who contribute to the making of films alike, real-life woodmen, that on the eve of the 2004 election no one could tell which of the imperial candidates would win—they both egged on their supporters with competing wet dreams of a pax Americana settling gaily over Iraq, Afghanistan (when this bombed over land was remembered at all by late 2004), and the long-forgotten adventures undertaken, say, when Ronald Reagan, the kindly grandfather of neo-Manifest Destiny, was quietly brokering the deaths of hundreds of thousands of peasants in Central America, acting on the false notion that the region was swimming in communism and that decolonization presented a measurable threat to the United States.

It begs the question: when will it stop? At a human level over two centuries the vanquishing and murder and humiliations of Indians and blacks and half-breeds and mulattos and Asians, even of white females, has been and remains America's most basic story and Hollywood's most prolific gravy train. It does not end there, either, because it is also a road movie, taking the bullying not only to family members (Mexico) and neighbors (Central America, Cuba) but to faraway communities such as Vietnam and outer space.

Reality Check

But can it really be that bad?

At least four common arguments refute it. First, there is the notion that the United States has vigorously led while effete Europeans have merely followed the sometimes fitful construction of just and increasingly more equalitarian societies. In short, America pioneered democracy as we know it and have come to love it. America has fought for freedom ceaselessly, as evidenced by its revolution, its erasure of slavery during the Civil War, its reaction to Pearl Harbor, to September 11, and to Saddam. America, further, has gone to bat countless times in the names of freedom and democracy, most notably in world wars but also against the perils of communism that took up a good portion of the twentieth century. In short, America ain't perfect, pshaw, but it is a damned sight freer and more democratic than the rest of the world. This is not simply talk. America leads by example. This is what Dubya means by expanding freedom in the Middle East. You know, you gotta break some eggs.

Second, there is the idea that in many nation-states a healthy, if not entirely desirable, friction exists between peoples of varying ethnic backgrounds. Again, America has led the way toward integration and improved multicultural relations—even though its ethnic makeup is far more complex than many other countries and thus the challenge has proved to be more formidable. It has not balkanized, though, nor is there any present threat of it doing so. America, let us remember, opened its doors to immigration and became a magnet for the dispossessed and marginalized of the planet. It threw open its generous arms to the world. That this process has engendered domestic chafing within the United States should surprise no one. I mean, grow up. You simply cannot eradicate ethnic jealousies over night—but they will pass, you can be sure. Witness the path of the black Irish, scorned and racialized when they came to the United States but now indistinguishable from so many other Euro-Americans (just like Spike Lee's Monty Brogan). Capitalism will see to it. And notice how time will heal all wounds. Ever heard of the Bohunks? Not anymore! And certainly not if you are under the age of 30. Spics and Dagos and Niggers and Polacks and Nips and Greasers and Gooks are a thing of the past, so many relics, like Archie Bunker's chair now resting in the

Smithsonian. The story of America is the story of improvement and growth.

Third, the United States has stood firm against imperialism for centuries. This is crucial. Born in the fires of an anti-imperialist conflagration, the American Revolution, the U.S. has been uniquely sensitive to the evils of colonialism. To wit, it has fought the scourge—first versus England and against Spain (over Cuba), countless aggressive Latin American would-be potentates, and the Nazis and Soviet Union (say, in Vietnam), Ronald Reagan's "evil empire," and Saddam. So, yes, the United States has engaged imperialism—but in a constant struggle to vanquish it, stupid.

Fourth, there is the pitch that the ebb and flow of history is the story of winners and losers. Wars are fought. That much is inevitable. Someone wins and someone loses. How can it be otherwise? That is just the way it is, the way people are. That the losers are expected to abide and even to adopt the ways of the winner is a story and practice as old as history itself. Examples abound—the Romans, the Aztecs, and on and on. Besides, America treats its visible minorities in ways far more progressive and decent than any other country (with the exception perhaps of Canada). So quit your griping and belly-aching.

Lavender Red, Lavender Blue

This catalog might be expanded easily and nearly endlessly. But its points stand in error and, like the frontier myth that feeds them, are never more than half true. Back to the list. Point one. The United States no more invented democracy and freedom than it serves as the best examples of promoting either. These practices vary considerably across time and space. Only mainstream Americana, willfully and hermetically sealed from the rest of the world by its own onanistic national myths, believes in such nonsense. Are Britons less free than Americans? Canadians? Germans? Japanese? Mexicans? Are they less democratic? In what other major democracy today was the leader elected, in the first case, after having won fewer votes than his opponent?[27] In what other major democracy today was the leader elected, in the second case, and according to reliable reports, after an election stolen by corruption?[28] While the myth holds that the frontier delivered up democracy, etcetera, etcetera, surely it was English culture that sowed the seeds for this phenomenon in the United States as it did in other frontier regions such as Canada and Australia. For that matter, the experience of frontier no more gave rise to democracy in the United States than it did in Australia, Brazil, Canada, or Russia. And ask yourself, was the United States really fighting for freedom and democracy during the cold war? Maybe such rubbish washes in the gated communities of Indianapolis or Des Moines or Tucson, but it surely does not in Tegucigalpa, or Managua, or Ho Chi Minh City, or Buenos Aires, or Sao Paulo, or Santiago, or Kabul, or Baghdad.

Point two. Multiethnic states frequently suffer ethnic strife, granted. This has been true of the United States—but also of Canada, England, France, and India. The United States has not excelled in developing ways and means to bridge a path from its mainstream to its various marginalized populations. It languored decades behind many countries in abolishing slavery, as witnessed by one of the key issues giving rise to the birth of Texas and its subsequent annexation to the United States. Meanwhile, its Jim Crow legacy certainly served as anything but a positive affirmation of its race relations. Remember Watts, 1965? Rodney King? The LA riots of 1992? Moreover, it has been most effective in denying visible minorities, especially indigenous peoples, access to equal opportunity. Just consider for a moment the unofficial segregation rampant in poor black and Latino neighborhoods today in large American cities, or the backlash against demonstrably successful affirmative action programs in the 1990s.

Point three. Yes, the United States has claimed to stand for anti-imperialism. In fact, this position makes a certain amount of sense, given the U.S. war for independence. Did the U.S. not, for example, fight the Nazis and were the Nazis not imperialists? And did the United States not struggle against the former Soviet Union and was it not also imperialistic? Yes and yes. But so what. Imperial powers have been duking it out for centuries—Spain versus Britain, Britain versus France, France versus Germany. Besides, the United States also has engaged in imperialist conquests of its own—versus Indians, Mexicans, black Americans, Vietnamese, Colombians, and so on. Again, aided and abetted by the frontier myth, in America historical truth has been and is nearsightedly envisioned. One fact, to me, stands above all others: the very geography of the 50 states. I mean, it is not as if indigenous peoples asked to be warred upon and to have their lands taken away. Right? Then how was the territory gained if not by force, a force reflecting cultural imperatives that in turn legitimized the taking of it in the first place? A force called imperialism. In effect, and in mood and in practice, the frontier myth granteth and the historical frontier taketh away.

Point four. Finally, the ebb and flow of history may be seen as the story of winners and losers. Maybe not. Since the middle of the twentieth century many in the West have prided themselves on the idea that notions about decency, tolerance, forbearance, freedom, opportunity, and so on are goals worth struggling, even fighting, for, irrespective of skin color or ethnic origin. The winner/loser paradigm belongs to another, more atavistic time. By its own logic it might be employed to re-sanction slavery because up until recent times such forms of unfree labor have been ubiquitous historically. Frankly, it is just a lousy idea.

Dilly Dilly

John Dewey once presciently warned against the American predisposition for fashioning what he termed "pernicious dualisms." The frontier myth operates on such an axis, conjuring up us versus them at every turn. This dynamic is neither healthy nor reasonable. Here is one example. In reality, the United States has fought imperialism tooth and nail at the same time as it has behaved imperialistically with considerable relish. On the surface, these facts do not fit easily. But fit they do. Together they fashion a fuller, more accountable, rendering of historical accuracy. Policymakers and politicians would do well to wake up to the reality of what Homi Bhabha terms splitting, that it is possible to hold two contradictory notions dear to one's heart and even to be motivated to action by both ideas simultaneously. It is what David Harvey refers to as the "dialectics" of American foreign policy.[29] Filmmakers such as the Coen brothers, Clint Eastwood, Howard Hawks, Stanley Kubrick, and John Sayles, among others, know this well and their films, *The Big Lebowski*, *Heartbreak Ridge*, *Full Metal Jacket*, *Red River*, and *Lone Star*, as discussed in this book, have much to offer on this topic.

In fact, Americans have such a tool at their disposal. It is called the frontier myth. And you can catch it. It's starring at a theater near you.

Notes

Chapter One: A Theory of American Evolution

1. From the poem, "Shine, Perishing Republic," by Robinson Jeffers, from *The Selected Poetry of Robinson Jeffers* (Stanford University Press, 2001), 23.
2. Thomas Flanagan, "Western Star," *New York Review of Books* XLVIII: 19 (November 29, 2001): 24.
3. Richard Slotkin, "Gunfighters and Green Berets: *The Magnificent Seven* and the Myth of Counter-Insurgency." *Radical History Review* 44 (1989): 65.
4. *Elizabeth*, dir. Shekhar Kapur, 1998.
5. *Citizen Kane*, dir. Orson Welles, 1941.
6. *Nixon*, dir. Oliver Stone, 1995.
7. *A Beautiful Mind*, dir. Ron Howard, 2001.
8. *Bill and Ted's Excellent Adventure*, dir. Stephen Herek, 1989.
9. *Malcolm X*, dir. Spike Lee, 1992.
10. *The Birth of a Nation*, dir. D.W. Griffith, 1915.
11. *JFK*, dir. Oliver Stone, 1991.
12. *Platoon*, dir. Oliver Stone, 1986.
13. *Green Berets*, dir. John Wayne, 1968.
14. *Glory*, dir. Edward Zwick, 1989.
15. *The Sting*, dir. George Roy Hill, 1973.
16. *Annie Hall*, dir. Woody Allen, 1977.
17. *Star Wars*, dir. George Lucas, 1977.
18. *Passion of the Christ*, dir. Mel Gibson, 2004.
19. See, for example, Lee Clark Mitchell, *Westerns: Making the Man in Fiction and Film* (Chicago: University of Chicago Press, 1996). Or see Janet Walker's introductory essay in Janet Walker, ed., *Westerns, Films Through History* (New York: Routledge, 2001), 1–24.
20. The best work begins with the dated yet prescient Henry Nash Smith, *Virgin Land: The American West as Symbol and Myth* (New York: Vintage Books, 1950). Also see John G. Cawelti, *The Six Gun Mystique* (Bowling Green: Bowling Green University Press, 1984); Richard Slotkin, *Regeneration Through Violence: The Mythology of the American Frontier, 1600–1860* (New York: Harper Perennial, 1973); and, Richard Slotkin, *Gunfighter Nation: The Myth of the Frontier in Twentieth Century America* (Norman: University of Oklahoma Press, 1998).
21. *Full Metal Jacket*, dir. Stanley Kubrick, 1987.
22. *Red River*, dir. Howard Hawks, 1948.
23. *The Big Lebowski*, dir. Joel Coen, 1998.
24. *Silverado*, dir. Lawrence Kasdan, 1985.
25. *High Noon*, dir Fred Zinnemann, 1952.
26. *A Fist Full of Dollars*, dir. Sergio Leone, 1964.
27. *Good, the Bad, and the Ugly*, dir. Sergio Leone, 1966.
28. *Dances with Wolves*, dir. Kevin Costner, 1990.
29. *Far and Away*, dir. Ron Howard, 1992.
30. *Man in the Wilderness*, dir. Richard C. Sarafian, 1971.

31. *Man Who Shot Liberty Valance*, dir. John Ford, 1962.
32. *Posse*, dir. Mario Van Peebles, 1993.
33. *Alien*, dir. Ridley Scott, 1979.
34. *The Ballad of Little Joe*, dir. Maggie Greenwald, 1993.
35. *Lone Star*, dir. John Sayles, 1995.
36. *Raiders of the Lost Ark*, dir. Steven Spielberg, 1981.
37. *About Schmidt*, dir. Alexander Payne, 2002.
38. *25th Hour*, dir. Spike Lee, 2002.
39. See Gore Vidal, *Perpetual War for Perpetual Peace* (New York: Nation Books, 2002).
40. *Heartbreak Ridge*, dir. Clint Eastwood, 1986.
41. *Alamo*, dir. John Wayne, 1960
42. *Hidalgo*, dir. Joe Johnston, 2004.
43. *Do the Right Thing*, dir. Spike Lee, 1989.

Chapter Two: The Imperial in Residence

1. Toni Morrsion, *The Bluest Eye* (New York: Plume, 1994), 126.
2. Richard Ford, *Independence Day* (New York: Random House, 2001), 5.
3. Henry Miller, *Tropic of Cancer* (New York: Grove Press, 1961), 8.
4. See, for example, William Darby, *John Ford's Westerns* (Jefferson, NC: McFarland & Company, 2006); J.A Place, *The Western Films of John Ford* (Secaucus, NJ: The Citadel Press, 1974).
5. Edward Buscombe, "The Idea of Genre in the American Cinema," in Barry Grant, ed., *Film Genre Reader* (Austin: University of Texas Press, 2003), 14. Andre Bazin makes a similar muddled assertion. See Andre Bazin, "The Evolution of the Western," in Bill Nichols, ed. *Movies and Methods* (Berkeley: University of California Press, 1976), 150–157.
6. *Titanic*, dir. James Cameron, 1998.
7. *Serpico*, dir. Sidney Lumet, 1973.
8. *Alice in Wonderland*, dir. Clyde Geronomi, 1951.
9. *Barney's Great Adventure*, dir. Steve Gomer, 1998.
10. See Mitchell.
11. Cawelti, 9.
12. Buscombe, 15.
13. Buscombe, 16.
14. Buscombe, passim.
15. Andrew Tudor, "Genre," in Grant, ed., 6–7.
16. Stuart Kaminsky, *American Film Genres* (Pflaum Publishing, 1974), 10.
17. Richard Collins, "Genre: A Reply to Ed Buscombe," in Nichols, ed., 163.
18. Douglas Pye, "Introduction," in Ian Cameron and Douglas Pye, eds., *The Book of Westerns* (New York: Continuum, 1996), 10–11.
19. Harris M. Lentz, *Western and Frontier Film and Television Credits, 1903–1995* (Jefferson, NC: McFarland and Company), 1.
20. Herb Fagen, *Encyclopedia of Westerns* (New York: Checkmark Books, 2002).
21. See, for example, Scott Simmons, *The Invention of the Western Film* (New York: Cambridge University Press, 2003).

22. Roland Barthes, *Mythologies* (New York: Noonday Press, [1957] 1972), 109–158.
23. *Unforgiven*, dir. Clint Eastwood, 1992.
24. *Blazing Saddles*, dir. Mel Brooks, 1974.
25. *Shane*, dir. George Stevens, 1953.
26. *The Oxbow Incident*, dir. William A. Wellman, 1943.
27. *Starship Troopers*, dir. Paul Verhoeven, 1997.
28. *The African Queen*, dir. John Huston, 1951.
29. Slotkin, *Regeneration*.
30. See the introduction penned by the editors, "The West, Westerns, and American Character," in Peter C. Rollins and John E. O'Connor, *Hollywood's West: The American Frontier in Film, Television, and History* (Lexington: University of Kentucky Press, 2005), 1–34.
31. See, for example, Peter Rollins and John O'Connor's attack on Richard Slotkin as "wrongheaded." In Rollins and O'Connor, *Hollywood's West*, 12.
32. For example, in an important contribution by leading scholars the historian James R. Grossman prematurely concluded in 1994 that "most academics had relegated him [Turner] to the periphery years ago." See James R. Grossman, ed., *The Frontier in American Culture: Essays by Richard White and Patricia Limerick* (Los Angeles: University of California Press, 1994).
33. Eldon Kenworthy, *America/Americas: Myth in the Making of U.S. Policy Toward Latin America* (University Park: Pennsylvania State University Press, 1995). Also see Fredrick Pike, *The United States and Latin America: Myths and Stereotypes of Civilization and Nature* (Austin: University of Texas Press, 1992); Cecil Robinson, *With the Ears of Strangers* (Tucson: University of Arizona Press, 1969), 15–30.
34. Frederick Jackson Turner, "The Significance of the Frontier in American History," in Frederick Jackson Turner, *Frontier and Section, Selected Essays of Frederick Jackson Turner* (Englewood Cliffs, NJ: Prentice-Hall, Inc., [1893] 1961), 37–62.
35. While I employ it as the most useful model, Turner's articulation of the frontier narrative was by no means singular. Instead, it should be seen as the most widely known, even persuasive because of its fame and the force of its cultural logic, but not the only. See Nash Smith, 291. Also see Slotkin, *Regeneration*.
36. See Ray Allen Billington, ed., *The Frontier Thesis, Valid Interpretation of American History* (New York: Holt, Reinhart and Winston, 1966). Billington's collection of essays usefully charts the emergence of scholarly opposition to Turner.
37. Patricia Limerick stands as the best example of such scholarship. See, for example, *Legacy of Conquest, The Unbroken Past of the American West* (New York: W.W. Norton, 1988). Also see her essay, "Turnerians All: The Dream of a Helpful History in an Intelligible World," *The American Historical Review* 100: 3 (June, 1995): 697–715. Richard Hofstadter penned a devastating critique of Turner's essay in "The Frontier as an Explanation," in his book, *The Progressive Historians: Turner, Beard, and Parrington* (New York: Knopf, 1968), 118–163. Also see Richard White, "The Imagined West," in *It's Your Misfortune and None of My Own: A New History of the American West* (Norman: University of Oklahoma Press, 1991), 613–632.
38. For a good summary and synopsis of this opinion, see Forrest McDonald, "Rugged Individualism, Frederick Jackson Turner and the Frontier thesis," *The World and I* (May, 1990): 539–551.

39. Graham Fuller, "Sending Out a Search Party for the Western," *New York Times*, March 5, 2000; Pat Dowell, "The Mythology of the Western: Hollywood Perspectives on Race and Gender in the Nineties," *Cineaste* 21: 1–2 (1995): 6–10.
40. Limerick, "Turnerians All."
41. See Richard Slotkin, *Gunfighter Nation* (University of Oklahoma Press: Norman, 1998), 1–2. Also see Erik Baard, "George Bush Ain't No Cowboy," *Village Voice*, September 28, 2004 (http://www.villagevoice.com/news/0439,baard,57117,1.html).
42. Turner, 37, 39, 51; Slotkin, *Regeneration*.
43. Turner, 39.
44. Turner, 38.
45. Turner, 43.
46. Turner, 39.
47. Turner, 61. Also see Turner, 46, 57.
48. *Hondo*, dir. John Farrow, 1953.
49. *First Blood* was the first of three films in which action star Sylvester Stallone played John J. Rambo, the angry and vengeful Vietnam veteran. See *First Blood*, dir. Ted Kotcheff, 1982.
50. Benjamin F. Wright, "American Democracy and the Frontier," *The Yale Review* (December, 1920): 320–365. Also see Peggy Pascoe, *Relations of Rescue: The Search for Female Moral Authority in the American West, 1847–1939* (New York: Oxford University Press, 1993); Patricia Nelson Limerick, *The Real West* (Boulder: University Press of Colorado, 1996); Richard White, *It's Your Misfortune and None of My Own* (University of Oklahoma Press, 1990).
51. Turner, 56–57.
52. See William Appleman Williams, *Empire as a Way of Life* (New York: Oxford University Press, 1980).
53. Ibid.
54. Fred Shannon, "A Post-Mortem on the Labor-Safety Valve Theory," *Agricultural History* 19 (January, 1945): 31–37. Also see Susan Armitage and Elizabeth Jameson, eds., *The Women's West* (Norman: University of Oklahoma Press, 1987); and see Billington.
55. See Carlton Smith, *Coyote Kills John Wayne* (Hanover, MA: University Press of New England, 2000), 1–3. Also see Peter C. Rollins and John E. O'Connor, eds. *Hollywood's Indian, The Portrayal of the Native American in Film* (Lexington: University of Kentucky Press, 1998).
56. Turner, 61.
57. See Pike, Robinson.
58. William Appleman Williams, "The Frontier Thesis and American Foreign Policy."
59. Susan K. Opt, "American Frontier Myth and the Flight of Apollo 13: From News Event to Feature Film," *Film and History* 26: 1–4 (1996): 40–51.
60. See Kenworthy.
61. Nash Smith. Also see Slotkin *Gunfighter Nation*, 5; Slotkin, *Regeneration*; Earle Pomeroy "Toward a Reorientation of Western History," *Mississippi Valley Historical Review* 41 (March, 1955): 579–600.
62. See Joseph Campbell, *Myths to Live By* (New York: Arkana, 1993).
63. Jeffrey Bartholet, *Newsweek*, August 13, 2001.

64. Ira Progoff, "Waking Dream and Living Myth," in Joseph Campbell, ed., *Myths, Dreams, and Religion* (Dallas Spring Publications, 1970), 176–195.
65. See Limerick, *Legacy*.
66. Theodore Adorno and Max Horkheimer, *Dialectic of Enlightenment* (New York: Continuum, [1944] 1987).

Chapter Three: The Empire's New Clothes

1. William Appleman Williams, *Empire*, 4.
2. Turner, 61.
3. *Full Metal Jacket*.
4. *City Slickers*, dir. Ron Underwood, 1991.
5. See Gore Vidal, "Introduction," in Edgar Rice Burroughs, *Tarzan of the Apes* (New York: Signet Classics, [1914] 1990).
6. Turner, 61. Also see Turner, 46, 57.
7. *Open Range*, dir. Kevin Costner, 2003.
8. See, for example, Randy Rasmussen, *Stanley Kubrick: Seven Films Analyzed* (Jefferson, NC: McFarland & Company, Inc., 2001); Thomas Allen Nelson, *Kubrick: Inside a Film Artist's Maze* (Bloomington: University of Indiana Press, 2000); James Howard, *Stanley Kubrick Companion* (London: B.T. Batsford, 1999).
9. *The Deer Hunter*, dir. Michael Cimino, 1978.
10. *Apocalypse Now*, dir. Francis Ford Coppola, 1979.
11. James Howard briefly synopsizes Vietnam War flicks and where *Jacket* fits chronologically. See Howard, 162–163.
12. See, for example, Thomas Doherty, "Full Metal Genre: Stanley Kubrick's Vietnam Combat Movie," in Mario Falsetto, ed., *Perspectives on Stanley Kubrick* (Toronto: G. K. Hall & Co., 1996), 307–316; Karen Rasmussen and Sharon D. Downey, "The Dialectical Disorientation in Vietnam War Films: Subversion," *Quarterly Journal of Speech* 77 (1991): 176–195; *Maclean's* magazine, "Unblinking Visionary," (March 22, 1999): 62; *Video Hound's Golden Retriever, 1997* (NYC: Visible Ink, 1997), 293; Louis Giannetti and Scott Eyman, *Flashback: A Brief History of Film* (Englewood Cliffs, NJ: Prentice-Hall, 1996), 348; Desson Howe, "Full Metal Jacket," review of *Full Metal Jacket. Washington Post* (June 26, 1987).
13. About as close as any criticism comes to linking *Jacket* to the mythical frontier (and it's not very close) is Mario Falsetto, who espies universalisms at work in the picture: "Although *Full Metal Jacket* concentrates specifically on the Vietnam experience, its primary concern is the examination of aspects of human behavior that any war or conflict might generate." See Mario Falsetto, *Stanley Kubrick: A Narrative and Stylistic Analysis* (Westport, CT: Praeger, 2001).
14. See Kenworthy, 1–53; Slotkin, *Regeneration*, 3–24; Richard Slotkin, "Dreams and Genocide: The American Myth of Regeneration." *Journal of Popular Culture* 5 (1971): 41.
15. See Falsetto, *Stanley Kubrick*.
16. See Richard Corliss, "Welcome to Vietnam, the Movie: II," review of *Full Metal Jacket, Time* (June 29, 1987); Richard Lacayo, "Semper Fi: Kubrick Sticks to His Guns," review of *Full Metal Jacket, Film Comment* 23:5 (1987): 11–14; Gerri Reaves,

"Full Metal Jacket and the Beast Within," *Literature/Film Quarterly* 16: 4 (1988): 226–236.
17. Pauline Kael, "Ponderoso," review of *Full Metal Jacket, New Yorker* (July 13, 1987): 75–76.
18. Roger Ebert, review of *Full Metal Jacket*, dir. Stanley Kubrick, *Chicago Sun-Times* (June 26, 1987).
19. Ibid.
20. Robert Castle and Stephen Donatelli, "Kubrick's Ulterior War," *Film Comment* (September/October, 1998): 24.
21. See Rasmussen and Downey.
22. Falsetto, *Stanley Kubrick*, 145.
23. Turner, 42.
24. Nelson also comments upon the conformity, the "rigid symmetry and order" carried out so effectively in the film's first act. See Nelson, 240.
25. William Appleman Williams, *The Contours of American History* (Chicago: Quadrangle Books, 1966). Also see Slotkin, *Regeneration;* Kenworthy, passim.
26. Turner, 61.
27. Probably the best filmic example was set in Vietnam and filmed by John Wayne, *The Green Berets* (1968), to be discussed at length later.
28. *Oxford American Dictionary* (New York: Oxford University Press, 1980), 210.
29. Williams, *Empire*, passim.
30. Noam Chomsky, *On Power and Ideology* (New York: Black Rose Books, 1987), 10.
31. See Herbert J. Storing, *What the Anti-Federalists Were For: The Political Thought of the Opponents of the Constitution* (Chicago: University of Chicago Press, 1981).
32. *Coming to America*, dir. John Landis, 1988.
33. *Moscow on the Hudson*, dir. Paul Mazursky, 1984.
34. *Coming Home*, dir. Hal Ashby, 1978.
35. Film reviewer Kathleen Maher, writing in the *Austin Chronicle* (May 29, 1992) called the film "adolescent," as did Roger Ebert in the *Chicago Sun-Times* (May 22, 1992).
36. John F. Kelly, review of *Far and Away*, dir. Ron Howard, *Washington Post* (May 22, 1992).
37. Critics generally agreed that Howard's epic ambitions for this film were undone most fundamentally by poor scriptwriting. Peter Travers, film critic for *Rolling Stone*, observed, "It's the sluggish, old-hat script that makes you feel the weight of the film's two hours and twenty minutes." *Rolling Stone* (December 8, 2000).
38. Roger Ebert, review of *Far and Away*, dir. Ron Howard, *Chicago Sun-Times* (May 22, 1992). Also see Hal Hinson's review in the *Washington Post* (May 22, 1992).
39. Joanne Kaufman, review of *Far and Away*, dir. Ron Howard, *People* (June 1, 1992).

Chapter Four: Being Not It!

1. Homi Bhabha, *The Location of Culture* (New York: Routledge, 1994), 132.
2. Octavio Paz, *The Labyrinth of Solitude* (New York: Grove Press, 1985), 370.
3. See Patricia Seed, *Ceremonies of Possession in Europe's Conquest of the New World, 1492–1640* (Cambridge: Cambridge University Press, 1995), 16–40.

4. Toronto *Daily Globe*, September 11, 1874.
5. Reviews in *Variety* and the *New York Times* concur. See *Variety* (March 23, 1962) and A.H. Weiler, review of *The Man Who Shot Liberty Valance*, dir. John Ford, *New York Times* (May 24, 1962) 29: 2.
6. Darby, 148.
7. See, for example, John Baxter, *The Cinema of John Ford* (New York: A.S. Barnes & Company, 1971).
8. Garry Wills, "John Wayne's Body," *New Yorker* (August 19, 1996): 43.
9. *High Noon*, which provides an interesting juxtaposition, a traditional Western, was released the same year.
10. See Robert Sklar, "Empire to the West: Red River," in John C. O'Connor and Martin Jackson, eds., *American History/American Film* (New York: Frederick Ungar Publishing Co., 1979), 167–181.
11. Todd McCarthy, *Howard Hawks* (New York City: Grove Press, 1997), 423.
12. See Joseph McBride, *Focus on Howard Hawks* (Englewood Cliffs, NJ: Prentice-Hall, 1972).
13. See Bosley Crowther, review of *Red River*, *New York Times* 31: 2 (October 1, 1948). Also see Donald C. Willis, *The Films of Howard Hawks* (Metuchen, NJ: Scarecrow Press, 1975), 43; the review of *Red River* in *Variety* (July 13, 1948); and Roger Ebert, review of *Red River*, dir. Howard Hawks, *Chicago Sun-Times* (March 1, 1998).
14. Joseph McBride, *Hawks on Hawks* (Los Angeles: University of California Press, 1982).
15. See Christopher Hitchens, *The Trial of Henry Kissinger* (New York: Verso, 2002).
16. See, for example, Lars Schoultz, *Beneath the United States: A History of U.S. Policy Toward Latin America* (Cambridge: Harvard University Press, 1998). Also see Pike.
17. Peter Travers, review of *Lone Star*, dir. John Sayles, *Rolling Stone* (December 19, 2000); Roger Ebert, review of *Lone Star*, *Chicago Sun-Times* (July 3, 1996).
18. Dennis West and Joan M. West, review of *Lone Star*, dir. John Sayles, *Cineaste* 22: 3 (Summer, 1996): 34. Also see Kenneth Turan, review of *Lone Star*, dir. John Sayles, *Los Angeles Times* (June 21, 1996).
19. Stanley Kaufman, review of *Lone Star*, dir. John Sayles, *New Republic* (August 5, 1996).
20. See Walter Russell Mead, *Power, Terror, Peace, and War: America's Grand Strategy in a World at Risk* (New York: Alfred A. Knopf, 2004) 59-103.
21. Arthur Asa Berger, *Media Analysis Techniques* (Thousand Oaks, CA: SAGE, 1998), 138.

Chapter Five: Ritual War

1. *New York Times Magazine* (January 14, 2000). The novel of the same name by Owen Wister upon which a handful of films titled *The Virginian* have been made, is widely considered to be the best or among the very best works of Western fiction. See Owen Wister, *The Virginian* (New York: Mass market paperbacks, [1902] 2002.

2. *New York Times* (March 5, 2000).
3. Ward Churchill, "Smoke Signals in Context," An Historical Overview, *Z Magazine* (November, 1998).
4. Gore Vidal has usefully attempted to chart this martial behavior. See Vidal, *Perpetual War*.
5. Turner, 61.
6. McBride, *Hawks on Hawks*, 120.
7. See Philip Taylor, "The Green Berets (Film in Context)," *History Today* (March, 1995).
8. See the Internet Movie data Base (IMDB: http://www.imdb.com/title/tt0063035/business).
9. See Wills, 38.
10. Renata Adler, review of *The Green Berets*, dir. by John Wayne, *New York Times* (June 20, 1968), 49: 1.
11. Charles Mohr, review of *The Green Berets*, dir. by John Wayne, *New York Times* (June 20, 1968), 49: 2.
12. Slotkin, "Gunfighters and Green Berets," 66.
13. Anonymous review of *The Green Berets*, dir. by John Wayne, *Variety* (June 12, 1968).
14. Michael Coy, review of *The Green Berets*, dir. by John Wayne, IMDB website (http://us.imdb.com) December 13, 1998).
15. Ibid.
16. Philip Taylor, "*The Green Berets*," *History Today* 45: 3 (March 1, 1995) 25.
17. John Wayne, quoted in Philip Taylor, "The Green Berets," in David. W. Elwood, ed., *The Movies as History: Visions of the Twentieth Century* (Trowbridge, UK: Sutton Publishing, 2000) 37.
18. See Wills.
19. Edward Gallafent, *Clint Eastwood: Actor and Director* (London: Studio Vista, 1994), 153.
20. See Roger Ebert, review of *Heartbreak Ridge*, dir. by Clint Eastwood, *Chicago Sun-Times* (December 5, 1986).
21. Rita Kempley, review of *Heartbreak Ridge*, dir. by Clint Eastwood, *Washington Post* (December 5, 1986).
22. Ibid.
23. Douglas Thompson, *Clint Eastwood Riding High* (Chicago: Contemporary Books, 1992), 105.
24. See Sigmund Freud, *Civilization and Its Discontents* (W.W. Norton and Company, [1930] 2005).
25. See Robert Baird, "Going Indian: Dances With Wolves (1990)," in Rollins and O'Connor, eds., *Hollywood's West*, 160.
26. Vine Deloria, "Comfortable Fictions and the Struggle for Turf," in Devon A. Mihesuah, ed., *Natives and Academics: Researching and Writing about American Indians* (Lincoln: University of Nebraska Press, 1998), 66.
27. Roger Ebert, review of *Dances with Wolves*, dir. by Kevin Costner, *Chicago Sun-Times* (November 9, 1990).
28. Review of *Raiders of the Lost Ark*, dir. by Steven Spielberg, "Norm of the Movies" (www.projet9.netc.net/norm/archives/archive-r/raiders -a htm).
29. *Schindler's List*, dir. Steven Spielberg, 1993.

30. Quoted in Taylor and Obrien, 105.
31. Dan Georgakas, review of *Dances with Wolves*, dir. by Kevin Costner, *Cineaste* 18: 2 (1991): 53.
32. Once internalized, orientalism naturalizes the Arab-as-Other, effectively engendering popular images in Western culture that have historically presented "orientals" as weak, retrograde, aggressive, warlike, sneaky, dirty, dishonest, feminine, and so on. See Edward Said, *Orientalism* (New York: Vintage Books, 1979).
33. Todd McCarthy, review of *The Big Lebowski*, dir. by Joel Coen, *Variety* (January 26, 1998).
34. Stanley Kaufman, review of *The Big Lebowski*, dir. by Joel Coen, *The New Republic* (April 6, 1998).
35. Susan Stark, review of *The Big Lebowski*, dir. by Joel Coen, *Detroit News* (March 6, 1998).
36. Stephen G. Wilson, review of *The Big Lebowski*, dir. by Joel Coen, IMDB (http://us.imdb.com/Title? 0118715).
37. Roger Ebert, review of *The Big Lebowski*, dir. by Joel Coen, *Chicago Sun-Times* (March 6, 1998).
38. Kenneth Turan, review of *The Big Lebowski*, dir. by Joel Coen, *Los Angeles Times* (March 6, 1998).
39. Richard Schickel, review of *The Big Lebowski*, dir. by Joel Coen, *Time* (March 2, 1998).
40. Jack Kroll, review of *The Big Lebowski*, dir. by Joel Coen, *Newsweek* (March 16, 1998).
41. Toronto *Globe and Mail* (September 25, 2006).

Chapter Six: Back to the Future

1. Clifford Geertz, *The Interpretation of Cultures* (New York: Basic Books, 1973), 14.
2. Salman Rushdie, *Fury* (Toronto: Vintage Canada, 2001), 51.
3. Diane Negra. *Off-White Hollywood: American Culture and Ethnic Female Stardom* (New York: Routledge, 2001), 59–60.
4. *Aliens*, dir. James Cameron, 1986.
5. *Alien 3*, dir. David Fincher, 1992.
6. *Alien: Resurrection*, dir. Jean-Pierre Jeunet, 1997.
7. *Close Encounters of the Third Kind*, dir. Steven Spielberg, 1977.
8. *Thelma and Louise*, dir. Ridley Scott, 1991.
9. See, for example, textbooks as different (as the titles suggest) as Gary B. Nash et al. *The American People: Creating a Nation and a Society* (New York: Longman, 2000) and Bernard Bailyn et al., *The Great Republic: A History of the American People* (New York: DC Heath & Co., 1992).
10. See, for example, Ivan Musicant, *Empire by Default: The Spanish-American_War and the Dawn of the American Century* (New York: Holt, 1998).
11. Roger Ebert, review of *Posse*, dir. by Mario Van Peebles, *Chicago Sun-Times* (May 14, 1993).

12. Hal Hinson, review of *Posse*, dir. by Mario Van Peebles, *Washington Post* (May 14, 1993).
13. Louis Black, review of *Posse*, dir. by Mario Van Peebles, *Austin Chronicle* (May 21, 1993).
14. See Marjorie Baumgarten, review of review of *The Ballad of Little Jo*, dir. by Maggie Greenwald, *Austin Chronicle* (November 5, 1993).

Chapter Seven: Lying Line Laying

1. Louis L'Amour, *The Ferguson Rifle* (New York: Bantam Books, 1973), 30.
2. Terry Eagleton, *Holy Terror* (New York: Oxford University Press, 2005), 65.
3. Zane Grey, *The Trail Driver* (New York: Harper Paperbacks, [1936] 1991), 197.
4. Richard R. Flores, *Remembering the Alamo: Memory, Modernity, and the Master Symbol* (Austin: University of Texas Press, 2002), 153.
5. Many studies of the Mexican-American War have been published. Among the best, see Robert W. Johannsen, *To the Hall of the Montezumas: The Mexican War in the American Imagination* (New York: Oxford University Press, 1988); John S. D. Eisenhower, *So Far from God: The U.S. War with Mexico, 1846–1848* (Norman: University of Oklahoma Press, 2000).
6. Any good history of Mexico makes this point clearly. See, for example, Michael C. Meyer, William L. Sherman and Susan M. Deeds, *The Course of Mexican History* (New York: Oxford University Press, 2005).
7. See Rodolfo Acuña. *Occupied America* (New York: Longman, 2003).
8. See Dee Alexander Brown, *Bury My Heart at Wounded Knee: An Indian History of the American West* (New York: Henry Holt & Company, 2003).
9. See Paul T. McCartney, *Power and Progress: American National Identity, the War of 1898, and the Rise of American Imperialism* (Baton Rouge: Louisiana State University Press, 2006).
10. Ramón Eduardo Ruíz, *Cuba: The Making of a Revolution* (Amherst: University of Massachusetts Press, 1968).
11. Review in Jay Robert Nash and Stanley Ralph Ross, eds., *The Motion Picture Guide, A–B, 1927–1983* (Chicago: Cinebooks, 1985), 34–35.
12. Flores, 160.
13. David Crockett, *A Narrative of the Life of David Crockett of the State of Tennessee* (Lincoln: University of Nebraska Press, [1834] 1987), xxxii.
14. Bosley Crowther, review of *The Alamo*, dir. by John Wayne, *New York Times* (October 27, 1960).
15. Flores, 157.
16. *Davy Crockett, King of the Wild Frontier*, dir. Norman Foster, 1954.
17. *The Alamo*, dir. John Lee Hancock, 2004.
18. *Death Wish*, dir. Michael Winner, 1974.
19. Bosley Cowther, review of *Davy Crockett, King of the Wild Frontier*, dir. by Norman Foster, *New York Times* (May 25, 1954).

Chapter Eight: Mirror, Mirror

1. Walt Whitman, *Leaves of Grass* (New York: Bantam Classics, 1983).
2. Milan Kundera, *Identity* (Harper Flamingo, 1998), 26.
3. Sherman Alexie, *The Toughest Indian in the World* (New York: Atlantic Monthly Press, 2000), 217.
4. *Pearl Harbor*, dir. Michael Bay, 2001.
5. *Independence Day*, dir. Roland Emmerich, 1996.
6. *The Last Samurai*, dir. Edward Zwick, 2003.
7. Mike Clark, review of *About Schmidt*, dir. by Alexander Payne, *USA Today* (January 29, 2003).
8. Roger Ebert, review of *About Schmidt*, dir. by Alexander Payne, *Chicago Sun-Times* (December 20, 2002).
9. Charles Taylor, review of *About Schmidt*, dir. by Alexander Payne, www. Salon.com (December 13, 2002).
10. Peter Travers, review of *About Schmidt*, dir. by Alexander Payne, *Rolling Stone* (November 28, 2002).
11. David Edelstein, review of *About Schmidt*, dir. by Alexander Payne, www.Slate.com (December 12, 2002).
12. Charles Taylor, review of *About Schmidt*, dir. by Alexander Payne December 13, 2002, www. Salon.com.
13. See, for example, Dan Dervin, "A Funny Thing Happened to Moses on the Way to the Promised Land: Midpoint in Bush's Second Term," *The Journal of Psychohistory* 34: 2 (Fall, 2006): 144–149.
14. *Pulp Fiction*, dir. Quentin Tarantino, 1994.
15. Ann Hornaday, review of *25th Hour*, dir. by Spike Lee, *Washington Post* (January 10, 2003).
16. Steven Rea, review of *25th Hour*, dir. by Spike Lee, *Philadelphia Inquirer* (January 10, 2003).
17. Rene Rodriguez, review of *25th Hour*, dir. by Spike Lee, *Miami Herald* (January 10, 2003).
18. David Edelstein, review of *25th Hour*, dir. by Spike Lee, December 19, 2002, Slate.com.
19. Roger Ebert, review of *25th Hour*, dir. by Spike Lee, *Chicago Sun-Times* (January 10, 2003).
20. The movie comprises 11 short films offered by directors from around the globe. See *11'09"01–September 11*, dir. Samira Makhmalfab, et al., 2002.
21. Mortensen starred as the character "Strider" in all three of the blockbuster installments dir. by Peter Jackson and based on the books by J.R.R. Tolkien. See *The Lord of the Rings: The Fellowship of the Ring* (2001); *The Lord of the Rings: The Two Towers* (2002); and *The Lord of the Rings: Return of the King* (2003).
22. See Brown; Larry McMurtry, *Oh What a Slaughter: Massacres in the American West, 1846–1890* (New York: Simon and Schuster, 2005).
23. Elvis Mitchell, review of *Hidalgo*, dir. by Joe Johnston, *New York Times* (March 5, 2004).
24. Roger Ebert, review of *Hidalgo*, dir. by Joe Johnston, *Chicago Sun-Times* (March 5, 2004).

25. For an excellent discussion of the construction of Indians in American culture see Scott Vickers. *Native American Identities: From Stereotype to Archetype in American Art and Literature* (Albuquerque: University of New Mexico Press, 1998).
26. Noam Chomsky, *Hegemony or Survival, America's Quest for Global Dominance* (New York: Henry Holt, 2004), 48–49.
27. This wasn't the first time, either. Consider the elections of 1824, where Andrew Jackson bested John Quincy Adams but lost the race, and 1876, where Samuel Tilden outpolled Rutherford Hayes but failed to win the presidency.
28. See, for example, the piece written by Robert F. Kennedy Jr., "Was the 2004 Election Stolen?" *Rolling Stone* (June 1, 2006).
29. David Harvey, *The New Imperialism* (New York: Oxford University Press, 2003), 30.

Filmography

11'09"01-September 11, dir. Youssef Chahine, et al. 2002.
25th Hour, dir. Spike Lee, 2002.
The African Queen, dir. John Huston, 1951.
The Alamo, dir. John Lee Hancock, 2004.
Alice in Wonderland, dir. Clyde Geronomi, 1951.
Alien, dir. Ridley Scott, 1979.
Alien: Resurrection, dir. Jean-Pierre Jeunet, 1997.
Alien 3, dir. David Fincher, 1992.
Aliens, dir. James Cameron, 1986.
Annie Hall, dir. Woody Allen, 1977.
Apocalypse Now, dir. Francis Ford Coppola, 1979.
Barney's Great Adventure, dir. Steve Gomer, 1998.
A Beautiful Mind, dir. Ron Howard, 2001.
Bill and Ted's Excellent Adventure, dir. Stephen Herek, 1989.
The Birth of a Nation, dir. D.W. Griffith, 1915.
Blazing Saddles, dir. Mel Brooks, 1974.
Citizen Kane, dir. Orson Welles, 1941.
City Slickers, dir. Ron Underwood, 1991.
Close Encounters of the Third Kind, dir. Steven Spielberg, 1977.
Coming Home, dir. Hal Ashby, 1978.
Coming to America, dir. John Landis, 1988.
Davy Crockett, King of the Wild Frontier, dir. Norman Foster, 1954.
Death Wish, dir. Michael Winner, 1974
The Deer Hunter, dir. Michael Cimino, 1978.
Do the Right Thing , dir. Spike Lee, 1989.
Elizabeth, dir. Shekhar Kapur, 1998.
First Blood, dir. Ted Kotcheff, 1982.
Glory, dir. Edward Zwick, 1989.
Green Berets, dir. John Wayne, 1968.
High Noon, dir. Fred Zinnemann, 1952
Hondo, dir. John Farrow, 1953.
Independence Day, dir. Roland Emmerich, 1996.
JFK, dir. Oliver Stone, 1991.
The Last Samurai, dir. Edward Zwick, 2003.
Lone Star, dir. John Sayles, 1996.
The Lord of the Rings: The Fellowship of the Ring, dir. Peter Jackson, 2001.

The Lord of the Rings: Return of the King, dir. Peter Jackson, 2003.
The Lord of the Rings: The Two Towers, dir. Peter Jackson, 2002.
Malcolm X, dir. Spike Lee, 1992.
Moscow on the Hudson, dir. Paul Mazursky, 1984.
Nixon, dir. Oliver Stone, 1995.
Open Range, dir. Kevin Costner, 2003.
The Oxbow Incident, dir. William A. Wellman, 1943.
Passion of the Christ, dir. Mel Gibson, 2004.
Pearl Harbor, dir. Michael Bay, 2001.
Platoon, dir. Oliver Stone, 1986.
Schindler's List, dir. Steven Spielberg, 1993.
Serpico, dir. Sidney Lumet, 1973.
Shane, dir. George Stevens, 1953.
Star Wars, dir. George Lucas, 1977.
Starship Troopers, dir. Paul Verhoeven, 1997.
The Sting, dir. George Roy Hill, 1973.
Thelma and Louise, dir. Ridley Scott, 1991.
Titanic, dir. James Cameron, 1998.
Unforgiven, dir. Clint Eastwood, 1992.

Bibliography

Acuña, Rodolfo. *Occupied America*. New York: Longman, 2003.

Adler, Renata. Review of *The Green Berets*, directed by John Wayne, *New York Times*, June 20, 1968.

Adorno, Theodore, and Max Horkheimer. *Dialectic of Enlightenment*. 1944. New York: Continuum, 1987.

Alexie, Sherman. *The Toughest Indian in the World*. New York: Atlantic Monthly Press, 2000.

Anonymous Review of *The Green Berets. Variety*, June 12, 1968.

Anonymous Review of the *Man Who Shot Liberty Valance*, directed by Howard Hawks, *Variety*, March 23, 1962.

Anonymous review of *Red River*, directed by Howard Hawks, *Variety*, July 13, 1948.

Armitage, Susan, and Elizabeth Jameson, eds. *The Women's West*. Norman: University of Oklahoma Press, 1987.

Baard, Erik. "George Bush Ain't No Cowboy." *Village Voice*, Septemer 28, 2004.

Bailyn, Bernard, et al. *The Great Republic: A History of the American People*. New York: DC Heath & Co., 1992.

Baird, Robert. "Going Indian: Dances With Wolves (1990)." In Peter C. Rollins and John E. O'Connor, eds. *Hollywood's Indian: The Portrayal of the Native American in Film*. Lexington: University of Kentucky Press, 1998.

Barthes, Roland. *Mythologies*. New York: Noonday Press, [1957] 1972.

Bartholet, Jeffrey. *Newsweek*. August 13, 2001.

Baxter, John. *The Cinema of John Ford*. New York: A.S. Barnes & Company, 1971.

Berger, Arthur Asa. *Media Analysis Techniques*. Thousand Oaks, CA: SAGE, 1998

Bhabha, Homi. *The Location of Culture*. New York: Routledge, 1994.

Billington, Ray Allen, ed. *The Frontier Thesis: Valid Interpretation of American History?* New York: Holt, Reinhart and Winston, 1966.

Brown, Dee Alexander. *Bury My Heart at Wounded Knee: An Indian History of the American West*. New York: Henry Holt & Company, 2003.

Buscombe, Edward. "The Idea of Genre in the American Cinema." In Barry Grant, ed. *Film Genre Reader*. Austin: University of Texas Press, 1986.

Campbell, Joseph, ed. *Myths, Dreams, and Religion*. New York: E. P.Dutton, 1970.

———. *Myths to Live By*. New York: Arkana, 1993.

Cameron, Ian, and Douglas Pye, eds. *The Book of Westerns*. New York: Continuum, 1996.

Carter, Forrest. *The Education of Little Tree*. Albuquerque: University of New Mexico Press, 1999.

Castle, Robert, and Stephen Donatelli. "Kubrick's Ulterior War." *Film Comment* (September/October, 1998): 24.

Cawelti, John G. *The Six Gun Mystique*. Bowling Green: Bowling Green University Press, 1984.

Chomsky, Noam. *Hegemony or Survival: America's Quest for Global Dominance*. New York: Henry Holt, 2004.

———. *On Power and Ideology*. New York: Black Rose Books, 1987.

Churchill, Ward. "Smoke Signals in Context: An Historical Overview." *Z Magazine* (November, 1998).

Clark, Mike. Review of *About Schmidt*, directed by Alexander Payne, *USA Today*, January 29, 2003.

Collins, Richard. "Genre: A Reply to Ed Buscombe." In Bill Nichols, ed. *Movies and Methods*. Berkeley: University of California Press, 1976.

Corliss, Richard. "Welcome to Vietnam, the Movie: II." Review of *Full Metal Jacket*, directed by Stanley Kubrick, *Time* (June 29, 1987).

Coy, Michael. Review of *The Green Berets*, directed by John Wayne, Internet Movie data Base (http://us.imdb.com).

David Crockett. *A Narrative of the Life of David Crockett of the State of Tennessee*. 1834. Lincoln: University of Nebraska Press, 1987.

Crowther, Bosley. Review of *The Alamo*, directed by John Wayne, *New York Times*, October 27, 1960.

———. Review of *Davy Crockett, King of the Wild Frontier*, directed by Norman Foster, 1954, *New York Times*, May 25, 1954.

———. Review of *Red River*, directed by Howard Hawks, *New York Times*, October 1, 1948.

Darby, William. *John Ford's Westerns*. Jefferson, NC: McFarland & Company, 1996.

Deloria, Vine. "Comfortable Fictions and the Struggle for Turf." In Devon A. Mihesuah, ed. *Natives and Academics: Researching and Writing about American Indians*. Lincoln: University of Nebraska Press, 1998.

Doherty, Thomas. "Full Metal Genre: Stanley Kubrick's Vietnam Combat Movie." In Mario Falsetto, ed. *Perspectives on Stanley Kubrick*. Toronto: G.K. Hall & Co., 1996.

Dowell, Pat. "The Mythology of the Western, Hollywood Perspectives on Race and Gender in the Nineties." *Cineaste* 21: 1–2 (1995) 6–10.

Eagleton, Terry. *Holy Terror*. New York: Oxford University Press, 2005.

Ebert, Roger. Review of *About Schmidt*, directed by Alexander Payne, *Chicago Sun-Times*, December 20, 2002.

———. Review of *The Big Lebowski*, directed by Joel Coen, *Chicago Sun-Times*, March 6, 1998.

———. Review of *Dances with Wolves*, directed by Kevin Costner, *Chicago Sun-Times*, November 9, 1990.

———. Review of *Far and Away*, directed by Ron Howard, *Chicago Sun-Times*, May 22, 1992.

———. Review of *Full Metal Jacket*, directed by Stanley Kubrick, *Chicago Sun-Times*, June 26 1987.

———. Review of *Heartbreak Ridge*, directed by Clint Eastwood, *Chicago Sun-Times*, December 5, 1986.

———. Review of *Hidalgo*, directed by Joe Johnston, *Chicago Sun-Times*, March 5, 2004.

———. Review of *Lone Star*, directed by John Sayles, *Chicago Sun-Times*, July 3, 1996.

———. Review of *Posse*, directed by Mario Van Peebles, *Chicago Sun-Times*, May 14, 1993.

———. Review of *Red River*, directed by Howard Hawks, *Chicago Sun-Times*, March 1, 1998.

———. Review of *25th Hour*, directed by Spike Lee, *Chicago Sun-Times*, January 10, 2003.

Edelstein, David. Review of *25th Hour*, directed by Spike Lee, December 19, 2002 (www.Slate.com).

———. Review of *About Schmidt*, directed by Alexander Payne, December 12, 2002 (www.Slate.com).

Eisenhower, John S. D. *So Far from God: The U.S. War with Mexico,1846–1848*. Norman: University of Oklahoma Press, 2000.

Ellwood, David, ed. *The Movies as History: Visions of the Twentieth Century*. Trowbridge, UK: Sutton Publishing, 2000.

Fagen, Herb. *Encyclopedia of Westerns*. New York: Checkmark Books, 2002

Falsetto, Mario. *Stanley Kubrick: A Narrative and Stylistic Analysis*. Westport, CT: Praeger, 2001

———. ed. *Perspectives on Stanley Kubrick*. Toronto: G.K. Hall & Co., 1996.

Flanagan, Thomas, "Western Star." *New York Review of Books*, November 29, 2001.

Flores, Richard R. *Remembering the Alamo, Memory, Modernity, and the Master Symbol*. Austin: University of Texas Press, 2002.

Ford, Richard. *Independence Day*. New York: Random House, 2001.

Freud, Sigmund. *Civilization and Its Discontents*. 1930. New York: W.W. Norton and Company, 2005.

Fuller, Graham. "Sending Out a Search Party for the Western." *New York Times*, March 5, 2000.

Gallafent, Edward. *Clint Eastwood: Actor and Director*. London: Studio Vista, 1994.

Geertz, Clifford. *The Interpretation of Cultures*. New York: Basic Books, 1973.

Georgakas, Dan. Review of *Dances with Wolves*, directed by Kevin Costner, *Cineaste* 18: 2 (1991).

Giannetti, Louis and Scott Eyman. *Flashback: A Brief History of Film*. Englewood Cliffs, NJ: Prentice-Hall, 1996.

Grant, Barry, ed. *Film Genre Reader*. Austin: University of Texas Press, 2003.

Grey, Zane. *The Trail Driver*. 1936. New York: Harper Paperbacks, 1991.

Groen, Rick. "An American Maverick." *The Globe and Mail*, March 22, 2002.

Grossman, James R. ed. *The Frontier in American Culture: Essays by Richard White and Patricia Limerick*. Los Angeles: University of California Press, 1994.

Harvey, David. *The New Imperialism*. New York: Oxford University Press, 2003.

Hinson, Hal. Review of *Far and Away*, directed by Ron Howard, *Washington Post*, May 22, 1992.

———. Review of *Posse*, directed by Mario Van Peebles, *Washington Post*, May 14, 1993.

Hitchens, Christopher. *The Trial of Henry Kissinger*. New York: Verso, 2002.

Hofstadter, Richard, "The Frontier as an Explanation." In Richard Hofstadter. *The Progressive Historians: Turner, Beard, and Parrington*. New York: Knopf, 1968.

Hornaday, Ann. Review of *25th Hour*, directed by Spike Lee, *Washington Post*, January 10, 2003.

Howard, James. *Stanley Kubrick Companion*. London: B.T. Batsford, 1999.

Howe, Desson. Review of *Full Metal Jacket*, directed by Stanley Kubrick, *Washington Post*, June 26, 1987.

Jeffers, Robinson. "Shine, Perishing Republic." In *The Selected Poetry of Robinson Jeffers*. Stanford University Press, 2001.

Johannsen, Robert W. *To the Hall of the Montezumas: The Mexican War in the American Imagination*. New York: Oxford University Press, 1988.

Kael, Pauline. "Ponderoso." Review of *Full Metal Jacket*, directed by Stanley Kubrick, *New Yorker*, July 13, 1987.

Kaufman, Joanne. Review of *Far and Away*, directed by Ron Howard, *People*, June 1, 1992.

Kaufman, Stanley. Review of *The Big Lebowski*, directed by Joel Coen, *New Republic*, April 6, 1998.

———. Review of *Lone Star*, directed by John Sayles, *New Republic*, August 5, 1996.

Kelly, John F. Review of *Far and Away*, directed by Ron Howard, *Washington Post*, May 22, 1992.

Kempley, Rita. Review of *Heartbreak Ridge*, directed by Clint Eastwood, *Washington Post*, December 5, 1986.

Kennedy, Robert F. Jr. "Was the 2004 Election Stolen?" *Rolling Stone*, June 1, 2006.

Kenworthy, Eldon. *America/Americas: Myth in the Making Policy Toward Latin America*. University Park: Pennsylvania State University Press, 1995.

Kroll, Jack. Review of *The Big Lebowski*, directed by Joel Coen, *Newsweek*, March 16, 1998.

Kundera, Milan. *Identity*. New York: Harper Flamingo, 1998.

Lacayo, Richard. "Semper Fi: Kubrick Sticks to His Guns." Review of *Full Metal Jacket*. *Film Comment* 23:5 (1987).

L'Amour, Louis. *The Ferguson Rifle*. New York: Bantam Books, 1973.

———. *Mustang Man.*. 1966. New York: Bantam Books, 1985.

Lentz, Harris M. *Western and Frontier Film and Television Credits, 1903–1995*. Jefferson, NC: McFarland and Company, 1996.

Limerick, Patricia. *Legacy of Conquest: The Unbroken Past of the American West*. New York: W.W. Norton, 1988.

———. *The Real West*. Boulder: University Press of Colorado, 1996.

———. "Turnerians All: The Dream of a Helpful History in an Intelligible World." *The American Historical Review* 100: 3 (June, 1995): 697–715.

Maclean's Magazine. "Unblinking Visionary [Stanley Kubrick obituary]." March 22, 1999.

Maher, Kathleen. Review of *Far and Away*, directed by Ron Howard, *Austin Chronicle*, May 29, 1992.

McAlister, Linda Lopez. Review of *The Ballad of Little Jo*. "The Woman's Show," WMNF-FM (88.5), Tampa, FL, November 13, 1993.

McBride, Joseph. *Focus on Howard Hawks*. Englewood Cliffs, NJ: Prentice-Hall, 1972.

McCarthy, Todd. Review of *The Big Lebowski, Variety*, January 26, 1998.

———. *Howard Hawks*. New York City: Grove Press, 1997.

McCartney, Paul T. *Power and Progress: American National Identity, the War of 1898, and the Rise of American Imperialism*. Baton Rouge: Louisiana State University Press, 2006.

McDonald, Forrest. "Rugged Individualism, Frederick Jackson Turner, and the Frontier Thesis." *The World and I*, May, 1990.

McMurtry, Larry. *Boone's Lick*. New York: Pocket Star Books, 2000.

———. *Oh What a Slaughter: Massacres in the American West, 1846–1890*. New York: Simon and Schuster, 2005.

Mead, Walter Russell. *Power, Terror, Peace and War: America's Grand Strategy in a World at Risk*. New York: Alfred A. Knopf, 2004.

Meyer, Michael C., William L. Sherman, and Susan M. Deeds. *The Course of Mexican History*. New York: Oxford University Press, 2005.

Mihesuah, Devon A., ed. *Natives and Academics, Researching and Writing about American Indians*. Lincoln: University of Nebraska Press, 1998.

Miller, Henry. *Tropic of Cancer*. New York: Grove Press, 1961.

Mitchell, Elvis. Review of *Hidalgo, New York Times*, March 5, 2004.

Mitchell, Lee Clark. *Westerns: Making the Man in Fiction and Film*. Chicago: University of Chicago Press, 1996.

Mohr, Charles. Review of *The Green Berets*, directed by John Wayne, *New York Times*, June 20, 1968.

Morrsion, Toni. *The Bluest Eye*. New York: Plume, 1994.

Musicant, Ivan. *Empire by Default: The Spanish-American War and the Dawn of the American Century*. New York: Holt, 1998.

Nash, Gary B., et al. *The American People: Creating a Nation and a Society*. New York: Longman, 2000.

Nash, Jay Robert, and Stanley Ralph Ross, eds. *The Motion Picture Guide, A–B, 1927–1983*. Chicago: Cinebooks, 1985.

Negra, Diane. *Off-White Hollywood: American Culture and Ethnic Female Stardom*. New York: Routledge, 2001.

Nelson, Thomas Allen. *Kubrick: Inside a Film Artist's Maze*. Bloomington: University of Indiana Press, 2000.

Nichols, Bill, ed. *Movies and Methods*. Berkeley: University of California Press, 1976.

O'Connor, John C., and Martin Jackson, eds. *American History/American Film*. New York: Frederick Ungar Publishing Co., 1979.

Opt, Susan K. "American Frontier Myth and the Flight of Apollo 13: From News Event to Feature Film." *Film and History* 26: 1–4 (1996): 40–51.

Pascoe, Peggy. *Relations of Rescue: The Search for Female Moral Authority in the American West, 1847–1939*. New York: Oxford University Press, 1993.

Paz, Octavio. *The Labyrinth of Solitude*. New York: Grove Press, 1985.

Pike, Fredrick. *The United States and Latin America: Myths and Stereotypes of Civilization and Nature*. Austin: University of Texas Press, 1992.

Place, J. A. *The Western Films of John Ford*. Secaucus, NJ: The Citadel Press, 1974.

Pomeroy, Earle, "Toward a Reorientation of Western History." *Mississippi Valley Historical Review* 41 (March, 1955): 579–600.

Progoff, Ira. "Waking Dream and Living Myth." In Joseph Campbell, ed. *Myths, Dreams, and Religion*. New York: E. P. Dutton, 1970.

Pye, Douglas. "Introduction." In Ian Cameron and Douglas Pye, eds. *The Book of Westerns*. New York: Continuum, 1996.

Rasmussen, Karen, and Sharon D. Downey. "The Dialectical Disorientation in Vietnam War Films: Subversion." *Quarterly Journal of Speech* 77 (1991): 176–195.

Rasmussen, Randy. *Stanley Kubrick, Seven Films Analyzed*. Jefferson, NC: McFarland & Company, Inc., 2001.

Rea, Steven. Review of *25th Hour*, directed by Spike Lee, *Philadelphia Inquirer*, January 10, 2003.

Reaves, Gerri. "Full Metal Jacket and the Beast Within." *Literature/Film Quarterly* 16: 4 (1988): 226–236.

Robinson, Cecil. *With the Ears of Strangers*. Tucson: University ofArizona Press, 1969.

Rodriguez, Rene. Review of 25th *Hour*, directed by Spike Lee, *Miami Herald*, January 10, 2003.

Rollins, Peter C., and John E. O'Connor, eds. *Hollywood's Indian: The Portrayal of the Native American in Film*. Lexington: University of Kentucky Press, 1998.

———. *Hollywood's West: The American Frontier in Film, Television, and History*. Lexington: University of Kentucky Press, 2005.

Ruiz, Ramon Eduardo. *Cuba: The Making of a Revolution*. Amherst: University of Massachusetts Press, 1968.

Rushdie, Salman. *Fury*. Toronto: Vintage Canada, 2001.

Said, Edward. *Orientalism*. New York: Vintage Books, 1979.

Schickel, Richard. Review of *The Big Lebowski*, directed by Joel Coen, *Time*, March 2, 1998.

Schoultz, Lars. *Beneath the United States: A History of U.S. Policy Toward Latin America*. Cambridge: Harvard University Press, 1998.

Seed, Patricia. *Ceremonies of Possession in Europe's Conquest of the New World, 1492–1640*. Cambridge: Cambridge University Press, 1995.

Shannon, Fred. "A Post-Mortem on the Labor-Safety Valve Theory."*Agricultural History* 19 (January, 1945): 31–37.

Simmons, Scott. *The Invention of the Western Film*. New York: Cambridge University Press, 2003.

Sklar, Robert. "Empire to the West: Red River." In John C. O'Connor and Martin Jackson, eds. *American History/American Film*. New York: Frederick Ungar Publishing Co., 1979.

Slotkin, Richard, "Dreams and Genocide: The American Myth of Regeneration." *Journal of Popular Culture* 5 (1971).

———. *Gunfighter Nation: The Myth of the Frontier in Twentieth Century America*. Norman: University of Oklahoma Press, 1998.

———. "Gunfighters and Green Berets: The *Magnificent Seven* and the Myth of Counter-Insurgency." *Radical History Review* 44 (1989).

———. *Regeneration Through Violence: The Mythology of the American Frontier, 1600–1860*. New York: Harper Perennial, 1973.

Smith, Carlton. *Coyote Kills John Wayne*. Hanover, MA: University Press of New England, 2000.

Smith, Henry Nash. *Virgin Land: The American West as Symbol and Myth*. 1950. Cambridge: Harvard University Press, 2005.

Stark, Susan. Review of *The Big Lebowski*, directed by Joel Coen, *Detroit News*, March 6, 1998.

Storing, Herbert J. *What the Anti-Federalists Were For: The Political Thought of the Opponents of the Constitution*. Chicago: University of Chicago Press, 1981.

Taylor, Charles. Review of *About Schmidt*, directed by Alexander Payne, December 13, 2002 (www.Salon.com).

Taylor, Philip, "The Green Berets (Film in Context)." *History Today*, March, 1995.

Taylor, Philip, and Daniel Obrien. *Steven Spielberg: The Man, His Movies and Their Meaning*. Harrisburg, PA: Continuum International Publishing Group, 1999.

Thompson, Douglas. *Clint Eastwood Riding High*. Chicago: Contemporary Books, 1992.

Travers, Peter. Review of *About Schmidt*, directed by Alexander Payne, *Rolling Stone*, posted on Rollingstone.com, November 28, 2002.

———. Review of *Far and Away*, directed by Ron Howard, *Rolling Stone*, posted on Rollingstone.com, December 8, 2000.

———. Review of *Lone Star*, directed by John Sayles, *Rolling Stone*, posted on Rollingstone.com, December 19, 2000

Tudor, Andrew, "Genre." In Barry Grant, ed. *Film Genre Reader*. Austin: University of Texas Press, 1986.

Turan, Kenneth. Review of *The Big Lebowski*, directed by Joel Coen, *The Los Angeles Times*, March 6, 1998.

———. Review of *Lone Star*, directed by John Sayles, *Los Angeles Times* June 21, 1996.

Turner, Frederick Jackson. "The Significance of the Frontier in American History." In Frederick Jackson Turner. *Frontier and Section*. 1893. Englewood Cliffs, NJ: Prentice-Hall, Inc., 1961.

Vickers, Scott. *Native American Identities: From Stereotype to Archetype in American Art and Literature*. Albuquerque: University of New Mexico Press, 1998.

Vidal, Gore. "Introduction." In Edgar Rice Burroughs, *Tarzan of the Apes*. 1914. New York: Signet Classics, 1990.

———. *Perpetual War for Perpetual Peace*. New York: Nation Books, 2002.

Video Hound's Golden Retriever, 1997. New York: Visible Ink, 1997.

Walker, Janet, ed. *Westerns: Films Through History*. New York: Routledge, 2001.

Weiler, A.H. Review of *The Man Who Shot Liberty Valance*, directed by John Ford, *New York Times*, May 24, 1962.

West, Dennis, and Joan M. West. Review of *Lone Star*, directed by John Sayles, *Cineaste* 22: 3 (Summer, 1996): 34.

White, Richard. *It's Your Misfortune and None of My Own: A New History of the American West*. Norman: University of Oklahoma Press, 1991.

Whitman, Walt. *Leaves of Grass*. New York: Bantam Classics, 1983.

Williams, William Appleman. *The Contours of American History*. Chicago: Quadrangle Books, 1966

———. *Empire as a Way of Life*. New York: Oxford University Press, 1980.

———. "The Frontier Thesis and American Foreign Policy." *Pacific Historical Review* 24 (1955): 379–395.

Willis, Donald C. *The Films of Howard Hawks*. Metuchen, NJ: Scarecrow Press, 1975.

Wills, Garry. "John Wayne's Body." *New Yorker* (August 19, 1996): 39–49.

Wilson, Stephen G. Review of *The Big Lebowski*, directed by Joel Coen, Internet Movie Data Base (http://us.imdb.com/Title?118715).

Wright, Benjamin F. "American Democracy and the Frontier." *The Yale Review* (December, 1920): 320–365.

Index